City of Victory

the story of Colchester - Britain's first Roman town

Lea and Stephen Chambers
June 1997

Philip Crummy

with 34 illustrations by Peter Froste

Colchester Archaeological Trust

Published in 1997 by the
Colchester Archaeological Trust,
12 Lexden Road,
Colchester CO6 1BN.

paperback ISBN 1 897719 04 3
hardback   ISBN 1 897719 05 1

Cataloguing in data / British Library

Designed and set by the
Colchester Archaeological Trust Ltd.
Scanning and film output by
David Holland Graphics, Colchester
Printed and bound by the
Bath Press, Bath

The Colchester Archaeological Trust gratefully
acknowledges grants towards the publication of
this book from the following:
Colchester Borough Council, Essex County
Council, the Friends of the Colchester Archaeological Trust, and the Essex History Fair.

The Trust is also indebted to all those individuals (listed on pages 156-7) who supported the
book by subscribing in advance to its publication.

Pictures
Front page - Roman pot.
Contents page - detail of
the Middleborough mosaic;
doorway of St Botolph's
Priory church.

Cover:
front - the Temple of
Claudius and the tomb-
stone of Longinus;
back - the face of
Longinus, the game board
from Stanway, and the
Balkerne Gate.

Contents

A picture lamp from Culver Street showing an eagle (the bird of the god Jupiter) with a small wreath or amulet in its beak.

Last-minute archaeological excavations (to the right of the lorry) in 1985 at the Culver Street site as the contractors dig out the new service basement under Culver Square.

INTRODUCTION

Britain today is broadly a nation of town-dwellers. The story of Colchester is therefore important to us all, because Colchester was a place where urban life in Britain began. It was the Romans who introduced towns to Britain and through them ensured their control of the country for almost four hundred years. The process began with Colchester which, the Roman historian Tacitus tells us, was a settlement of ex-soldiers whose role was 'to protect the country against revolt and familiarise the provincials with law-abiding government'. But it was even more than that, for ultimately the town was a mechanism by which the Britons were to be bundled into the Roman way. To the Romans, towns were expressions of what they regarded as civilised life. To the Britons, at first they were the bastions of their oppressors but, as the years went by and the distinction blurred between the invader and the invaded, towns became a central feature of an evolving and distinctive 'Romano-British' way of life.

Some archaeologists argue over whether or not certain pre-Roman communities in Britain should be regarded as urban. The arguments revolve around how urbanism can be defined and how it can be recognised in the archaeological record. Fully-fledged urban communities cannot be found before the Romans but sometimes archaeologists describe some settlements as 'proto-urban' to imply the existence of a kind of embryonic town. As we shall see, such a description could be applied to Iron Age Colchester as it was in the years leading up to the Roman invasion, but really this is all rather academic. The first true towns in Britain were built by the Romans, and Colchester was the most senior and most important of the earliest Roman towns in the country.

Although to you and me the new town at Colchester would have seemed very primitive (rather like a frontier town in the Wild West of America), it would nevertheless obviously have been what we call a town. Its population would have been held together, not by kinship as in more primitive groupings of people, but by a desire to share in a communal way of life which offered opportunities for the individual's pleasure or gain. There would have been commerce (shops, markets, inns), personal and technical services of various kinds, public services (eg water and drainage), entertainment, and social activities (eg in theatres, amphitheatres, and public baths). To us, the place would have looked like a town with its grid of streets, all neatly surfaced with gravel. Its houses would have been easily recognisable as such being rectangular, with windows, doors, and tiled roofs. To the native Britons who had never seen a town before, Colchester would have

Part of a small mosaic from the Middleborough site.

Open day at the Middleborough site in 1979.

Archaeological excavations from the air.
Above: the Lion Walk site in 1973 from the south.
Below: the Culver Street site in 1982 from the north.
Opposite, bottom right: the Balkerne Lane site in 1974 from the west.

been quite alien and, no doubt, a stunning place to visit for the first time.

One reason why Colchester is such a rewarding place to study is its association with famous people of the past. Claudius, Boudica, Cunobelin, Caratacus, Edward the Elder, and Athelstan are some of the major historical figures associated with the town's history. The first three in particular are key players. Under Cunobelin, Colchester became the major settlement in south-east Britain (if it was not so already). Claudius captured Colchester in person and a few years later authorised the construction there of what may have been intended as the first capital town of Britain. A decade or so

later Boudica and her followers destroyed the place by fire during the native uprising against the Roman invaders.

What happened in Colchester is a microcosm of what happened in the Roman province at large. Chart Colchester in Roman and later times and you will get a good impression of what was happening in much of the rest of Roman Britain. In this book we shall construct a history of Colchester starting with the pre-Roman settlement in the days of Cunobelin and his predecessors. We shall trace how Claudius and his army conquered the settlement and made Colchester, first as a military base and then as a civic centre, the strategic focal point of their conquest of the rest of Britain. We shall see how the plan nearly fell apart when native resentment under the leadership of

Aerial view of the walled town centre of Colchester in October 1985, showing the town wall and gates, and the sites of the main excavations of the 1970s and 1980s:

A... Balkerne Gate

B... Balkerne Lane

C... Butt Road

D... Culver Street

E... the Gilberd School

F... Lion Walk

G... Maidenburgh Street

H... Middleborough

The course of the town wall is shown in red.

Boudica boiled up into open revolt with disastrous consequences for the town. We will see how the town was rebuilt and how it was to flourish for two hundred years. Gradual decline set in, with the end coming somewhat obscurely about four hundred years after its foundation under the emperor Claudius. We shall examine the evidence for the inhabitation of the former Roman town by the Saxons and the eventual evolution of the Norman town from the ruins of the Roman settlement under the great Norman baron Eudo Dapifer. We shall see how the Normans broke up and reused much of the old Roman town to make buildings which are as interesting and important as those they destroyed.

The Romans are often much admired for their technology and their 'civilised' way of life. They brought literacy, technological innovation and an urban way of life to a country occupied, in their view, by a backward and primitive people. But we should never forget that the Roman invasion of Britain was unwanted, and that only by their overwhelming military superiority did the Romans manage to overrun most of the country and, to a large extent, smother a culture and a people that had just as much right to survive as their own. Archaeologists can (and do) endlessly discuss and debate the finer points of the Roman military machine without a thought of what it all means in human terms. That is perfectly proper: compassion and prejudice have no place in the analytical process. But equally we should resist our instinct to admire the victor whatever the contest. The scale and ferocity of

the Boudican uprising is clear proof, if clear proof be needed, that the Roman invasion of Britain and the subjugation of the conquered people which followed were events that must have caused immeasurable human misery and resentment.

Like the modern town, Roman Colchester was constantly changing. Dig at most places within the walled area and you will find the remains of not one but maybe as many as five Roman buildings, one on top of the other. When digging large sites like Balkerne Lane, we try to rationalise these changes so as to express them as a series of plans showing the development of the site and its buildings throughout the whole of the Roman period and later (usually up to around AD 1700). Having studied individual areas, the challenge is then to use our understanding of the development of the individual sites to try and construct a sequence for the development of

the town as a whole. The large-scale excavations of the 1970s and 1980s at Balkerne Lane, Lion Walk, and Culver Street have helped make this possible for Colchester. The details of this work are to be found as technical reports in archaeological publications elsewhere (see page 154) but here we present this information in the form of reconstruction paintings by Peter Froste. There are four series of these, one covering the fortress and the town which grew out of it, and three series showing details for the Balkerne Lane, Lion Walk, and Culver Street sites respectively. Each series is drawn from the same viewpoint which, in the case of the fortress and town series, is the same as that of the aerial photograph of the modern town on the previous page. As far as possible the detailed reconstructions (for the three sites) are based on the results of the excavations and represent three-dimensional interpretations of the site plans that can be found in the archaeological reports already referred to.

Much of the evidence which comes from excavation can be very detailed and difficult to describe in a direct, uncluttered way. More to the point the evidence often either contradicts earlier conclusions or fails to provide neat single explanations for any specific problems. In fact the more we dig, the more sophisticated and complicated become our interpretations, and the less confident we feel about the little that we can claim to understand. *City of Victory* is an attempt to summarise how we currently view the history of Britain's first true town. Some will disagree with various aspects of the story and no doubt in time some of it will prove to be wrong. But such is the nature of archaeology.

Top: remains of the Roman theatre uncovered in Maidenburgh Street in 1984. Above: 3rd-century cremation in a pot at the Butt Road cemetery. Below: pots in a 3rd- or 4th-century grave in the former grounds of St John's Abbey, found in 1972.

Right: recording the remains of buildings at Balkerne Lane destroyed during the Boudican revolt.

The sequence of paintings tracing the development through the ages of the town and the three main excavated sites (Balkerne Lane, Culver Street and Lion Walk) are to be found on pages 42-3, 62-3, 98-9, 100-101, 126-7, and 138-9.

STRONGHOLD OF THE BRITISH WAR GOD

Julius Caesar

Practically all our knowledge of the Britons comes either from archaeological sites and finds or from the little that the Romans wrote about them in the surviving histories. Unfortunately the Britons themselves had little use for writing. They had an extensive oral literature which relied on well developed memory skills. They had highly trained bards who were the repositories of Celtic folk-lore, poetry, legends and history. Some of these traditions survived in Wales and Ireland where they were later written down by monks. Ancient Welsh manuscripts compiled in this way may have been used as source material for early medieval writers such as Geoffrey of Monmouth and others. It is here that Shakespeare found the inspiration for his play *Cymbeline*, the name and main character of which is our very own Cunobelin. Historians cannot avoid writing from their own perspective and the Roman (and Greek) writers were no different in having their own agendas. Despite their bias, the information passed to us by the Roman historians has the advantage that their authors were either contemporary with the events and people they described or wrote about them not long afterwards.

Of all the histories, one of the most remarkable is that by Julius Caesar, in which he describes at some length and in some detail his version of his conquest of Gaul. Caesar's history is very relevant here because of the snippets of information he provides about the Britons and, in particular, the Trinovantes, the tribe which occupied the area of Britain around Colchester.

Although Caesar's campaign was a hundred years before Claudius' conquest of Britain, he did land twice on these shores.

The first visit was really a disaster for Caesar. Stiff resistance on landing combined with the subsequent near loss of all their ships because of bad weather meant that the Romans returned to Gaul without any significant penetration of inland Britain. The following year, Caesar returned with more than 800 ships and a bigger army. British resistance united under a war-like king called Cassivellaunus. It is not known what tribe he belonged to but it seems likely that he was Catuvellaunian (in which case he was probably an ancestor of Cunobelin).

Julius Caesar.

This passage (unlike the play generally) does have some correspondence with the accepted history as described by Julius Caesar. Cymbeline is Cunobelin and Cassibelan is Cassivellaunus. Although not necessarily Cunobelin's uncle, Cassivellaunus may be an ancestor. There is however no basis for the tribute being three thousand pounds.

> **Cymbeline.** Now say what would Augustus Caesar with us?
> **Lucius.** When Julius Caesar—whose remembrance yet
>   Lives in men's eyes, and will to ears and tongues
>   Be theme and hearing ever—was in this Britain,
>   And conquer'd it, Cassibelan thine uncle,—
>   Famous in Caesar's praises, no whit less
>   Than in his feats deserving it,—for him
>   And his succession, granted Rome a tribute,
>   Yearly three thousand pounds, which by thee lately
>   Is left untender'd... Shakespeare, *Cymbeline*: III.i

*Celtic face
on bronze coin of
Cunobelin, c AD 10-20.*

The defence of Camulodunum.
*Warriors charging through an
entrance in one of the dykes to
attack the enemy, while their
families watch anxiously from the
top of the dyke rampart.*

A pretext for Caesar's expeditions to Britain seems to have been an alleged murder of a British king by another. During his second expedition, envoys from the Trinovantes (a tribe described by Caesar as 'about the strongest in south-east Britain') appealed to him to protect one of the murdered man's sons called Mandubracius against the apparent culprit, Cassivellaunus, and to send him home as their new king. Earlier Mandubracius had apparently fled to the continent and put himself under the protection of Caesar.

After much fighting, Caesar tracked down Cassivellaunus' stronghold and captured it. Cassivellaunus then sought and accepted terms of surrender which involved the supply of hostages, an annual tribute to Rome, and an undertaking not to molest Mandubracius and the Trinovantes again.

From Caesar we learn that the population of Britain was very large and grouped according to tribes, and that the country was thickly studded with homesteads resembling those of the Gauls. He said that the most 'civilised' people lived in Kent and that the tribes on the coast had originally come to plunder and make war but had since settled permanently, often retaining the names of the tribes from which they originated. Cattle were numerous and, for money, the British used copper and gold coins and iron ingots of fixed weights. Other details are given about the Britons' way of life but there is no way of being certain how generalised or accurate any of them are.

Most interesting is his account of the Britons' highly skilled use of chariots in warfare. Each chariot would convey its warrior to a suitable spot in the battlefield. Here he would jump down and engage the enemy on foot while the chariot was withdrawn to a safe distance until needed further. The Britons practised with their chariots and became so skilful that they could run along the chariot pole, stand on the yoke, and get back into the chariot while the horses were moving at speed. Clearly

10

the Britons used chariots in large numbers—when describing his second British campaign, Caesar claimed that, even after most of the British troops had been disbanded, there were still about four thousand charioteers left. As we shall see, the use of chariots in such numbers helps explain the size and complexity of the earthworks which protected Colchester in the Iron Age and early Roman periods.

Also of relevance to understanding Colchester is Caesar's account of the capture of Cassivellaunus' stronghold. This, says Caesar, was very well fortified by a combination of earthworks and natural features, including forest and marsh. When he arrived with his army, the stronghold was filled with many men and cattle. He attacked the site on two sides but it was so large that many Britons were able to escape out the other sides. Such a description could almost have been applied to Colchester, and it goes some way to showing how the dykes were meant to work. But more of this later.

The Trinovantes

Britain was divided up into tribal areas and Camulodunum lay within the territory of the Trinovantes, the tribe which Caesar had attempted to protect against Cassivellaunus. The generally-accepted picture of Britain just before the Claudian conquest shows the territory of the Trinovantes roughly corresponding to most of modern Essex and southern Suffolk. Maps of this kind are based on the distributions of various coin-types which unfortunately are not properly understood. The maps are unlikely to be precise and probably reflect more accurately administrative areas in the Roman period than the distribution of tribes in the immediate pre-Roman times. Caesar hinted at the presence of many more tribes than are generally reckoned on when he

named five otherwise unknown tribes in his account of his dealings with the Trinovantes. He also named four kings in Kent, which is an area usually thought of as being that of the Cantiaci. It is not much to go on but, if there were indeed many more tribes in Britain than is thought, then the area of the Trinovantes would probably have been much smaller than is generally believed. The Trinovantes must certainly have occupied what is now north-east Essex, because Tacitus (a Roman historian) describes how the Trinovantes lost their land to the Roman settlers at Colchester. However there is no way of knowing how far the tribal territory extended out from Camulodunum.

Like other tribes in Britain, the Trinovantes are likely to have lived in farmsteads and in groupings based on kinship. Excavation of these sites has been limited so that at present it is not known what a typical Trinovantian occupation site looked like. Certainly there is a class of farmstead which consisted of houses (nearly always round) within a sub-rectangular compound formed by at least one defensive bank and ditch. This would have been the main living- and working-area. Beyond the compound would have been the fields and pasture. The latter would have been reached by droveways along which the animals were herded. The droveways were simply unsurfaced tracks formed by two ditches, one to each side, which prevented the animals from wandering off. Although probably too far west of Colchester to have been Trinovantian, a good example of this kind of site was excavated in 1987 at Stansted in north-west Essex. Here, inside a sub-square ditched enclosure, the remains of eleven or so round buildings were found plus a small structure which is interpreted as a shrine.

The comparative rarity of sites of this kind suggests that they were the homes of high status Britons and that most people lived in undefended settlements. A very large example of this kind of site lay at the heart of Camulodunum and

Two late Iron Age pedestal urns from the Lexden cemetery. Found in 1904.

Map of Iron Age Britain indicating tribal territories. Note the neighbouring Trinovantes and Catuvellauni.

Map labels: Caledonii, Vacomagi, Taexali, Venicones, Damnonii, Votadini, Selgovae, Novantae, Brigantes, Parisi, Deceangli, Cornovii, Corieltauvi, Ordovices, Iceni, Demetae, Catuvellauni, Silures, Dobunni, Trinovantes, Atrebates, Dumnonii, Durotriges, Cantiaci

11

Right: the farmstead (trapezoidal in shape) at Gosbecks where Cunobelin lived, as revealed by marks in ripening crops. The square marks in the top right-hand corner of the photograph indicate the site of the possible funerary enclosure (page 27) and the later Roman temple and portico (page 104).

clearly was of the highest rank. Indeed the presence of a large farmstead of just this type explains the origin and nature of Camulodunum. The settlement used to be regarded as a kind of early town. This interpretation was influenced by the findings in the 1930s at the Sheepen site which turns out to have been industrial in character. But the presence of the farmstead makes it clear that Camulodunum was no different to other sites after all, except that it was much larger and had additional defences in the form of dykes.

Inset: a conjectural reconstruction of an Iron Age round-house.

Camulodunum and its dyke system c AD 10 in relation to the countryside, rivers, and sea.

The extent of woodland and the number and distribution of settlements on the map is highly speculative, and is based on aerial photographs of cropmarks, known sites, and heathland and woodland as shown in 18th-century and later maps.

The map shows how poorly placed Camulodunum was to exploit waterborne transport for trade.

The town centre of Colchester today lies immediately east of the Sheepen site, south of the River Colne.

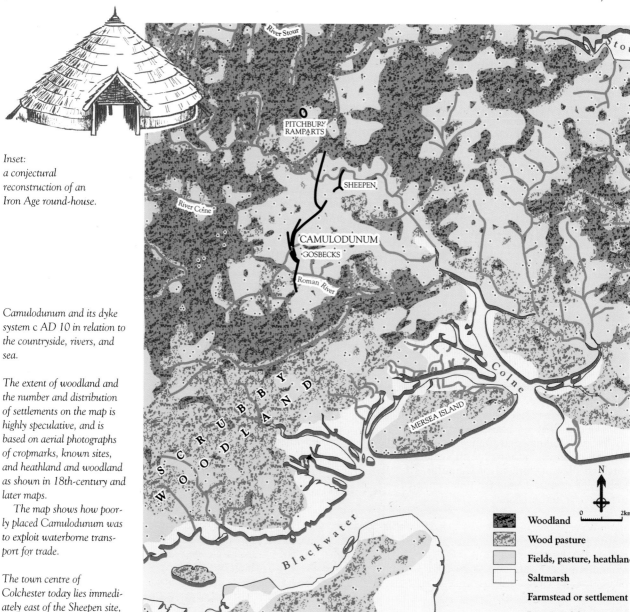

Legend:
- Woodland
- Wood pasture
- Fields, pasture, heathland
- Saltmarsh
- Farmstead or settlement
- Iron Age dyke

Iron Age fortress

Camulodunum in its Iron Age form overlapped with the arrival of the Romans by about two decades. This account covers the history of the settlement up to *c* AD 60 and anticipates some of the events which are described later in the book.

Camulodunum covered an area of around ten square miles, mainly between the valleys of the Colne and the Roman River but with some extension beyond both. It was a flat, rural landscape of pasture and woodland with some groups of cultivated fields, all bound together by sinuous earthen defences known today as 'dykes'. Cattle would probably have been the commonest animal, but sheep, pigs, goat, and deer could have been found in the woodland and in the open pasture and outfields. And in the fields, ditched to exclude grazing animals, there would have been many of the crops familiar to us today such as wheat, barley, oats, peas, and beans. There would have been little clusters of houses and other structures dotted around the area with at least two major concentrations, one at Gosbecks and the other at Sheepen. Many of the habitation sites would have had their own cemeteries, prominent among which would have been the burial mound at Lexden (the Lexden Tumulus). There would have been sacred areas in the form of clearings in the woodland, and ditched fields out in the open. Shallow-draughted boats would have been brought up the Colne to a landing area at Sheepen. The various elements of the settlement would have been linked by networks of ditched droveways which provided routeways for animal and man alike.

Camulodunum takes its name from the earthworks which protected it. They form the largest group of their kind and period in Britain. If placed end to end they would have measured over 12 miles in length. The settlement was known as Camulodunum (its Romanised form), meaning the stronghold or fortified place (*-dunum*) of Camulos, the Celtic god of war. The name thus conveyed power and strength and was appropriate to the scale of its defences.

Each dyke consisted of a V-shaped ditch with a simple bank behind, made from the upcast, constructed in such a way that the inner face of the ditch continued as the outer face of the bank. The dykes varied in size. The largest of them (the Lexden Dyke/Moat Farm Dyke, Kidman's Dyke, Berechurch Dyke and Gryme's Dyke) had ditches which were 13

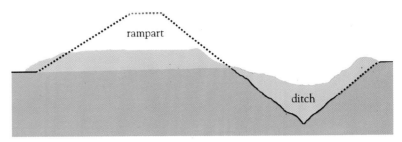

Section through a dyke, based on an excavation of the Lexden Dyke in Bluebottle Grove in 1987.

Below: the Lexden Dyke in 1932: a section through a well-preserved part of the defences of Camulodunum. The man is standing on the front face of the rampart overlooking the ditch in the foreground. This is the first recorded excavation of one of Colchester's ancient dykes.

feet or more deep so that the combined bank and ditch created an unbroken slope measuring 25 feet or so. This would have been an impossible obstacle for chariots and a formidable one for warriors on horseback.

Most of the dykes faced west to provide protection against attack from that direction. Prettygate Dyke had a ditch to either side of its bank, and Triple Dyke consisted of three small dykes side by side. The dykes mostly run transversely valley to valley (north to south) to provide sequential lines of defence, but a few were placed laterally (some U-shaped in section) so that they provided barriers between entrances of some of the transverse dykes. Such variations and oddities were probably designed to control the

movement of chariots, and, to a lesser extent, mounted warriors. At places where the rivers could be crossed easily, the dykes continued beyond the Colne and Roman River presumably to prevent opponents from circumventing the lines of north-south dykes.

Berechurch Dyke is unusual in that it faces eastwards. It is generally regarded as having provided Camulodunum with protection against sea-borne forces, although it was more likely intended as a defence against a land-based assault from the south-east.

There were gaps or entrances in the dykes to allow passage through them. It is uncertain whether or not these entrances contained wooden gates. If not, they were presumably blocked in times of need with fallen trees. There is also some evidence of vertical timber faces on the rampart of part of at least one dyke (the Lexden Dyke), although it is doubtful if such an arrangement was common elsewhere.

The dykes were probably also useful for the management of stock. Coupled with the Colne and the Roman River, the dyke system could have been used to confine large numbers of grazing animals and also give them some protection against theft. Cattle raiding may have been a problem in the late Iron Age just as it was, for example, across the Scottish and Welsh borders at later times in history. However, the arrangement of dykes on the western side of Camulodunum as sequential and consistently west-facing shows clearly that they were intended primarily as defensive structures. Moreover, the addition of new dykes in the Roman period (as we shall see) proves that the dykes were not built as an empty display of wealth and authority but had a real defensive role to play.

The system of dykes was developed piecemeal over a century or so. There does not seem to have been a master plan: each new addition was simply meant as an improvement on what was there already. The sequence can be deduced to an extent from how the dykes lie in relation to one another and in particular from the relationships between them where they intersect. The most informative place is at the south end of the Lexden Dyke where excavations in the 1940s and 1950s showed that this dyke was post-dated by the Prettygate Dyke and pre-dated by the Heath Farm Dyke. The Heath Farm Dyke appears to have been the earliest of the earthworks and Gryme's Dyke the latest.

Simplified plan of the dyke system protecting Camulodunum. Note that some of the dykes were built in early Roman times.

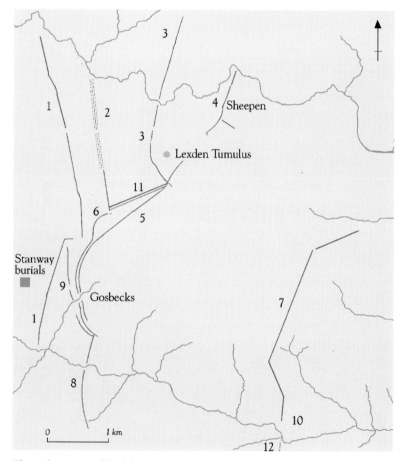

The modern names of the dykes are:

1... *Gryme's Dyke (early Roman)*
2... *Triple Dyke (early Roman)*
3... *Lexden/Moat Farm Dyke*
4... *Sheepen Dyke*
5... *Heath Farm Dyke*

6... *Kidman's Dyke*
7... *Berechurch/Barnhall Dyke*
8... *Oliver's/Layer Dyke*
9... *Gosbecks Dyke*
10... *Layer Dyke*
11... *Prettygate Dyke*
12... *Abberton Dyke.*

It is difficult to say when Camulodunum was founded. The answer to the problem lies at the farmstead at Gosbecks which only excavation will reveal. The name Camulodunum first appears on early coins of Tasciovanus, dated by most numismatists to around 20-15 BC. Thus not only did the settlement exist by then, but it was sufficiently well developed defensively to merit the description of 'fortress'. The earliest archaeological evidence for its existence comes from a cemetery at Lexden. Here, within an area of about 75 m across, around twenty-seven pots have been found from at least ten different graves. The group is fairly consistent in composition, and the absence of a distinctive type of pottery known as 'Gallo-Belgic' suggests that it dates to before c 15 BC, the date of the earliest known occurrence of the name Camulodunum. Clearly the settlement was in existence by around 25 BC, but how much earlier is uncertain and, crucially, there is as yet no way of telling if the settlement was in existence by the mid 1st century BC at the time of Caesar's encroachments into Britain. It would be surprising if it were not, but the evidence is not available to say either way.

Works depot

One feature which Camulodunum did share with later urban communities was some zoning of areas in terms of activity. Gosbecks was primarily agricultural whereas the Sheepen site seems to have been Camulodunum's industrial and commercial base. The latter was carefully positioned by the river to take advantage of waterborne transport and, like Gosbecks, it had its own defences, which here took the form of a single dyke (the Sheepen Dyke). Before the Romans came, it was a manufacturing area under Cunobelin which included his coin-mint. After the conquest, activities intensified and it appears to have been some kind of works depot, possibly undertaking among other things contracts for the army.

Sheepen was excavated in the 1930s with some work in one area following in 1970. Finds were prolific: hundreds of coins and other metal objects, much glass and bone, and tons and tons of broken pottery. A trackway snaked across the site in pre-Roman days and was surfaced with gravel in the Roman manner after the conquest. Workshops lined the road before and after the conquest, and there was plenty of evidence of industrial activities until at least AD 60 when the site was destroyed by fire during the Boudican revolt. Metal-working was easy to detect through the remains of structures such as ovens and hearths and finds such as waste products, crucibles, raw materials, and specialist tools and equipment. Iron-working (smithing but maybe not smelting) and casting in copper-alloys seem to have been widespread. Casting in bronze and brass was carried out on a large scale using either ingots and sheet metal or suitable broken or scrap-metal objects. Some of the products were decorated with enamel. Leather was in great demand, particularly after AD 43 by the Roman army which used large quantities of the material for such things as tents, sails, and horse gear. Cattle bones were the commonest type of bone at Sheepen which, together with what

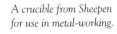

Brass ingot for use in metal-working (90 by 15 cm). Found on the Sheepen site.

A crucible from Sheepen for use in metal-working.

Copper-alloy stamp from Sheepen. Possibly for leather-working. 5 by 6 cm.

Part of the very extensive excavation of the ancient industrial site at Sheepen in the 1930s.

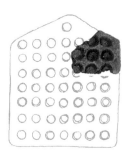

A fragment of coin flan mould found at Sheepen in 1971.

Gosbecks

Below: the farmstead and its field system at Gosbecks (the name 'Gosbecks' is relatively modern).

appears to be a leather-working stamp, suggests that hides were a significant product. Pottery and tile were made on the site. Tools associated with trade and physical labour include smith's tongs, fragments of steelyards and balances, weights, a pair of iron shears, bill hooks, and iron 'shoes' from the ends of wooden spades. Iron shackles are especially evocative, and point to the use of slaves on the site. (Less likely, equipment such as this could have been made here.)

Fragments of broken military equipment were very common. Bits of body armour in the form of studs, belt fittings, and even iron chain mail were plentiful and there were parts of swords, daggers, spears, and shields. Most spectacular of all were the remains of helmets, including a sackful of them which had been dumped in a pit. It was thought at one time that much of this material was being made on the site, and that some of it was even the product of last-minute preparations on the eve of the Boudican assault on the town. However, it is now recognised that the military equipment was most likely scrap metal, brought to the site some time after

AD 43 for re-working.

Of all the metal-working activities on the site, one of the most significant must be the manufacture of Cunobelin's coins. Hundreds of fragments of so-called 'coin moulds' have been recovered, mainly from the southern part of the site. None are complete, but each mould seems to have consisted of a slab of clay with fifty circular moulds for coin blanks. The holes were arranged as seven rows of seven with the fiftieth in the centre of one side. The coin-blanks were cast in the moulds and then struck first on one side and then the other to make the coins. Analyses of Celtic coins have shown that the moneyers were very skilled at controlling the weight and the metallurgical content of the coins. There has been much argument over how the coin-blanks were made. It seems most likely that the metal was not poured into the holes in molten form but was placed there as nuggets or powder after being weighed. It was then heated either in an oven or with the use of a blow-pipe and a charcoal block.

Many things would have been made on the site which have not left tangible traces. For

The Iron Age features in blue: dykes, farmstead, droveways and fields.

Roman features in orange: fort, theatre, temple, portico, and road with adjacent enclosures and streets.

Plan compiled from aerial photographs and limited excavation.

Roman fort

Iron Age dyke

Iron Age dykes

road

pond

temple

road?

farm-stead

theatre

droveway

0   400 metres

example, wood-working in any form is hard to detect, and so are activities linked with the preparation of food.

With the construction of at least four temples, Sheepen seems to have become a sanctuary after the Boudican revolt. The later history of the site has strong echoes of Gosbecks. The location of the site near the river means that commerce as opposed to manufacturing may have been a major activity there, just as it seems to have been at Gosbecks. As at Gosbecks, we can imagine that markets were held regularly at Sheepen with all sorts of agricultural and manufactured goods being on sale, and that the site had been the venue for such markets right from its foundation in Iron Age times.

Cunobelin's farm

The excavations at Sheepen in the 1930s were spectacular and produced finds on a scale and of a quality not expected. The coin moulds in particular proved influential in the site being identified with Cunobelin. It was thought that he founded the site and made it the centre of his 'capital'. However as the

years have passed, the importance of Gosbecks in relation to Camulodunum as a whole has become more and more apparent, and it is now clear that the key to understanding the nature and development of the settlement lies at Gosbecks rather than at Sheepen. Major Roman features (the theatre, temple and portico, and the road to the Roman town) were recognised at Gosbecks and partly investigated between the 1930s and the early 1950s. But it was the dry summers of the mid 1970s which provided cropmarks with a clarity not seen before. And it was these cropmarks which enabled the buried archaeological features to be more thoroughly mapped and consequently better understood than was previously possible.

The cropmarks show that the focal point of the site was a native farmstead of a type which has been recognised elsewhere in Essex and beyond but is here exceptionally large. The farmstead was of the sort already described above for Stansted. It took the form of a trapezoidal-shaped area which was defended by a deep ditch and bank. Inside there would have been round-houses in

Two sides of a gold coin of Cunobelin (about one and two-thirds actual size). One side shows an ear of barley and CAM for Camulodunum. The other shows a horse and CUN for Cunobelin.

Impression of Cunobelin's farmstead at Gosbecks in c AD 40. The picture shows round-houses, and droveways leading to fields. Viewed from the north-west.

Iron Age 'fire dogs' with stylised bulls' heads. From Mount Bures, near Colchester. Used for cooking over an open fire.

which Cunobelin and his family lived, with other buildings (maybe including some square or rectangular in shape) being used for the farm. The compound was connected in the south-west corner to a network of droveways and fields. The fact that the network led to the compound suggests that animals were kept inside it. They would have been driven down the droveways, past all the small fields around the compound, and out to large areas of pasture beyond.

Size alone does not distinguish the Gosbecks farmstead from other examples. The farmstead and its areas of fields and pasture were also protected by dykes. These substantial earthworks underline the high status of Camulodunum. Moreover they show that the whole operation was profitable enough to allow the investment of what must have been thousands of man-hours in producing something which did not yield a tangible return in terms of consumable or marketable goods.

The earliest of these earthworks was the Heath Farm Dyke. This was fairly modest in size, being only around 3 m (10 ft) from the bottom of the ditch to the top of the bank. However, it was over two miles long, so what it lacked in size it made up for in length. The dyke protected the Gosbecks settlement in an arc following the east side of a little valley which provided the site with its all-important water-supply. Later, the defences were improved with the provision of three more dykes (Kidman's Dyke, Gosbecks Dyke, and Gryme's Dyke), the last of which we shall see being apparently of Roman date.

But Gosbecks must have been more than a large farmstead. We can only speculate what other activities took place there, although, as we shall see, the major Roman structures on the site indicate what is likely to have happened there in pre-Roman times. For the time being, we can note that Gosbecks was probably a major place of assembly with important administrative, commercial, and religious functions for the region before and after the Roman conquest. Markets and fairs were probably held here and it may have been a meeting place where important matters affecting the Catuvellauni and presumably the Trinovantes were debated by senior men of both tribes.

Hillfort

Rather absurdly, Pitchbury is classed as a hillfort despite not being on a hill. It is so-called because, like the hundreds of hillforts which sit on the tops of many of the highest peaks in the hilly parts of the country, it was completely enclosed by its defences. However, being in north-east Essex, the absence of any decent hills means that instead it had to be built overlooking the side of a valley. The dykes of Camulodunum worked differently and were more suited to a less profiled landscape. They blocked rather than encircled, and thus provided cross-country barriers which were intended to complement and bring out the defensive potential of the natural topography.

Pitchbury lies to the north-west of Camulodunum and appears to predate it. The hillfort is oval shaped and is around 5 acres in size. At first it was protected by a single large ditch and bank, similar in

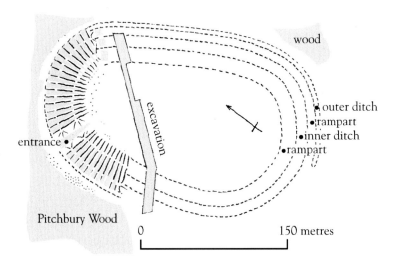

wood

excavation

outer ditch
rampart
inner ditch
rampart

entrance

Pitchbury Wood

0   150 metres

Plan of ramparts of Pitchbury hillfort, showing the site of the 1973 excavation.

proportions to the largest of the Colchester dykes, but this was later supplemented by the addition of a smaller bank and ditch around part of its circuit. It is not clear when Pitchbury was built but, from the little dating and other evidence that exists, a date in the 1st century BC seems to be the most likely.

Despite two excavations (one in 1933 and another in 1973), the hillfort remains a puzzle. On neither occasion was much evidence found to indicate occupation on any scale. The interior has been continually ploughed for many years, and no doubt much of the evidence for occupation has been lost as a result. Nevertheless, finds were very limited which would not have been the case had people lived there in any numbers for substantial lengths of time. Unlike Pitchbury, many true hillforts contain the remains of large numbers of houses and were extensively occupied. Perhaps Pitchbury was built simply as a place of refuge in times of need. Certainly, being on comparatively flat land, it would have been easy to move large numbers of people and animals into it quickly. It may also have been used seasonally.

As regards finds from the hillfort, perhaps the most interesting is a fine flint knife discovered in 1973. Ironically, this is not a late Iron Age object but was lost in the Neolithic period about two thousand years before the hillfort was built.

Kings and tribal conflict

Coins are a rich source of information about the history of Camulodunum. The first coinage in Britain came from Gaul; it was gold and in circulation by around the end of the 2nd century BC. The earliest coinage made in Britain was of cast bronze and appeared around 100 BC. The first British gold coinage appeared around 70 BC with the first of the so-called 'dynastic' coinage appearing just after the middle of the same century. These coins are particularly informative, since they usually bear the names of the kings who issued them and sometimes the name of the place where they were struck. The names are abbreviated and, intriguingly, in Latin (and exceptionally Greek) lettering. The coinage betrays the hand of skilled moneyers since weight and metallurgical composition, although showing gradual debasement with time, was controlled with great precision. Numismatists have studied the development of the designs of the coinage and, with the help of the changes in weight and composition, have been able to sequence and date it.

The names, mints, dates, and distributions of the coins, supplemented by evidence from written and other sources, have been used to construct a political history of the period in terms of kings and their dynasties. In the case of Camulodunum, the result is more complicated than for any other British site. Moreover attempts have been made to elaborate this history by linking various of the supposed changes of rulers at Camulodunum with physical developments there such as the building of dykes, burials, and so on. The results of the exercise, or at least the dynastic elements of it, have been widely accepted although, as we shall see, there are aspects of the story which are hard to believe.

Central to the conventional view of the

Gold coin (a Whaddon Chase type), which may be an issue of Cassivellaunus.

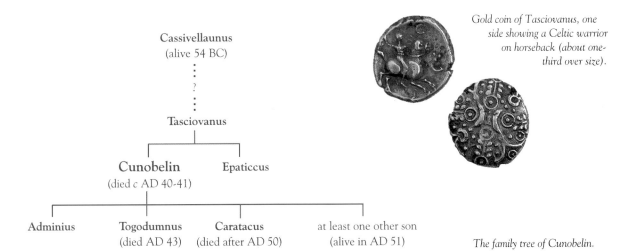

Cassivellaunus
(alive 54 BC)

⋮
?
⋮

Tasciovanus

Cunobelin   Epaticcus
(died c AD 40-41)

Adminius   Togodumnus   Caratacus   at least one other son
           (died AD 43)   (died after AD 50)   (alive in AD 51)

The family tree of Cunobelin.

Gold coin of Tasciovanus, one side showing a Celtic warrior on horseback (about one-third over size).

history of Camulodunum is that it was held by a sequence of kings, each of whom in turn drove out his predecessor. The dykes are seen as a physical expression of a violent and turbulent past which was bound up with rivalry between the Trinovantes and their neighbours (or at least their presumed neighbours), the Catuvellauni. The Catuvellauni seem to have been a warlike tribe occupying a territory centred around what is now the St Albans area and apparently corresponding (very roughly) to what is now Hertfordshire. It is possible that Cassivellaunus, the man credited by Caesar as leading the British opposition to his second expedition into Britain, was in fact Catuvellaunian. If so, rivalry between the two tribes must have extended back to at least the mid 1st century BC when Cassivellaunus was accused of killing the king of the Trinovantes and father of his presumed successor, Mandubracius. There is however no convincing evidence that Cassivellaunus really was Catuvellaunian, although Caesar's description of the location of his territory makes it sound as if he was.

Depending on which numismatist's chronology you accept, the practice of putting personal names on coins started around 15 to 25 years after the episode mentioned by Caesar involving Mandubracius and Cassivellaunus.

The first king to do this was Addedomaros. He is believed to have been Trinovantian. He never included the name of the mint on his coins but their distribution is thought to centre around the Colne valley, suggesting that his base was at Camulodunum. The first person to put the mint name on his coins was a Catuvellaunian called Tasciovanus who struck almost all of his coins at Verulamium (St Albans). However, most significantly, Tasciovanus issued a few coins mint-marked as Camulodunum early in his reign. These coins are taken to suggest that he held the place for a short period and that he drove the Trinovantes out of Camulodunum. Unfortunately at this point the story becomes more complicated because there is some disagreement among numismatists about dates and who followed whom. One interpretation is that Addedomaros' later coins overlapped those of Tasciovanus and therefore he must have regained control. Another view is that he predated Tasciovanus altogether. Either way, they were succeeded by a king called Dubnovellaunus who, again depending on the numismatist concerned, was either Trinovantian (and thus referred to as 'Dubnovellaunus-in-Essex') or was the king of that name who had expanded northwards from his existing territory in Kent where he issued coins. Finally, around AD 5, Cunobelin produced the first of his coins, which, from the beginning, he mint-marked as Camulodunum. Importantly, on a few of his coin-types, he stated that he was 'TASC FIL' (or variations of this) meaning 'son of Tasciovanus'. Only Cunobelin and Tasciovanus put the name Camulodunum on their coins, there being no names of mints on the others. And only Cunobelin used 'FIL' (from the Latin *filius*) on the Camulodunum coins to indicate his ancestry.

It is hard to accept the idea inherent in this interpretation that Camulodunum was continually changing hands as a result of warfare. Camulodunum was essentially a large farm with substantial industrial and commercial elements, all of which would have needed careful and skilful management. Capture Camulodunum and you presumably captured something which was not only prestigious but also an agricultural and commercial asset. The population of Camulodunum was probably not very large since its inhabitants are likely to have been dependent on the king in some way or other. They probably consisted mainly of members of Cunobelin's

Map showing the distribution of coins of Cunobelin and his brother Epaticcus.

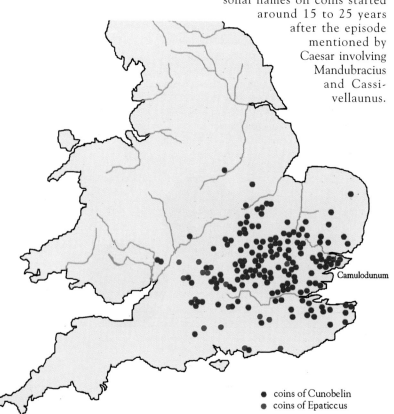

Camulodunum

● coins of Cunobelin
● coins of Epaticcus

extended family, mercenaries, agricultural workers and craftsmen of various sorts including of course moneyers. If each king had driven out his predecessor, then presumably the existing population would have been lost each time and the incomer would have been faced with the problem of how to build up from scratch what must have been a complicated and demanding operation.

This argument suggests that we should try to explain the history of Camulodunum in ways which involve fewer radical changes of ownership. Yet although, as we have already seen from Tacitus, Camulodunum was undoubtedly in Trinovantian territory, we can hardly doubt that Cunobelin and his father, Tasciovanus, were Catuvellaunian since two of Cunobelin's sons, Caratacus and Togodumnus, were thus described by the Greek historian Cassius Dio. How then can we explain the fact that Camulodunum, despite being in Trinovantian territory, had clearly been in Catuvellaunian hands?

One explanation is that Camulodunum was a Catuvellaunian settlement from the beginning, founded by a land-locked tribe anxious to gain a coastal trading post. Its extensive defences suggest that its presence was an unwelcome intrusion into somebody else's territory. The fact that different series of coins were being struck in parallel at Camulodunum and at Verulamium by different rulers need not rule out both being Catuvellaunian. Similar situations certainly occurred elsewhere. Cunobelin's brother, Epaticcus, issued coins in the Berkshire region early on in Cunobelin's reign and Adminius, one of Cunobelin's sons, did the same in Kent towards the end of his father's life. However such a situation would mean that Dubnovellaunus-in-Essex and Addedomaros were also both Catuvellaunian, if indeed both had struck coins in Camulodunum as is generally believed.

It is mostly speculation of course, but if Camulodunum was indeed a Catuvellaunian colony, then it seems very unlikely that it was an isolated settlement. There would presumably have been other smaller 'satellite' settlements in the surrounding area with the effect that a substantial tract of land would have been colonised. Below we shall see how land around Camulodunum was later acquired by the Roman settlers at the expense of the Trinovantes. It is not known how far the area of settlement extended out from Camulodunum, but it might have been anything up to 10 miles or so judging by similar arrangements abroad. Clearly any early Catuvellaunian acquisition of land from the Trinovantes could not have been that extensive if what remained was still sufficient to be termed Trinovantian so close to the later Roman town. The Catuvellaunian enclave, if it really existed, would thus appear to have been comparatively small.

Nevertheless, the explanation that Camulodunum was, and always was, a Catuvellaunian colony is an attractive one, especially if, as is possible, Cassivellaunus was Catuvellaunian too. One implication of the murder of Mandubracius' father as described by Caesar is that his place as king was taken, if not by Cassivellaunus himself, then at least by one of his supporters. Caesar does not mention Camulodunum and gives no hint as to where Mandubracius or his father lived. We may wonder therefore if Camulodunum lay at the root of these problems and was in effect a 'cuckoo in the nest'. In other words, Camulodunum was a Catuvellaunian plantation of c 50 BC into Trinovantian territory. Mandubracius and his father lived elsewhere.

Despite everything, Cunobelin remains a shadowy figure about whom little is known, especially when compared to someone like Claudius. We know that Cunobelin belonged to the Catuvellauni tribe. We also know that his father was Tasciovanus and that he had at least four sons (Caratacus, Togodumnus, Adminius, and at least one other). He must have been a very wealthy man since it has been estimated that he struck around a million gold coins. A Roman writer (Suetonius) described Cunobelin as 'King of the Britons'. Clearly he was a very powerful figure who achieved some kind of control and supremacy over the warring tribes of south-east England—so much so that his death was a trigger for fresh inter-tribal conflict which was to provide both an excuse and an opportunity for the Roman invasion itself. Otherwise that is all that we know. We have no idea what he looked like or how long he lived. We know nothing of the women in his life and we know little of his achievements or what he was like as a person. It is in Camulodunum that we come closest to him. Yet, ironically, few—perhaps even none—of the dykes at Camulodunum were his doing. With one or two possible exceptions such as the Sheepen Dyke, those dykes that he did not inherit seem to have been made under the Romans after his death.

Gold coin of Dubnovellaunus (above) and gold coin of Addedomaros (below) (about one-third over size).

21

The simplest of the Iron Age burials at Camulodunum consists of a pot containing a dead person's cremated remains. The pot would be buried in a small pit and there was no mound or chamber. Burials like these are most common in the Lexden area (page 11), although examples have been found elsewhere in the settlement. Sometimes the burial included more than one vessel. The Lexden 'mirror' grave is exceptional in that it consisted of six pottery vessels, a bronze cup, a bronze pin and a hand mirror. It was found not far from the Lexden Tumulus in 1904.

Below are the fragments of the Iron Age mirror from the Lexden 'mirror' grave. The mirror is made of copper alloy and the reflective surface was achieved by polishing. The reconstruction shows the decorated back plate.

Burial places fit for kings

We are beginning to see in Colchester evidence for a remarkable series of aristocratic burials not recognised anywhere else in Britain. They find their closest parallels in rich chambered tombs which have been discovered abroad, in north-west Europe, and they confirm the high status of people who lived in Camulodunum two thousand years ago. The picture at Colchester is still not clear but there are three important sites which, although different to each other in many important respects, are likely to prove to be broadly the same in character. They are the Lexden Tumulus, the funerary site at Stanway, and a ditched enclosure on the site of the Roman temple at Gosbecks. These seem to be the burial places of kings and their relatives. We will examine each of the sites in turn.

The **Lexden Tumulus** clearly indicates the importance of Camulodunum in the late 1st century BC. Excavation of the mound in 1924 uncovered the remains of a most remarkable burial group. Many of the objects appeared to have been ritually broken at the time of burial, with only a small proportion of the pieces being buried. This is a pity because, if the group had been complete, the burial would be one of the great treasures of British archaeology. Even so, the quality and variety of the objects together with their manner of burial show that the tumulus must have been the resting place of someone of considerable wealth and importance. The person cannot be identified but, for what it is worth, the date seems to fit Addedomaros, who, as we have just seen, was one of the British kings at Camulodunum.

The mound is around 70 feet in diameter and stands to a height of around five feet. Originally it must have been higher and more clearly defined on the ground than it is now. The excavators thought that the mound had been surrounded by a shallow ditch but, as a result of a small excavation in 1973, there is some doubt over whether this ditch existed. The mound was thrown up over a large oval-shaped pit which contained the remains of a wide range of expensive personal and domestic objects. The deceased had been cremated and the remains placed in small heaps over the western half of the pit floor. Like the bones, most of the objects were carefully placed on the floor of the pit although some ended up in its backfill. The distribution of the objects on the pit floor suggests that they had been inside a large wooden burial chamber which has completely decayed.

The collection of objects is quite extraordinary. Cast figurines were rare in Britain before the Roman conquest but there were many examples of these items in the tumulus. There are little copper-alloy figurines of a cupid, a boar, a bull, and a griffin, all of which may have been parts of larger pieces. The lower part of the griffin is curved, suggesting that it was part of a vessel such as a large flagon. All that remains of a metal bowl are two copper-alloy fittings in the form of vine leaves, which were used to fix on loop handles. A small copper-alloy pedestal probably served as a stand for a figurine. The latter must be missing because none of the existing figurines would have fitted it. The most impressive objects include chain mail and a leather jerkin. The chain mail was made of thousands of interlinked iron rings, each about 5 mm across. It was fitted with silver studs and copper-alloy buckles and hinges. The jerkin was presumably worn under the chain mail to protect the skin. In addition, there must have been at least one exotic garment of textile or leather. It (or they) included silver trefoil-shaped ornaments and embroidery with gold tissue. A tantalising find was a copper-alloy foot, which seems to have been one of the feet of a stool or other piece of furniture. Some fragments of iron rods may have come from the same folding-stool. This would have been a significant object since the stool was a symbol of authority. There was also a drop-handle and decorative copper-alloy sheeting inlaid with roundels of red glass. These items must been belonged to a casket or chest. Other decorative fittings include large cup-shaped studs and some slender pins with heads inlaid with red glass. These may have been parts of furniture, such as a stool. Many of the objects are even more difficult to identify, particularly the iron objects of which there is quite a range. Of particular note is a copper-alloy axehead which must have been some sort of cult object. Its presence in the grave is remarkable since the axehead is Middle Bronze Age in date and thus was already over 1,000 years old when buried. Moreover it had been mutilated (presumably ritually 'killed') with a large gouge down the length of one side, and it had been wrapped in cloth.

The group seems to have originally included at least 17 amphoras. It is not known if any of the vessels had been placed intact in the grave since the fragments were in a part of the grave which had been disturbed in antiquity. The purpose of this intrusion is unclear but it may have led to the vessels being broken up, if they were not so already.

Of all the objects in the grave, the most significant is the silver medallion. It was made by cutting out the head of Augustus from a cast copy of a Roman coin. The medallion is important on two counts. Firstly it tells us something about the date of the grave. The coin was struck between 18 and 16 BC which means that the grave cannot predate that date. Secondly the presence of an effigy of a Roman emperor itself is of great significance. The dead person and whoever buried him would undoubtedly have known who was shown on the coin. This indicates not only that the people involved were not anti-Roman, but even that they were well disposed towards them.

It was the Trinovantes rather than the Catuvellauni who were protected by the Romans by treaty at the time of Julius Caesar. Thus the presence of a medallion showing the head of a Roman emperor might

be a reason to suppose that the Lexden Tumulus was the burial place of a member of the Trinovantes, and that therefore Camulodunum could not have been simply a Catuvellaunian colony as suggested above. However relationships with the Romans were not so clear cut. Augustus himself recorded in a document, substantially completed by AD 7 and known as 'Res Gestae', how two British kings had fled to him for help. One of the men was called Dubnovellaunus. He was probably the same Dubnovellaunus who was king at Camulodunum, possibly in succession to whoever had been buried in the Lexden Tumulus. Moreover an appeal to the Roman emperor Caligula by Adminius, son of Cunobelin, shows that (albeit fifty or so years later) a member of the Catuvellauni could come to rely on Roman patronage.

At **Stanway**, not far west of Gosbecks, there lay a remarkable burial site which involved four large wooden mortuary chambers and the ritual breaking of objects as at the Lexden Tumulus. The burials date from the late 1st century BC to c AD 60—in other words they belong to the period when the native stronghold of Camulodunum was at its most important, and they overlapped the arrival of the Romans by two decades or so.

Each chamber had been placed symmetrically in a large enclosure which was up to 80 m across and demarcated by a ditch. There is some evidence that each chamber was covered by an earth mound, like the Lexden Tumulus. In all, there were five

The silver medallion from the Lexden Tumulus. 25 mm in diameter.

The excavation of the Lexden Tumulus in 1924. Much of the early work was done by tunnelling into the mound (behind the two trees).

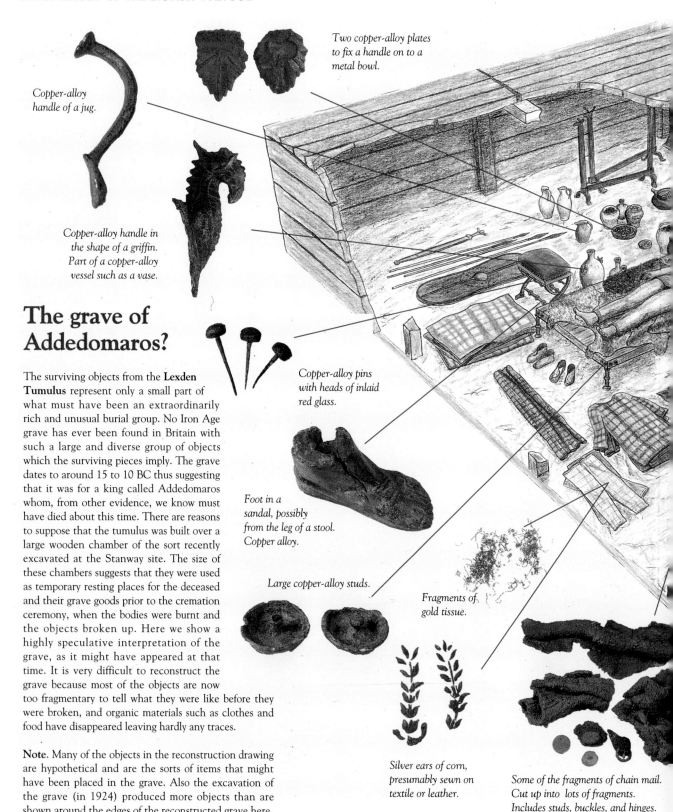

Copper-alloy handle of a jug.

Two copper-alloy plates to fix a handle on to a metal bowl.

Copper-alloy handle in the shape of a griffin. Part of a copper-alloy vessel such as a vase.

The grave of Addedomaros?

The surviving objects from the **Lexden Tumulus** represent only a small part of what must have been an extraordinarily rich and unusual burial group. No Iron Age grave has ever been found in Britain with such a large and diverse group of objects which the surviving pieces imply. The grave dates to around 15 to 10 BC thus suggesting that it was for a king called Addedomaros whom, from other evidence, we know must have died about this time. There are reasons to suppose that the tumulus was built over a large wooden chamber of the sort recently excavated at the Stanway site. The size of these chambers suggests that they were used as temporary resting places for the deceased and their grave goods prior to the cremation ceremony, when the bodies were burnt and the objects broken up. Here we show a highly speculative interpretation of the grave, as it might have appeared at that time. It is very difficult to reconstruct the grave because most of the objects are now too fragmentary to tell what they were like before they were broken, and organic materials such as clothes and food have disappeared leaving hardly any traces.

Note. Many of the objects in the reconstruction drawing are hypothetical and are the sorts of items that might have been placed in the grave. Also the excavation of the grave (in 1924) produced more objects than are shown around the edges of the reconstructed grave here.

Copper-alloy pins with heads of inlaid red glass.

Foot in a sandal, possibly from the leg of a stool. Copper alloy.

Large copper-alloy studs.

Fragments of gold tissue.

Silver ears of corn, presumably sewn on textile or leather.

Some of the fragments of chain mail. Cut up into lots of fragments. Includes studs, buckles, and hinges.

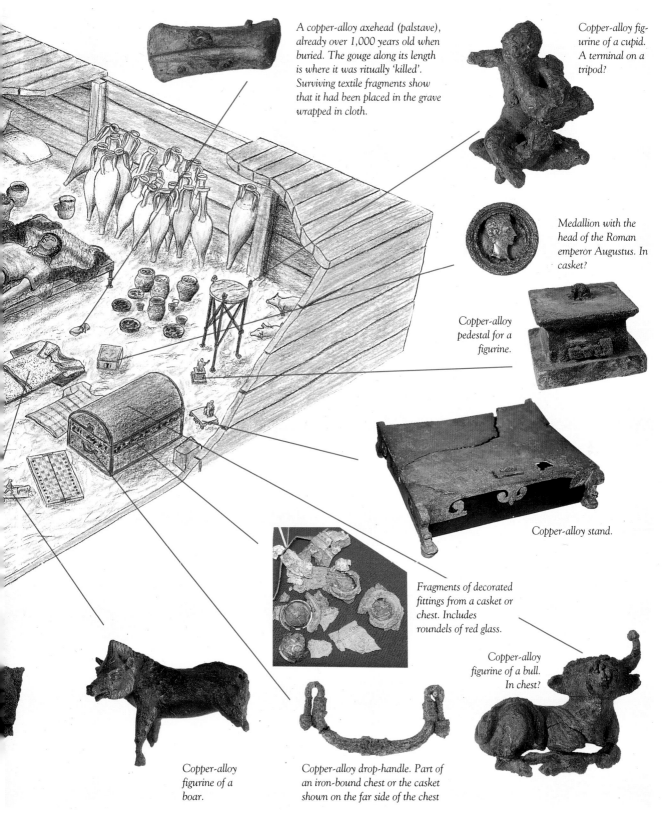

A copper-alloy axehead (palstave), already over 1,000 years old when buried. The gouge along its length is where it was ritually 'killed'. Surviving textile fragments show that it had been placed in the grave wrapped in cloth.

Copper-alloy figurine of a cupid. A terminal on a tripod?

Medallion with the head of the Roman emperor Augustus. In casket?

Copper-alloy pedestal for a figurine.

Copper-alloy stand.

Fragments of decorated fittings from a casket or chest. Includes roundels of red glass.

Copper-alloy figurine of a bull. In chest?

Copper-alloy figurine of a boar.

Copper-alloy drop-handle. Part of an iron-bound chest or the casket shown on the far side of the chest

enclosures laid out as two rows, one of three and the other of two. The smallest of the enclosures seems to have been the earliest and was the nucleus of a small farmstead, to which the funerary enclosures were later added one by one. Each of the four funerary enclosures had an entrance in the centre of the east side, presumably to face the rising sun. The chambers were large enough to accommodate a body laid out on a couch or bed and surrounded by many of the deceased person's worldly possessions. The bodies and their grave goods may have been kept in their respective chambers until the cremation ceremony, when it seems that all the objects and perhaps also the chamber were ritually destroyed.

Unfortunately only a small proportion of the objects found their way into the back-filled remains of the chambers, and there is no way of telling how representative they are

Impression of the Stanway burial site in c AD 60, in the Iron Age landscape. Viewed from the north-east.

of the original collection. Two of the graves contained the remains of a table service (drinking vessels and plates in pottery), and one of them included parts of a broken necklace showing that the dead person had been female. It is doubtful if any of these graves were the burial places of a king or queen. But undoubtedly this was such an unusual method of burial that the people concerned are likely to have been related to Cunobelin in some way. The largest of the chambers dates to around AD 25 so it is probable that Cunobelin himself was present at the ceremony. The owner of the necklace died around AD 60 and could conceivably have been his niece, daughter, or even his wife.

The breaking of the grave goods is reminiscent of the Lexden Tumulus although the broken remnants in the Stanway graves are more mixed up. As at the Lexden Tumulus, the evidence points strongly to the objects

being broken as part of the burial ritual.

A small number of other people were buried in and around the otherwise empty enclosures. These secondary burials did not involve ritual breaking so the grave goods are much better preserved because they are more or less intact. Two of these graves are particularly impressive. The 'warrior' grave is notable for a spear and possible shield, and the 'game' grave for the remains of an extraordinary wooden gaming board complete with pieces set out as if the game was just starting. Some of these graves (including the two just mentioned) post-date the arrival of the Romans and consequently are of considerable interest for what they imply about the relationships between at least one branch of the British nobility and their newly-arrived Roman overlords. There is also some remarkable evidence that the secondary burials were of people who had been high-ranking aides rather than relatives of the persons for whom the chambers had been constructed. We shall return to both these matters in due course (page 67).

The third site is the most enigmatic yet is of great interest because it could be where the great Cunobelin himself was buried. As we shall see later (page 104), the temple at **Gosbecks** was built in Roman times inside a great square ditched enclosure. Like the Stanway enclosures, it had an entrance in the centre of the east side. The ditch was very substantial (11 feet deep), perhaps befitting Cunobelin and, at least in the Roman period, it had no bank. There is no direct evidence to suggest that this was a Stanway-type funerary enclosure but it clearly has much in common with a site in St Albans which is the only other high status burial site of this kind known in Britain outside Colchester. Here the remains of a substantial wooden mortuary chamber lay inside a large rectangular enclosure. The grave goods were very rich and included a chain mail (like the Lexden Tumulus), but they had been broken up and dispersed at the time of the cremation. Later a temple of the same type as that at Gosbecks had been built in one corner of the enclosure. The similarity between Gosbecks and

Glass beads from a necklace. Found in the burial chamber in Enclosure 4 at the Stanway site.

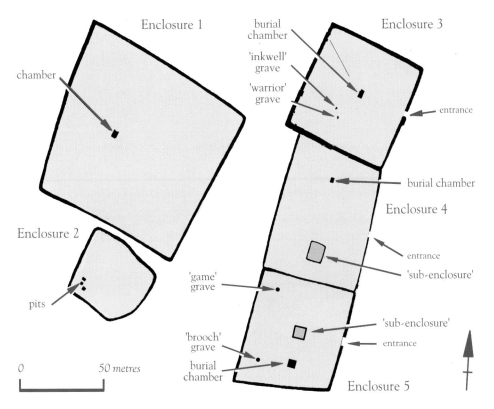

Plan of the burial enclosures at Stanway, near Gosbecks.

Enclosure 3 was excavated in 1992 and Enclosure 5 in August/September 1996.

the St Albans site and the proximity of the Gosbecks enclosure to the farmstead where Cunobelin is likely to have lived suggest very strongly that the square ditched enclosure does indeed indicate the site of his burial place.

Taken together, these three sites in Camulodunum underline the special nature of Colchester in the years leading up to the Roman invasion. The kings at Camulodunum are among the earliest Britons for whom names survive. They belong to that difficult period where prehistory shades into history, which is one reason why the archaeological remains at Colchester are as important as they are.

Copper-alloy pedestal base from the backfilled remains of the chamber in Enclosure 3. This is an unusual object from an Iron Age burial, and it is reminiscent of the finds in the Lexden Tumulus.

Excavation in 1992 of the chamber in Enclosure 3 at the Stanway site. One half of the backfill has been removed to expose the remains of the timbers which formed the top of the chamber.

THE
ROMAN INVASION

Claudius

Claudius has a special association with Colchester. The only time he left Italy after becoming emperor was in effect to travel to Camulodunum. The round trip took six months and he could only have stayed a few days here, but Camulodunum was his destination where he turned and returned home after having led his army into the conquered British settlement. The foundation of the Roman town at Camulodunum would also have been done with his express authority, and the place would have included his name in its official title. Moreover it was also centre of the cult of Claudius in Britain, if not in his lifetime, then immediately afterwards. The focal point of the cult was the great Temple of Claudius which was built in the eastern part of the town and where he was worshipped as a god.

Compared to Cunobelin, there is a great wealth of information about Claudius. He was born Tiberius Claudius Drusus Nero Germanicus in Lugdunum, now Lyon in France, in 10 BC. Ancient historians ridiculed Claudius and called him ignorant and malicious, but modern scholars tend to regard him as shrewd and able. He was disabled in some way, perhaps as a result of cerebral palsy. His head and hands shook slightly. He dragged his right foot from a weakness that may also have affected his right hand. His mother is said to have referred to him as being 'a monstrosity of a human being, one that Nature began and never finished'. His voice was cracked and barely intelligible, and when he was angry, he supposedly would snarl and slobber and his nose would run. But he was not mentally backward. On the contrary he was able to write a history which was apparently good enough for Tacitus to make use of as source material a few decades later. The family seems to have shielded him from public attention and never saw him as a potential emperor.

In AD 41, he succeeded his nephew Caligula (Gaius) who, as an insane and vicious tyrant, was murdered by officers of his own guard. Claudius was found hiding in the palace and his guards proclaimed him emperor.

Claudius turned out to be one of Rome's best rulers who was an able administrator in civil and military affairs. Mauretania (now Morocco and western Algeria), Judaea (now Israel), and Thrace (now part of Greece) were all made Roman provinces under Claudius and, of course, a successful start was made on the conquest of Britain. He is famous for giving the people of Rome 'water and winter bread' (from *I, Claudius* by Robert Graves). There were about one and a half million people in the city whose welfare in part depended on importing grain (hence the reference to bread) and pure water. The grain mainly came from Egypt, and to facilitate its importation Claudius had a new harbour built at Ostia which was the port for Rome. The

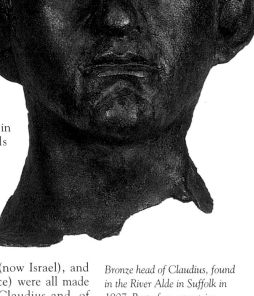

Bronze head of Claudius, found in the River Alde in Suffolk in 1907. Part of an equestrian statue.

work included new granaries and the establishment of a force of 500 men to protect them. He dramatically improved the city's water supply, mainly by completing two aqueducts (totalling 94 km in length) and providing them with a set of lavish basins in the city. As a result, all seven hills of Rome were supplied with clean water and the system as a whole was said to be the most remarkable of its kind in the world.

Another of Claudius' great building projects was also aimed at reducing food shortages. The Fucine was the largest lake in central Italy. It had no visible outlet and was liable to fluctuate in height suddenly and flood the countryside. The idea was to drain the lake into a nearby river, and thereby not only stop the flooding, but also provide 600 square km of new farmland comparatively close to Rome. The water from the lake was to flow down a man-made channel which was over 5 km long and passed under a mountain. The project took eleven years to finish and, reputedly, a workforce of 30,000 men, although a modern estimate reduces the latter by a factor of ten. The tunnel was opened in AD 51 but it never really worked.

Claudius had four wives, the last being his own niece, Agrippina the Younger (great-granddaughter of the emperor Augustus). Apparently he was poisoned in AD 54, presumably by Agrippina, thus paving the way for Nero, her son by an earlier marriage, to become emperor in his stead.

Caligula's aborted invasion

Claudius' invasion in AD 43 marked the end of a period almost a century long during which the Romans had not attempted an invasion of Britain. Claudius' grandfather, Augustus, had considered such a venture on three different occasions between 34 and 26 BC but for various reasons preparations were abandoned. The idea was resurrected by Caligula who had succeeded his grand-uncle Tiberius as emperor in AD 37. In AD 40 or 41, Cunobelin exiled his son Adminius who, to judge by the distribution of his coins, was based in the Kent area. Adminius fled to the Continent with a small band of followers and submitted to Caligula in the hope of his help. He is said to have persuaded the emperor that the time was ripe for an invasion of Britain, although something of the sort may already have been in Caligula's mind. In any event, troops were assembled on the beach at Boulogne. Caligula gave

the signal for battle and then suddenly ordered his troops to fill their helmets and tunics with sea shells because they were spoils of war. Later at Boulogne he built a lighthouse (which survived until AD 1544), supposedly as a memorial to the event. It is hard to judge what really happened because of the way the episode was mocked by ancient historians. However, the Claudian invasion in Britain was a huge undertaking which needed much advance planning and preparation. If nothing else, Caligula's activities provided at the very least a modest dress rehearsal for its initial stage. It probably set in motion various preliminary steps for the movement of troops and supplies that Claudius would mobilise two years later in his expedition to Britain.

The invasion under Claudius

The loyalty of the senate and army was dubious and Claudius, as a new emperor, was very insecure. Within a year or so of his promotion, there was an attempted coup by the governor of Dalmatia which found substantial support among members of the senate. Clearly Claudius needed a military conquest to establish his credibility, and the time seemed right for just such a venture in Britain. Cunobelin's death between AD 40 and 43 seems to have triggered off yet more inter-tribal troubles which resulted in yet another important fugitive seeking help from Rome. This time it was Verica, king of the Atrebates, who appears to have been driven out by Caratacus (a son of Cunobelin).

Just as Adminius had been operating a few years before in what is now Kent, Caratacus seems to have been based in what is now the Berkshire region, the area immediately to the east of Atrebatian territory. Caratacus and his brother Togodumnus were clearly in aggressive mood since, according to Cassius Dio, they had already managed to subjugate a section of the Dobunni tribe who were to the north and west of the Atrebates. The time for invasion seemed right since the internal feuding would weaken and divide the opposition. Moreover, if the invasion were delayed, there was the danger that the brothers would weld together an enlarged kingdom which could offer even stronger resistance to Roman expansionist ambitions than they could expect now.

The invasion army assembled presumably at Boulogne (Gesoriacum) under its commander Aulus Plautius, and seems to have

Bronze bust presumed to be of the emperor Caligula. Found in Colchester in the 19th century.

consisted of around 40,000 soldiers. There were four legions, each of about 5,000 men. They were the II Augusta and XIV Gemina and probably the IX Hispana and XX. The legions were infantry troops containing substantial numbers of Italian-born soldiers. They were accompanied by about the same number of auxiliary troops. These were units of soldiers which were raised in the provinces and could be allowed to keep something of their national equipment and method of fighting. Although mainly infantry, they included units of cavalry and archers. There is no list of the auxiliary troops involved in the invasion force, but it possibly included Ala I Thracum which was raised in Thrace (roughly corresponding to modern Bulgaria) and soon to be stationed in Colchester.

Before the invasion had hardly begun, there was trouble: troops mutinied, refusing to cross the Ocean which they believed to be a great river encircling the known world. Many of the soldiers had never seen a tidal sea before, only the Mediterranean which of course is without tides. Plautius appealed for help to Claudius who was still in Rome, and Narcissus, a very senior civil servant, was sent to persuade the troops to change their minds. Given that he was also a former slave and the soldiers knew it, Narcissus did surprisingly well and the troops obeyed their orders without further trouble.

Dio said that the army was split into three divisions to avoid having 'an opposed landing', although his added comment that bad weather interfered with the crossing leaves us wondering where and in what conformation they actually landed in the end. There are several theories. Currently the most popular view is that the whole army disembarked at Richborough in Kent, where excavations on the site of the later Roman fort have revealed an earlier Claudian beach-head. This was a linear earthwork, dug transversely across the headland to protect it. The beach-head incorporated a double ditch which, as we shall see, is reminiscent of the Triple Dyke at Colchester. Other theories have the army landing in three places (Dover, Lympne, and Richborough), or as a single force in the Chichester area, in what would have been the territory of the recently deposed king Verica.

In any event, the delay caused by the mutiny turned out to be to the Romans' advantage, because the Britons gave up waiting and the Romans were able to land unopposed. At first the Britons seem to have deliberately avoided fighting in the hope that the Roman army would use up its supplies. But in the end there was no set-piece battle but a series of engagements by which the Roman army gradually gained the upper hand. At first Caratacus was defeated, and then his brother Togodumnus, and then a section of the Dobunni tribe surrendered (quite how or why is not known). Then the Britons dug in their heels over what must have been a key river crossing. Nobody knows which river was involved, but the Medway in Kent or the Arun in Sussex are currently the most favoured. The whole episode lasted two days and at one point the Britons appeared to be having some success. However, eventually they retreated, this time to a crossing place over the Thames. The fighting which ensued resulted in many losses on both sides including, it would appear, Togodumnus himself. The fact that Dio acknowledged that the Romans lost a large number of men shows that the fighting was fierce and bloody.

By this stage the Roman army had crossed the Thames and presumably now had Camulodunum in its sights. However, according to Dio, the death of Togodumnus had stiffened the British resolve to resist, presumably by causing wavering groups to join

A model of a war elephant of the sort faced by the Romans. It has a crenellated tower chained on its back. Note the way the rider encourages the animal to obey his commands by giving it tit-bits from a pouch in his lap.

Two alternative theories about the routes taken by Plautius and the Roman army during the invasion of Britain in AD 43. Claudius joined the force at the Thames and continued with it on to Camulodunum.

the cause. This worried Plautius and, supposedly, made him unwilling to proceed further. Instead he decided to secure his position and send for the emperor. There is some debate as to whether Plautius then withdrew to the south bank of the Thames or whether he stayed put. Either way, he had a long time to wait for Claudius (perhaps six weeks or so) and presumably he would have been active during this time in building camps, clearing roadways, and generally patrolling and securing what he had gained so far.

The call for Claudius must always have been part of the plan. Dio implies that he left Rome on receiving Plautius' message but he must have left much earlier, perhaps on hearing of the army's successful landing in Britain. He departed by boat from Ostia, sailed up the Italian coast and round to Massilia (Marseilles), and then he went by

Claudius subduing Britannia; from the city of Aphrodisias in Turkey.

road and river, perhaps via the Saône and then the Seine, to meet up with the troops and equipment which were being assembled at Boulogne. He arrived in Britain with a substantial force which would have included detachments of the élite Praetorian Guard and a number of elephants. His entourage was unusual for such circumstances in that it included an exceptional number of distinguished senators. Claudius was taking a great political risk in leaving those of influence in Rome and beyond to machinate in his absence. The high-flyers that he brought with him would serve as persuasive witnesses to his glory while being unable to cause any mischief back home.

At various times since 280 BC, the Roman army had been faced with elephants in battle and had occasionally used them themselves. Elephants could be very effective. Their trumpeting and their scent could spook the enemies' horses and their very presence severely intimidate the opposition. A group of twenty to forty charging elephants must have been a terrifying sight if they were heading straight for you. However the problem was that if the elephants panicked in battle (as they often seemed to do, particularly when wounded), they could do more damage to their allies than their enemies. Worse still, the enemy could frighten the animals so that they turned and stampeded back through their own lines. The Carthaginian elephant drivers were supposed to kill their elephant if it got out of control by hammering a chisel into the base of its skull. The idea of using animals as weapons of war was not new. Unsuccessful experiments had been tried with bulls, boars, and lions but these creatures proved even worse at distinguishing between friend and foe.

It is not known how many elephants Claudius brought with him. To judge by the recorded occurrences of elephants in warfare at other times, he may have had something like twenty to forty rather than hundreds or just two or three. When on the march, Hannibal had his elephants at the head of his column (with his cavalry) because it scared the natives who were unfamiliar with such beasts. Claudius may have done the same. They may also have been used as pack animals.

The fall of Camulodunum

When Plautius stood by at the Thames waiting for Claudius, he gave the Britons time, several weeks at least, to prepare for the attack on Camulodunum that was to come. But we cannot identify any hasty additions to its defences. Berechurch Dyke and Gosbecks Dyke are two obvious candidates but the dating evidence is absent. Perhaps preparations were limited to rounding up all the animals and blocking up the entrances in the dykes or, of course, the Britons may not have expected the Romans to find the place so quickly and single it out for capture. Equally, there is as yet no identifiable archaeological evidence of an assault by Claudius on the British stronghold. Given the speed of events once Claudius arrived, it might be surprising if there was any. Had it been a protracted affair, then perhaps the Romans would have built siegeworks or encampments which we could find and recognise.

Although by this time Cunobelin was dead, the political significance of Camulodunum must still have been considerable for Claudius to target it in this way. It must surely have been the base of the major figure of influence in the south-east. However it is not clear who succeeded Cunobelin at Camulodunum. The current consensus favours a breakup of Cunobelin's 'kingdom' with the area north of the Thames including Camulodunum going to Togodumnus. The southern area is seen as belonging to Caratacus because those few coins which he is known to have issued suggest a base for him in the Hampshire area immediately before the invasion. Adminius is seen as a non-runner as he had fled the country a few years earlier because of his dispute with his father, and the fourth son (who was captured with Caratacus) is never mentioned because he seems to have been eclipsed by his more famous brothers.

This is likely to be too simplistic an explanation which hinges on an oversimplified view of what is meant by 'kingdom'. Dio indicated something of the true situation when he said that after defeating Caratacus and Togodumnus who were Catuvellauni, Plautius won over by agreement a section of the Dobunni tribe which was subject to the two men. There are a number of interesting points about this statement: that just a 'section' of the tribe was involved, implying the existence of autonomous or at least semi-autonomous sub-groupings within it, that the grouping was 'subject' to Caratacus and Togodumnus, and that Caratacus and Togodumnus are mentioned together as if they

were equals in a joint personal arrangement which took second place to being Catuvellauni. Thus Cunobelin's 'kingdom' would have been the product of similar relationships with various other tribes (and/or sub-groupings within them) over the south-east whereby they were obligated to the rulers of the Catuvellauni in some way, either by force, intimidation, or hostage-taking. Moreover from Dio's statement we can guess that this obligation, and thus presumably other obligations like it, would have involved assisting the Catuvellauni in times of war. Thus Cunobelin's kingdom would not have been something that could be carved up, but on his death there may well have been a need for Caratacus and Togodumnus to try and reaffirm many of the tribal relationships that had existed under their father.

As we have seen, the coin distributions of Epaticcus (Cunobelin's brother), Adminius, and indeed Cunobelin himself are centred away from the Catuvellaunian home territory in the Hertfordshire region. It is uncertain what these distributions mean but generally they are thought to indicate usage through trade and domination of other tribes by the Catuvellauni. However an explanation which (as far as I am aware) has never been considered is that they largely reflect usage within the Catuvellauni themselves, and that these coin distributions in general reflect the scale and penetration of their migrations. In other words the distributions seem to show how members of the Cunobelin family, each with a section of the Catuvellauni, would settle in the territories of other tribes. We can imagine that the section of the Dobunni referred to by Dio was similar in its structure in that it was a branch of that tribe with its own chief. The friction between the migrating Catuvellauni and the tribes resident in the areas into which they moved may not always have led to war, so that the domination of the south-east by the Catuvellauni could have come about through a combination of new settlements and treaties which bound the subordinate parties to them. The leader or 'chief-of-chiefs' of the Catuvellauni would thus have been in effect 'king' of much of the south-east. Cunobelin enjoyed this status which explains how the Roman writer Suetonius could describe him (inaccurately nevertheless) as 'King of the Britons'. Plainly Cassivellaunus, a hundred years earlier, had also been a chief-of-chiefs and so too presumably was Cunobelin's father, Tasciovanus.

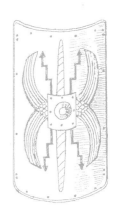

Shield of a Roman legionary soldier of the mid 1st century AD.

The fact that a section of the Dobunni could make terms in their own right with the Romans shows that they did not have to defer to their own chief-of-chiefs. Hence Cunobelin probably had less power than did, for example, a medieval king of England, because his authority is likely to have rested on his position as head of a council made up of chiefs of the Catuvellauni and perhaps even of other tribes such as the Trinovantes which the Catuvellauni had subsumed.

According to Dio, when Claudius met up with Plautius he took command of the whole expeditionary force, crossed the Thames, defeated a force of Britons, and 'captured Camulodunum, the royal seat of Cunobelin'.

The size of the army which bore down on Camulodunum would have depended on various factors: the size of the invasion army itself, the size of any subsequent reinforcements particularly those that came with Claudius, the extent to which the army was campaigning elsewhere, and what resources had to be used to secure the rearward lines of support. There is a suggestion that at least one division (under Vespasian) was not with Claudius, and there may have been others. However, at the very least, we can suppose that most of the army came with the emperor, and that, at a guess, the strike force was made up of 30,000 or more men.

It is not known what resistance, if any, Claudius encountered when he reached Camulodunum. However, he later gave a show, in the Campus Martius in Rome, which took the form of the siege and capture of a town (no doubt Camulodunum), and the surrender of British kings. Claudius presided over the show wearing his purple campaigning cloak.

If such an event did happen at Camulodunum, then it must have been over fairly quickly. The Romans had various devices to help them capture defended towns and the like. The equipment which Dio mentions as coming with Claudius could well have included some suitable siege weapons, brought in expectation of the need to storm Camulodunum. The Romans used towers and moveable 'sheds' which protected soldiers while they backfilled defensive ditches or dismantled walls. There were also rams of various sizes for battering down walls and catapults which could, among other things, fire red-hot bolts and set fire to entrances blocked with fallen timber. Lighter pieces like ladders and cranes could be made by the soldiers more or less on the spot but heavier equipment had to be brought in.

We need to remember Caesar's account of his capture of the stronghold of Cassivellaunus. He found it filled with people and cattle and attacked it on two sides at once, causing the Britons to make good their escape out the other sides. The attack seems to have been swift and decisive. The story seems likely to have been the same at Camulodunum. Tens of thousands of trained Roman soldiers, with or without charging elephants, was far too much for the Britons to resist. If Caratacus had been present, then he must have managed to escape because, as we shall see, he was to play an important role in the British opposition to the Romans over the next seven or eight years.

Once Camulodunum had been captured, Claudius and his army would have set out a temporary camp. It would have been protected by specially dug earthworks and close to a supply of water for the men and the animals.

How the Roman army made Camulodunum into their own stronghold.

Map showing the locations of the temporary encampment of Claudius and the invasion force (conjectural), the legionary fortress, the fort at Gosbecks, and the supply base at Fingringhoe (conjectural).

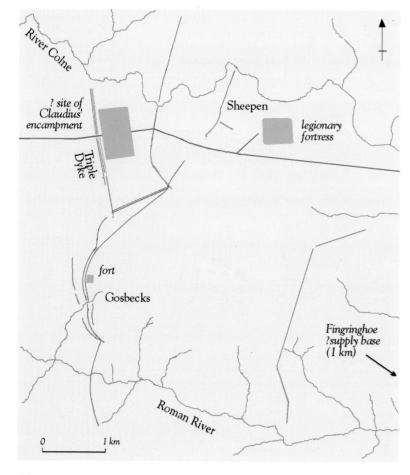

The Roman soldiers would have been encamped eight to a leather tent. The tents would have been set out neatly and regularly according to a predetermined plan which was set out on the ground before the main body of the troops arrived. Everybody would know where to go because the intended positions of each of the units would have been indicated by colour-coded flags attached to spears stuck in the ground. At the centre and thus in the safest place would have been the imperial tents for the emperor and his senatorial colleagues. No doubt close by would have been detachments of the Praetorian Guard who were there to protect the emperor and his entourage. We do not know how large the imperial accommodation would have been, but Julius Caesar had a tent 200 foot square when campaigning in Gaul a hundred years earlier.

It is possible to estimate very roughly the sort of area that the encampment would have covered by using the information handed down to us by the Roman military writer Hyginus on how such an encampment might be laid out. Without going into much detail, we can note, for example, that each century was to be allotted a space of 120x30 feet which was divided up into ten spaces, each 12 feet long and 30 feet wide. Eight places were occupied by *contubernia* (tent parties of eight men) with the remaining two being for the centurion. This arrangement only provided accommodation for sixty-four soldiers, since the other sixteen were deemed to be on night duty. (At this time, there were eighty rather than a hundred soldiers to a century.) The width of each space provided ten feet for the tent, five feet for the arms, and nine feet for the beasts of burden. There were six centuries to a cohort and each cohort was allocated 21,600 square feet made up as 60x360, 90x240 or 120x180 feet, which is in accord with the area just described for the centuries.

There is no clear evidence to indicate the site of the encampment. The most likely spot is immediately behind the Triple Dyke which enclosed the strip of land between the river Colne and the outermost dyke to the south (Prettygate Dyke). The earthwork was about 45 m across and 1.5 km long and did not consist of one bank and ditch as was normal for the dyke system, but in effect was three dykes, one placed immediately in front of the other. The earthwork was in two dead straight sections which were slightly out of alignment with each other. There was a

Soldiers on campaign were accommodated eight men to a leather tent.

Below: highly speculative plan of Claudius' encampment.

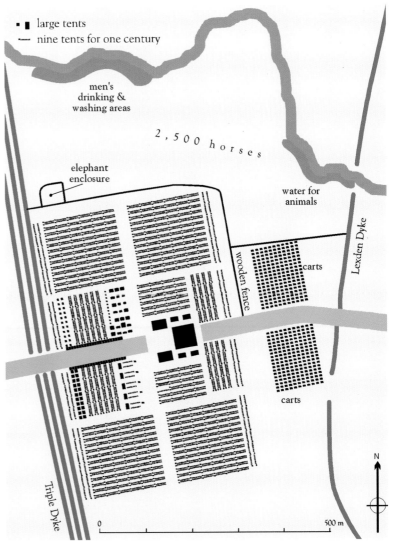

■ large tents

nine tents for one century

men's drinking & washing areas

2,500 horses

elephant enclosure

water for animals

wooden fence

Lexden Dyke

carts

carts

Triple Dyke

0   500 m

N

narrow gap between the two for an entrance at the place where the modern London Road crosses the line of the dyke. There is a possibility that the Triple Dyke started off as a single bank and ditch (the Shrub End Dyke) but was later tripled. It thus protected the invasion while at the same time providing easy access to the river for water for the soldiers and the animals. In addition to building Triple Dyke, the army also seems to have added a ditch along the south side of the Prettygate Dyke. In its original form, Prettygate Dyke faced north with its ditch on the north side of the bank. By adding a ditch on the south side, the earthwork was then capable of protecting the troops on the north.

The Triple Dyke.

Possibly dug by the invading army under the supervision of Claudius. The excavation shown in the photograph was carried out in 1961.

A measured section across the surviving ditches is shown below. There would have been three banks, one on the east side of each ditch, but these have been destroyed in this part of the dyke.

There is no close dating evidence for the construction of the Triple Dyke, or indeed for the conversion of the Prettygate Dyke. Nor is there firm evidence that the two events were contemporary. However, from the ground plan of the dyke system as a whole, it would seem that the Triple Dyke was built after the Lexden Dyke but before Gryme's Dyke. As we shall see later, Gryme's Dyke appears to be early Roman in date and may have been constructed up to twenty years or so after the invasion in AD 43. The Triple Dyke and the Prettygate Dyke are both dead straight and this appears to be a characteristic of the Roman dykes. Given all this, the most obvious date for the Triple Dyke is AD 43, but it is tentative.

The Triple Dyke has only been excavated once, when a trench was dug across it in 1961 by Professor Christopher Hawkes. He believed the earthwork to be of Roman military origin, because of so-called 'shovel slots' along the bases of the ditches which were supposedly caused by soldiers cleaning them out. The ditch around the legionary fortress, which we shall be coming to later, did not have a similar slot so it is doubtful if this feature really can be taken to be indicative of the Roman army. Christopher Hawkes found very little in the ditches apart from the remains of a Roman shoe. The leather had decayed completely, but fifteen iron hobnails survived in their original positions to show the shape of the shoe. There was some talk at the time of this being the remains of a soldier's boot. If the Triple Dyke really was built by the invasion army, then there might have been as many as 60,000 boots or more close by! However, the boot was not on the base of the ditch but lay about a foot up in the early silt. Thus it could have been lost or discarded by a soldier in AD 43, but if it was, then the shoe must have found its way into the ditch silt at a later stage.

Dio tells us that, having captured Camulodunum, Claudius went on to obtain the submission of a number of tribes, some by force and others by diplomacy. Presumably he accepted these submissions in his encampment behind the Triple Dyke. He then returned home after a stay of only sixteen days in Britain. The round trip had taken six months. The Senate voted him the title of Britannicus and gave him permission to hold a victory parade in Rome. They also decided that there should be an annual festival to mark the victory and that two triumphal

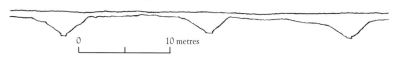

0   10 metres

arches should be erected, one in Rome and the other in Gaul (presumably at Boulogne). His family was to benefit too. His wife at that time (Messalina) was given the right to a front seat in the theatre and to use a carriage in the city, and his son was given the title Britannicus, which became his usual name.

The submission of tribes by diplomacy led to the establishment of 'client' kingdoms where tribes could maintain some degree of independence in return for loyalty to Rome. Tacitus described them as 'instruments of servitude'. Effectively this allowed the Romans to concentrate on the tribes that resisted, such as the Catuvellauni and the Trinovantes, and gave them the option of taking over the client kingdoms at a later date if they wanted to.

Although neither triumphal arch now stands, enough of the main inscription of the arch in Rome still survives to allow full reconstruction of the text. It does corroborate Dio to some extent in that the surviving part includes a reference to British kings, no doubt in relation to their submissions to Claudius. It used to be thought that eleven kings were involved, but a recent re-examination of the inscription shows that the precise number is uncertain. The arch was dedicated in AD 51-2, eight years after the event, so that some of the kings may have

been later additions. None are named but candidates are queen Cartimandua of the Brigantes, Verica of the Atrebates, Boduocus of the Dobunni, Prasutagus of the Iceni, and perhaps as a late addition, Caratacus, also of the Catuvellauni. Leaders of the Coritani and the Cornovii tribes may also have asked for terms.

There is a question mark over whether Claudius ever saw any action during his visit to Britain. Was it all a set-up job and was Plautius told to hang back at the last minute to let Claudius come to Britain and take the credit for capturing Camulodunum? Claudius was after all physically weak and without any military experience. He could hardly have been much more than an observer whatever happened, and he was in the country for only a very brief time. The Roman writer Suetonius contradicts Dio's account of Claudius' direct involvement in the campaign and says that he conquered part of the island within a few days and without battle or bloodshed. This seems unduly dismissive, particularly in view of the number and calibre of the senatorial witnesses. Certainly Claudius' intervention could not have been set up by Plautius as a low-risk, prestige-making event for his master if the army really did stop its advance at the Thames, sixty miles from their goal. If there had not been

The surviving fragments of the main inscription on Claudius' triumphal arch in Rome recording the conquest of Britain. The exact wording is uncertain.

This reconstruction reads: 'The senate and Roman people [dedicated this] to Tiberius Claudius Caesar Augustus Germanicus, son of Drusus, Pontifex Maximus, during his eleventh tenure of Tribunicia Potestas, Consul five times, hailed as Imperator twenty-two times, Censor, Pater Patriae, because he received into surrender eleven kings of the Britons conquered without loss and he first brought the barbarian peoples across the Ocean under the authority of the Roman people'.

A recent reassessment of the surviving fragments by Professor A.A. Barrett has cast doubt on the number of kings referred to in the sixth line.

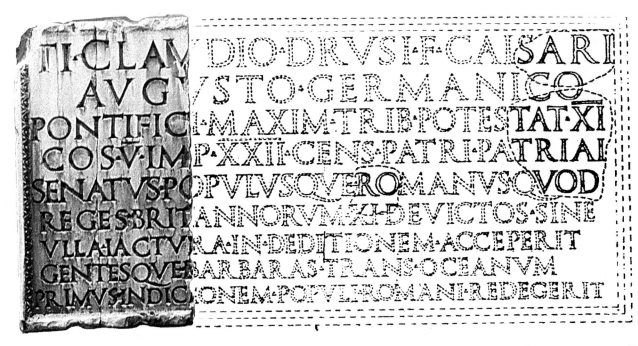

A gold coin with a representation of Claudius' victory arch in Rome. The arch has 'DE BRITANN' inscribed on it and it is surmounted by an equestrian statue of Claudius.

any more serious fighting, then that would have been a matter of luck rather than planning. Plautius would surely have expected more fighting with, at the very least, some stout resistance at Camulodunum itself. They were, after all, about to enter the territory of the Catuvellauni, the backbone of the British opposition. Dio's remark that Claudius brought some equipment with him hints that it was all part of a strategy in which initially Plautius was to travel light and be fast-moving and Claudius was to follow up at the appropriate point with heavier gear and the elephants. Arguably, what accompanied Claudius was an integral part of the invasion force, not just an inflated imperial bodyguard. And the antics in the Campus Martius point to the true purpose of the newly reinforced army, if indeed they did not reflect something of what actually happened.

Reconstruction drawing of the arch in Rome recording Claudius' victory in Britain. By the 16th-century antiquarian Piero Ligorio. The front of the arch was covered with sculptures. The arches to either side belong to an aqueduct incorporated in the triumphal arch.

STRONGHOLD OF THE ROMAN WAR MACHINE

Consolidation

After the departure of Claudius, the Roman task force was split up into units, each made up of a legion and some of the auxiliaries. Each was under the command of a legionary legate. The XIV Gemina and perhaps IX Hispana were to occupy the lands of the Catuvellauni, the XX was to deal with the Trinovantes, and the future emperor, Vespasian (who may already have been operating south of the Thames) was sent further west and south with the II Augusta. Gradually the army worked its way west and northwards so that within about four years the whole of the south-east of England was under Roman control, either directly by the army or with the co-operation of friendly kings in 'client' kingdoms.

After the bulk of the army moved on, at least two units seem to have been left behind in Colchester. The main one was the Twentieth Legion (XX) which in due course was to build a fortress for itself, and the other seems to have been an auxiliary unit from Thrace (now what is roughly Bulgaria). As we shall see, there may have been others to account for the fort at Gosbecks and a possible stores depot area at Fingringhoe.

The presence of a legionary fortress somewhere close to the town centre was suspected for many years, but it took the excavations at Lion Walk and Culver Street to show that it had stood in the area now occupied by the western half of the town centre. Tacitus seems to imply an association between the Twentieth Legion and the town when he wrote that the legion was transferred to the west and a colony of veterans founded at Colchester. He does not say that the two events are linked, but they occur in the same passage as if they might have been. More

The memorial of Marcus Favonius Facilis, a centurion of the Twentieth Legion. It stood on the side of the 'Street of Tombs', which was the main approach road to Colchester from the west. Found in 1868.

The inscription reads:

Here lies Marcus Favonius Facilis, son of Marcus, of the Pollian tribe, centurion of the XXth Legion. Erected by Verecundus and Novicius, his freedmen.

Military equipment

Part of the secret of the military success of the Roman army lay in its armour and weaponry. Being largely of metal, many of their tell-tale fragments are found on sites which were once inhabited by Roman soldiers. Here are just a few of the many such objects from Colchester.

a An iron spear or lance head. Found on the Culver Street site.

b Reconstructed helmet. Found at the Sheepen site in the 1930s.

c Buckle carved of bone. Includes a copper-alloy pin. Found at the Lion Walk site.

d A copper-alloy belt-plate and buckle. Inlaid with niello (in this case copper sulphide). Found at the Culver Street site.

e Front part of an iron dagger scabbard inlaid with brass and enamel. Found on the Gilberd School site.

f Two copper-alloy studs from the Lion Walk site.

g Iron boss of shield. From the Gilberd School site.

h Copper-alloy camp kettle. From the Sheepen site. Found in the 1930s.

i Hinge from body armour. From the Balkerne Lane site.

—and from the Lion Walk site:

j Copper-alloy buckle.

k Copper-alloy binding for the edge of an oval shield.

specific evidence came in 1868 with the discovery of the magnificent tombstone of the Roman soldier Marcus Favonius Facilis who, we learn from the inscription, had been a centurion of the Twentieth. This was the first of two marvellous memorial stones to be discovered in the town. The second (found in 1928) was the tombstone of Longinus Sdapeze, an officer with the First Thracian Cavalry. Facilis was presumably a serving soldier when he died because there is no indication in the inscription that he had retired. The same applies to Longinus, because he had only served fifteen years before his death, which would be too short a period of service. Thus the tombstones appear to tell us the names of two units stationed in Camulodunum. One conclusion to draw from them is that Facilis and the Twentieth Legion were in the fortress and Longinus and his unit were in the fort at Gosbecks.

However, as with archaeology generally, nothing is that simple or easy. As we shall see the fort at Gosbecks may be too small for a cavalry unit, in which case it could have been brigaded in the fortress along with the legion that was based there. Moreover, even if it were certain that both were serving soldiers, the presence of these tombstones still cannot be taken as unequivocal evidence that the units were stationed at Colchester since either man could have died here while on temporary duty during the early years of the colony. To complicate matters further, either man could have been part of a small garrison in or near the colony in the AD 50s, since Tacitus says that there was just such a unit at Colchester at the time of the revolt. On balance it would appear that the garrison of the fortress was very likely the Twentieth Legion, but the presence and the location of the First Thracian Cavalry is more problematic.

Before we move on to consider the fortress and the fort, we need first to pause to describe the composition of the Roman army at this time.

The Roman army

The backbone of the Roman army was the legions. These were infantry troops raised (at this time) mainly in Italy. The legionaries were Roman citizens who served for 25 years before being discharged with a lump sum or a grant of land. There were 27 legions in Claudius' day. Each one was made up of ten units called cohorts, each of which consisted of six centuries. Each century was under the command of a centurion, and (confusingly) was made up of eighty rather than a hundred soldiers. There were thus sixty centurions, the most senior being the *primus pilus* who, in addition to commanding the first century of the first cohort, had wider responsibilities.

The legionary commander was known as a *legatus legionis*. He would normally have been a senator in his thirties who would serve in the post for only three or four years as a step in a career that might lead to a provincial governorship, and with it, a commander of several legions depending on the province involved. Under him came the most senior of the six tribunes attached to a legion. After a short posting, he would ultimately hope to return to the army as a legionary commander and this was in effect his military apprenticeship. The other tribunes were young men who, again after a comparatively short period of service, would hope to attain high positions in the civil service or the command of an auxiliary cavalry unit. When the legate and the senior tribune were both absent, command would be assumed by the quartermaster (*praefectus castrorum*). He would be a man in his fifties or so who had been a centurion, and had risen through their ranks to become a *primus pilus* before reaching his present post which was the highest he could hope to achieve.

The legion also included a body of horsemen perhaps numbering 120. They acted as dispatch riders and scouts rather than as a cavalry unit.

The legionary headquarters had a staff of clerks and orderlies to deal with what must have been a substantial amount of paperwork and routine administration. The senior officers had their own aides and each century was provided with their own office staff.

The military success of the Roman army depended as much on its engineering and building skills as it did on its military prowess. As good generals know, managing the peace is as important as managing the war that precedes it. Indeed much of the success of the Roman army rested on the very considerable range of skills which the legionary commander could call on from within his ranks. A 2nd-century document underlines this point by listing such specialist tradesmen and others as: surveyors, architects, pilots, water engineers, shipwrights, medical orderlies and dressers, clerks, farriers, horse-trainers, glassfitters, arrowsmiths, coppersmiths, blacksmiths, helmet-makers, swordcutlers, bowmakers, wagon-makers, roof-tile-makers, trumpet-makers, horn-makers, plumbers, stone-cutters, lime-burners, charcoalburners, woodcutters, and butchers. It is easy to see from a list like this how it was possible for the Roman army to grant retired veteran soldiers land in newly-conquered lands and to expect them to create viable towns such as at Camulodunum.

The expansion of the empire opened up vast sources of recruitment for the Romans. These non-Roman troops were known as *auxilia*—aids to the citizen legionaries. On honourable discharge, they were granted Roman citizenship, and their sons could enlist in the legions. Some of the diverse peoples conquered by the Romans were able to bring to the army qualities and special fighting skills in which the Romans were weak. This was particularly important

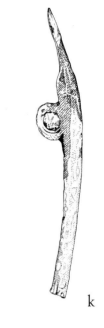

k

j

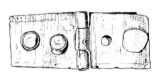

i

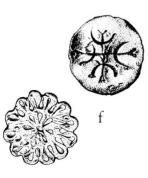

f

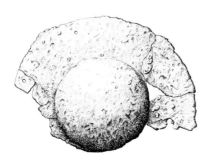

g

h

The legionary fortress in AD 48, viewed from the south-west.

Details based on excavation.

Left: the Balkerne Lane site, viewed from the south-west, and showing the workshops and other flimsy buildings lining the road leading up to the west gate (porta decumana).

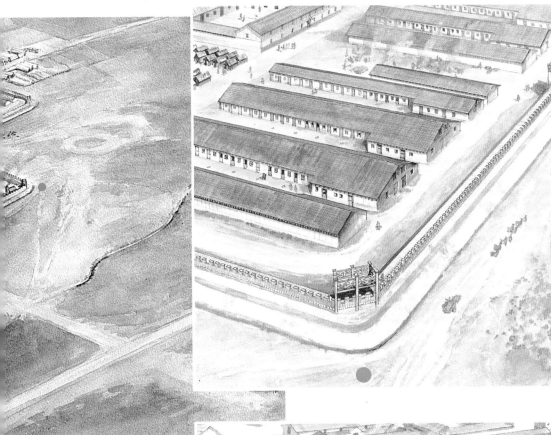

Above right: the Lion Walk site, viewed from the south-east, and showing the south-east corner of the fortress and the south-west corner of its annexe.

Right: the Culver Street site, viewed from the south-west, and showing the south gate (porta principalis dextra) and barracks and other buildings lining the south end of the main north-south street (via principalis) of the fortress.

Note: dots have been added to the drawings to help the reader orientate them one to the other.

for the cavalry. Although the Romans made able foot-soldiers, their own cavalry could not compete with opposition such as mounted nomadic tribesmen from North Africa who were brought up in the saddle. Thus cavalry raised in the provinces became invaluable, as did specialist units like slingers and archers. In Claudius' time, there were three types of auxiliary unit (cavalry, infantry, and a combination of cavalry and infantry), all of which were about 500 men strong. As we have seen, the tombstone of Longinus suggests that one of these cavalry units was based in Camulodunum.

The Gosbecks fort

A small fort was built at Gosbecks in the heart of Camulodunum. It was tucked up against the innermost of the defences and was less than 350 m from Cunobelin's farmstead. It was sited to control the area without being too disruptive.

The fort is known only from aerial photographs of cropmarks. These clearly show the layout of the fort. Long straight lines indicate continuous trenches into which the soldiers dropped posts to form the walls of the buildings and the inner and outer faces of the defensive bank. Circular spots show lines of pits between buildings and to the rear of the rampart. Other pits show the positions of post holes for the gates into the fort.

The fort was about four acres in size

measured inside its ramparts. Too little is known about it to determine its type of garrison. To judge by forts elsewhere, the fort would probably have accommodated around 500 auxiliary soldiers (one cohort). The most obvious unit for it is the First Thracian Cavalry to which Longinus belonged, although cavalry units seem generally to have needed more room than this. The streets had to be wider to allow the unit to assemble on their mounts, and presumably extra space would have been needed for stabling and fodder, unless the animals were catered for outside the defences.

Three gates were joined by two streets to make a T-shaped plan. It is possible that there was no gate on the west side of the fort. Although it is difficult to make out individual buildings in the aerial photographs, it is clear that they were mostly long and thin (as was normal) and that they were aligned east-west. The clearest of the buildings is the headquarters (*principia*) which is in the centre of the fort and is square in plan with an inner courtyard. It faced the east gate.

The legionary fortress

The new legionary base at Camulodunum was to be the first of its kind in Britain. As a building project there had been nothing like it before in Britain in terms of scale, logistics, speed, and innovation. Thousands of trees had to be cut down and vast quantities of sand, gravel and clay dug up and brought by cart and boat from the surrounding areas. Mortar, a material that we all take for granted, was probably being used here for the first time in Britain, bringing with it not just mortared foundations and walls but also, for some buildings in the fortress, strange vaults and perfectly plastered surfaces.

Part of the success of the Romans lay in their highly developed administrative skills. Military conquest depended as much on those qualities as it did on the ability to fight on the battlefield itself. The construction of the legionary fortress would have needed planning and the management of resources and men on a scale never seen before in this country. The task had to be done at great speed, and it would have been more difficult than normal because it was to be built in a newly-conquered land where there were no readily-available stockpiles of suitable materials apart from those across the water in Gaul. Practically overnight Camulodunum would have lost its predominantly rustic tranquillity

Plan of the Gosbecks fort possibly established in AD 43. The plan shows some of the buildings which can be deduced from cropmarks.

north gate

Heath Farm dyke

principia

street

east gate

south gate   0   50 metres

and become a huge and very busy building site. As much as possible of the materials needed for the fortress would have been obtained locally. Timbers would have been needed by the thousand for the walls and roof trusses of the buildings, and for the wooden parts of its defences. Large quarries would have been opened up to provide the clay, sand, and gravel needed for the walls, ramparts, tiles, and gravelled streets. Chalk would have had to be brought in (perhaps from Kent) to make the lime for mortar. Charcoal would have been needed in huge quantities to fire the tile kilns. Iron nails by the million would probably have been brought ready-made from abroad given the absence of local iron ore.

The fortress had to be carefully sited. It had to be inside Camulodunum's defences, but on unoccupied land to minimise the disruption. It had to be near the river to use waterborne transport and yet be high enough to command a good view of the surrounding area. It had to guard the main river crossings into the native settlement, and it had to be close to a good supply of water.

The site which met all these requirements was a spur of land immediately downstream from the Sheepen site where in c AD 44 work on building the base began. The longitudinal axis of the fortress was placed on an east-west ridge formed by the steep slope down to the river Colne on the north and a more gentle slope to the south. The fortress was deliberately aligned on true north so that it faced east with the principal gate (*porta praetoria*) facing seaward.

On the east side of the fortress was a large annexe. Its precise size and position have yet to be established but it appears to have been about a third of the size of the original fortress enclosure. This is an unusual feature for a Roman fortress and unfortunately there are few indications as to its purpose.

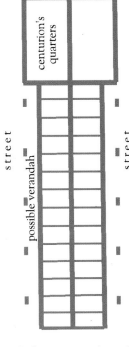

Right: plan of a pair of Roman barrack blocks at the Gilberd School site.

Left: the excavation of part of the defences of the annexe of the legionary fortress, at the Lion Walk site. Viewed from the north. In the background there is a trench across the width of the backfilled V-shaped ditch. In the foreground is the stump of the rampart. The remains of an oven set in the inside face of the rampart are visible in the near foreground (marked x).

0   200 metres

Plan of the legionary fortress at Colchester. Also shows the largest parts of the buildings which have been excavated so far.

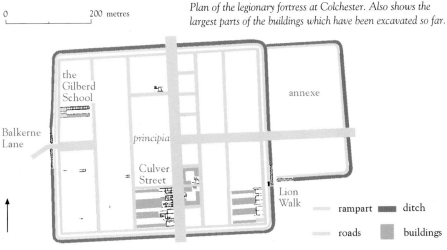

the Gilberd School

Balkerne Lane

principia

Culver Street

annexe

Lion Walk

rampart	ditch
roads	buildings

The layout of the fortress is sufficiently well known to determine how it was designed. The plan was formulated in terms of round figures and the planning of the buildings was secondary to the street system. In other words, the buildings were made to fit the street plan rather than vice versa.

The defences of the fortress and its annexe were of identical construction. The ditch was V-shaped and about 2.5 m deep and 5.0 m wide. The rampart was made of sand faced with blocks of sun-dried sandy clay. The topsoil had been removed and the ramparts built over a layer of timbers laid across their full width. The street around the inside of the defences (*via sagularis*) was set back 9.0 m from the inner face of the rampart. No *via sagularis* has been recognised in the annexe and nothing is known of the gates of the fortress other than their locations.

Although the plan of the fortress is broadly known, few of its buildings have been examined and, of these, none have been more than half uncovered. There would have been at least 60 barrack blocks—more if an auxiliary unit was garrisoned with the legion—and stables for the horses of the cavalry unit which the legion would have included. Only barracks have been identified so far, but there would have been many other kinds of building such as granaries and other store buildings, workshops, latrines, a hospital, and the legionary commander's house (*praetorium*). Although no two fortresses had the same plan, there is a consistency in their layouts which enables us to predict the probable locations of some of the buildings. Similarly the positions of the barracks can be anticipated to some extent, and something can be said about the status of each cohort according to its location in the fortress.

It was customary for the most senior of the cohorts to be placed to the left of the *principia* when viewed from the front. This means that the barracks found at Culver Street should all have belonged to the First Cohort. Because of their seniority, the accommodation given to the First Cohort underwent evolutionary changes in the later part of the 1st century. The number of centurions was reduced to five, but each was given a double century and a correspondingly larger set of quarters to reflect the increased responsibility which this brought. Although these changes seem to have occurred a little later than the fortress at Colchester, the barracks at Culver Street show that development of some sort had already started. Although still six in number, the barracks were larger than any of the others in the fortress, with one being noticeably larger than the rest.

In the centre of the fortress, taking pride of place, there would have been the headquarters building (*principia*). Unfortunately nothing of it has yet been excavated but we can be sure that the building stood over and to either side of what is now the westernmost 80 m or so of the High Street. The *principia* was a complicated building which served as the administrative centre and focal point of the whole establishment. It took the form of

The barracks

The corner of one of the barracks at the Culver Street site. The building was reused in the new town and subsequently destroyed during the great fire of AD 60/1, which explains its good preservation (see page 79).
Below right: diagram showing construction of the wall.

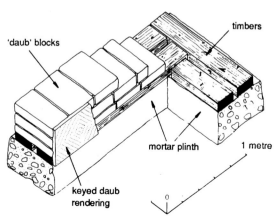

a square yard surrounded on three sides by stores and offices of the quartermaster and his staff. Dominating the fourth side of the square was a great lofty hall aligned north-south and spanning the full width of the building. The hall would have been aisled and lit by windows high up in the walls. At one end there would have been a platform (*tribunal*) from which the commander could address the troops, and along its west side there would have been a range of rooms, the central one of which was the *sacellum* or shrine of the standards. Each century had its own standard which would have been kept in the *sacellum*, along with those of any other units resident in the base. The other rooms in the range were administrative offices for the headquarters. The entrance to the *principia* would have been in the centre of its east side, where the main north-south street across the fortress (*via principalis*) met the central east-west street (*via praetoria*) leading to the east gate.

Excavations at Lion Walk, Culver Street, and the Gilberd School in the 1970s and 1980s provided information about the barracks. Each of these buildings was at least 69 m long and provided the accommodation for a century of soldiers. About one third of the length of each barrack was taken up by the centurion who occupied his own semi-detached block at the end of the building. Some of the rooms in the barracks were heated with hearths placed against a wall. The floors were rudimentary, being nearly always of sand or sandy clay, but at least two in the centurion's quarters at Culver Street were of wooden planks.

The only other buildings which were examined are two large buildings which fronted on the east side of the *via principalis*. Typically there would have been eight of these large buildings lining the entire length of the street. Six of them would have been occupied by tribunes (a class of officer) so that the chances of at least one, if not both, of these two buildings having been so used are high. Hearths and some shallow burnt pits in one of these buildings had been used for metal-working in brass. This suggests that the building may have been a workshop rather than a tribune's house or perhaps that part of a tribune's house was used for metal-working.

The annexe of the fortress would have been used as an area for stores and, more importantly, may conceivably have contained

Parts of two possible tribune houses with intersecting street in the legionary fortress. From the Culver Street site.

The trenches indicate the positions of walls. The voids in the trench (example illustrated left) show the positions of posts which were placed in the trenches prior to their being backfilled. The posts formed the framework of the walls. When the buildings were demolished, the posts were cut off at ground level and the buried ends left to rot.

building   street   building

*Claudian
coin (dupondius)
from Culver Street.*

*A hoof print (of an ox or cow)
and wheel ruts in a patch of mud
on an unmetalled street of the
early fortress. Found at the
Culver Street site.*

the large set of baths which the fortress would have needed for the comfort of the soldiers. Any legionary baths would almost certainly have been kept for civilian use in the new colony, but so far the site of this building has remained elusive.

The buildings of the fortress were well made and involved several different construction techniques. The load-bearing walls of the barracks had three main structural components: a mortar-and-stone plinth, a pair of oak ground-plates, and a superstructure of coursed sandy-clay blocks. Most of the internal walls of the barracks consisted of a timber frame where the ground-plate was bedded directly on top of the natural sand and where the panels between the uprights were filled with wattle and blocks made of sandy clay.

In contrast, at least three of the large buildings lining the east side of the *via principalis* were built in a manner which is typical of the Roman army. First trenches were dug up to a metre deep along the lines of the intended walls. Substantial posts of roughly square section were then dropped into the trenches as they were backfilled. The gaps between the posts were filled with sandy-clay blocks, and the finished walls were left unplastered.

A much simpler form of construction is associated with buildings outside the base. Here the walls were formed by applying sandy clay as a daub to a frame made by hammering a row of stakes into the ground and then weaving wattles round them.

The streets of the fortress, like those of the later Roman town, were made of compacted gravel. However this metalling of the streets was not a priority in the fortress since there are examples of streets between barracks which were never treated in this way. In one place, wheel ruts and a hoof print were impressed in a thin patch of sandy soil underlying the earliest metalling, indicating use of the street when it was no more than a muddy track.

The fortress was big as Roman fortresses go (50 acres), and the barracks were comparatively narrow and closely set so that there would undoubtedly have been more than enough room for a normal complement of buildings. Either the base was designed to hold much more than a single legion or it was to contain additional buildings, possibly for Plautius and his staff.

There are some puzzling aspects to the military occupation. In the 1960s a deep ditch and a rampart were found about 175 m apart within what can now be recognised as the site of the fortress. Although no evidence was found to link the two discoveries, both appear to be so early in date that they must have been parts of a fort which preceded the fortress. However this is far from certain.

Another puzzle is the empty space in the fortress. Compared with fortresses elsewhere, the amount of such space here appears to have been substantial, and this suggests that the fortress was unfinished. This would not be surprising since the fortress at Inchtuthil in Perthshire was abandoned incomplete after about four years in AD 87. The fortress at Camulodunum must have been occupied for much the same length of time and therefore it too could have been left unfinished. It

The Claudian coin mint at Colchester

Large numbers of copper-alloy coins were struck at unidentified mints in the north-western provinces of the Roman Empire as imitations of Claudian coins produced in Rome. More coins of this type have been found in Colchester than anywhere else in Britain, and a study of this group of them by Robert Kenyon has led him to suggest that a mint was operating in Colchester in the days of Claudius and some years later.

could also have taken longer to build than the one at Inchtuthil because the army had not been in Britain long enough to build up stockpiles of building materials to bring up from the rear. On the other hand, most of the required materials were close by, and the resources saved in transport would offset those needed to collect and process the materials which would otherwise have been stockpiled.

The early port

Another important site existed at a landing area further downstream at Fingringhoe, where quarrying in about 1930 produced Roman military equipment and substantial quantities of pottery and coins. The discoveries were too poorly investigated and recorded to tell us much about the true nature of the site. However Claudian finds and the riverside location of the site suggest that it may have started off as a military store base. This would have taken the form of a small fort similar in appearance and size to the fort at Gosbecks, except that the principal type of building would have been granaries and other kinds of store buildings rather than barracks.

Fingringhoe lies on the Colne estuary at a point just down river of where the river broadens and deepens before reaching the sea. The Colne is too narrow and shallow a waterway to have allowed much penetration of shipping inland as far as the fortress and later Roman town except perhaps at spring tides. Thus Fingringhoe would have been

well placed to provide the much-needed landing facilities although it is unclear what form these would have taken. There may have been a wooden dock at Fingringhoe for large ships, although the mud flats would have required dredging. More likely perhaps is that large ships were moored off Fingringhoe and their cargo was transferred to smaller boats for transportation further upriver. Certainly this technique was employed here later, as it is known that in the 1570s seagoing vessels were moored at Rowhedge or Wivenhoe so that their cargoes could be conveyed by small boat to the Hythe.

To the Romans living in Britain, particularly during the early years of the province, it must have seemed as if the sea was their umbilical cord—their lifeline with civilisation as they understood it. Thousands of tons of goods must have passed each year through Colchester via the Colne. These would have been not just exports of agricultural and other produce, but imports such as pottery, wine, foodstuffs, and more exotic items from various parts of the Roman empire which in their way would have helped make life more bearable.

Below: a colour-coated bowl of a type which was common in the fortress.

Below: the Fingringhoe site today is a wooded nature reserve. It overlooks the flat marshland to the south, and it is the first piece of high ground on the west bank of the Colne upriver of the mouth of the estuary. (The mouth of the estuary is to the left.)

The memorial of Longinus Sdapeze

The missing face. Found in 1996. It fits its place on the tombstone perfectly.

The inscription reads:
Here lies Longinus Sdapeze, son of Matycus, dupli-carius of the First Squadron of Thracian Cavalry, from the district of Sardica, aged forty, with fifteen years' service. His heirs had this erected in accordance with his will.

Longinus was an officer in a troop of cavalry. He came from Sardica in Thrace (the modern Sofia in Bulgaria). His beautifully carved monument shows a mounted Roman cavalry officer victorious over a naked Celtic warrior cowering on his shield. The tombstone was found face down in pieces near Lexden Road in 1928. The freshness of the carved surfaces and the absence of the face and other key features seemed to indicate that it had been thrown down by furious Britons during the Boudican uprising of AD 60/1. Missing bits include the face of the soldier, his right foot, his right hand and the metal lance which it would have held, the right nostril of his horse, and the right hand of the sphinx on the top of the monument.

In 1996 James Fawn and the Colchester Archaeological Group investigated the site of the tombstone and discovered many stone chippings. Some of these are carved and include the face and other missing carved pieces. Evidence from this excavation casts doubt on the theory that the monument was damaged in AD 60/1.

CLAUDIUS' CITY OF VICTORY

The conquest continues

Compared with Julius Caesar's campaign in Gaul a hundred years earlier, the conquest of Britain was hard going. In the space of around eight years, Caesar had managed to conquer most of the mighty tribes of Gaul as well as fit in expeditions to Britain and Germany. In fact he had managed to complete the conquest in the first two years, the remaining time being spent largely on dealing with various revolts. Yet six years after Claudius had taken Camulodunum, the Roman army in Britain had barely managed to penetrate more than 150 miles or so. They had reached the south-west and had moved northwards along the east side of the country to reach Lincolnshire. Of course it is true that Caesar's army was bigger than that of Claudius—twice the size—but then Gaul was far bigger than Britain and had a much larger population. It is generally supposed that progress in Britain was limited not because of military difficulties but because the initial intention was just to conquer lowland Britain. But their real difficulties lay in the Welsh mountains where the terrain was making the Silures and the Ordovices difficult to subdue.

By this stage Plautius had been replaced as governor. He had returned to Rome in AD 47 to enjoy an 'ovatio', a triumphant entry into that city only marginally less grand than the triumphs accorded to victorious emperors. His place in Britain was taken by Publius Ostorius Scapula who, from the moment of his arrival until his death four years later (supposedly because of exhaustion), was faced with one problem after another. Scapula's major preoccupation was with the tenacious tribes inhabiting the Welsh mountains. Unfortunately for the Romans,

they had formed an alliance with Cunobelin's son Caratacus who, presumably at the head of a large force, had been pushed westwards as the Roman army moved across the country.

The Roman historians are practically silent on Caratacus' activities between Claudius' visit to Britain and AD 51 when we are told something of his final battle in the Welsh mountains. Nevertheless we can be fairly sure that throughout this time Caratacus and his men would have been unrelenting in their opposition to the Romans. His army could have been substantial and consisted of a mix of Celtic nobles skilled on horseback and in chariots and many ordinary Britons prepared to risk their lives and livelihoods fighting the Romans. Caratacus, like his father Cunobelin, would have been a very rich man, so it is likely that he used some of his wealth to employ mercenaries. According to the Romans, Caratacus became a great hero, a king made famous by his many exploits against the Romans. No doubt his activities must have been a major factor in the slow progress of the Roman campaign.

Scapula needed more troops on the frontier to deal with Caratacus and the Welsh problem. None could be obtained from the Continent so a major reorganisation in Britain was necessary. Accordingly the Twentieth Legion was brought over from Camulodunum to a new base in the Gloucester region. Ideally the void which the move created should have been filled with more troops. After all, it was only six years since Camulodunum had been captured, and the construction of a fortress there shows that the Romans intended a much longer military occupation. To build a fortress was no light investment in terms of materials and

Figure of Victory from a Roman monumental arch.

51

human resources and the base at Camulodunum could hardly have been long finished; indeed, as already explained, there is some evidence that the job was never completed at all. In the absence of additional troops, the next best course of action was to replace the army base at Camulodunum with a Roman town populated with retired Roman soldiers. Although not nearly as militarily strong as a legionary fortress, the settlement would nevertheless, according to Tacitus, provide a strong Roman presence in the area and provide a model for the natives of the Roman government and the Roman way of life. In truth the Roman army in Britain was overstretched and, as we shall see, the idea that the colony of ex-soldiers could be an effective substitute for the Twentieth Legion was a gamble which misfired and nearly allowed the Britons to rid themselves of their foreign oppressors.

Ironically the Twentieth Legion was moved from Camulodunum to fight Caratacus who had come from here in the first place. At that time he was fighting alongside the Silures, the tribe occupying the south of Wales, but soon he was to transfer his activities to the territory of the Ordovices in the north of that country. According to Tacitus, Caratacus decided to make a stand. The battle was to become famous and enter Welsh folklore, with several hills in Wales and the west Midlands being claimed as its site. Tacitus gives some topographical clues about its location. He said that the site was next to a river where there were some cliffs and sloping ground which the Britons protected with a stone wall. Some archaeologists believe it took place near Newtown in the Severn valley, but nobody knows for certain.

Tacitus does not tell us anything about the numbers of troops involved. Graham Webster, in his book *Rome against Caratacus* (page 30), estimates that Scapula could have had an army of 20,000 to 25,000 men and that a force of this size could have coped with up to four or five times that number of Britons. Scapula attacked from the other side of the river. The crossing was successful but the Romans sustained considerable losses from missiles. The soldiers then protected themselves from the aerial bombardment by interlocking their shields over their heads to form a cover (known as a *testudo*). Thus, in comparative safety, the soldiers were able to take down the Britons' defensive wall with their hands and picks. Hand-to-hand combat

followed. Overwhelmed, the Britons had to retreat, but many were massacred as they fled. Tacitus was graphic on the point: those that were not killed with the swords and spears of the legionaries were to die by the broadswords and lances of the auxiliaries. Caratacus' wife and daughter were captured and his brothers (none of whom are named) surrendered. The families of Britons had the habit of watching battles from the sidelines, which would explain the capture of Caratacus' wife and daughter. Caratacus managed to escape, and sought refuge with Cartimandua, leader of the Brigantes who occupied much of the north of what is now England. Unfortunately, fearing trouble herself, she promptly handed Caratacus in chains over to the Romans.

Caratacus' protracted struggle against the Romans had brought him a notoriety which spread into Europe as far as Italy, and Claudius intended to make as much as he could out of the capture of the famous king who had caused his army so much trouble. Caratacus and his family were taken to Rome where, in chains, they were to be marched into the parade ground of the Praetorian Guard and put on public display as trophies of war. Huge crowds gathered to watch the procession. Claudius and his latest wife Agrippina were seated there, each on a dais. The Guard was marshalled under arms, a rare event in itself and an indicator of the significance of the spectacle which was to follow. First to arrive were Britons who had either been captured during Caratacus' last battle or had been with him when he was betrayed by Cartimandua. This group is likely to have included close aides of Caratacus—many would have been of aristocratic rank. The Britons were accompanied by a display of booty from the war. Then followed Caratacus' family—his wife, daughter and brothers—and then finally came Caratacus himself. For a man who had known considerable power and personal wealth, this was a degrading and humiliating experience—in chains like a criminal, before the Roman emperor and in front of thousands of gloating Romans. Nevertheless, according to Tacitus, Caratacus gave a speech which so moved Claudius that he pardoned Caratacus and his family and ordered the removal of the chains there and then. It was all rather similar to what had happened about one hundred years earlier when the great Gallic leader

'I had horses, men, arms and wealth. Are you surprised I am sorry to lose them? If you want to rule the world, does it follow that everyone else welcomes enslavement? If I had surrendered without a blow before being brought to you, neither my downfall nor your triumph would have become famous. If I execute me, they will be forgotten. Spare me, and I shall be an everlasting token of your mercy!'

Part of the speech made by Caratacus to Claudius and the people of Rome according to Tacitus.

Vercingetorix was captured after the siege of Alesia during Caesar's conquest of Gaul. The big difference was that Julius Caesar had Vercingetorix executed. Tacitus tells us what Caratacus was supposed to have said. It is of course imaginary and says more about Tacitus and his views of the Roman Empire than about Caratacus—ancient writers liked to spice up their histories with grand rhetoric of the kind he credits to Caratacus.

Nothing more is said about Caratacus and his family. The pardon would have let them live out their lives in Rome, but even an exiled Caratacus would have been a danger to the Romans as long as there was a free Britain. We can only wonder if Tacitus' happy ending is as reliable as his version of Caratacus' speech.

Colonia Victricensis

No doubt when it looked as if the building works were to quieten down with the completion of the fortress, it was all given fresh impetus with the decision to relocate the Twentieth Legion and create a colony out of their redundant fortress. The new phase of work may not have been on quite the scale of the fortress but it would have been substantial nevertheless. In the first year or two, the work would have been overshadowed by the drama involving the Twentieth and Caratacus which started in Wales and ended in Rome. The streets of the new town must have buzzed with excitement at the news of the capture of Camulodunum's famous son. With Caratacus out of the way, the Romans in Camulodunum would have set about their task with added gusto.

The new town was a colony, which by this stage was the foremost type of Roman city. It was a chartered town which meant that it would have its own set of laws (*lex coloniae*) set out in written form and approved by Claudius. In a legal sense, it was a self-governing extension of Rome on foreign territory, which is why property in it could only be held by Roman citizens. Roman citizenship was a much sought-after status which was not restricted to people from Rome. In Claudius' day (and for the next 150 years or so), you needed to be a Roman citizen to become a legionary soldier. This was not the case with the less-well paid auxiliary soldiers although these men received this status on retirement with the effect that their offspring could join a legion.

Colonia Victricensis was presumably run by a town council (*ordo*) of a hundred and magistrates who were appointed from within its number. Eligibility for membership on the council would have depended on a minimum level of property ownership. Like local authorities today, the magistrates and the council were responsible for such things as the public water supply, roads, public latrines, the town defences, law and order, tax collection, tolls, and public buildings.

There is some uncertainty about the name of the town. Many modern writers refer to the place as Camulodunum—as indeed did some ancient writers—but this name is not strictly correct. Easily the most authoritative source for its name comes from the 2nd-century tombstone in Rome of a man called Gnaeus Munatius Aurelius Bassus. The monument records how, after completing several senior commissions in the army, he had been in charge of the roll of the Roman citizens (the census officer) of 'Colonia Victricensis which is in Britain at Camulodunum'. Clearly the careful precision of the language shows that there was a distinction between the Roman colony and its Iron Age predecessor, and that each still retained its own name. Interestingly it also implies that the people of Rome were more likely to have heard of Camulodunum than Colonia Victricensis, which would explain why someone like Tacitus could rather sloppily refer to the Roman town as 'Camulodunum'. Sometimes the name of the Roman town was shortened to simply 'Colonia' which ultimately presumably led to the name 'Colchester' itself, meaning probably 'Colonia camp'. Since the colony was founded during the reign of Claudius, it is likely to have incorporated his name in its official title. Thus, although there is no record as such, the colony may have been called something like 'Colonia Claudia Victricensis'. Thus 'Colonia Victricensis' may itself be an abbreviation. Some scholars have complicated the issue further by

The base of the tombstone in Rome of Gnaeus Munatius Aurelius Bassus, who, earlier in his career, had been the census officer in Colchester. His inscription reads as follows:

Gnaeus Munatius Aurelius Bassus, son of Marcus of the Palatine tribe, Procurator of the Emperor, Prefect of the Armourers, Prefect of the Third Cohort of Archers, Prefect again of the Second Cohort of Asturians, Census Officer of the Roman Citizens of Colonia Victricensis which is in Britain at Camulodunum, Overseer of the Nomentum Road, Patron of the same municipality, Priest for life, *Aedile* with magisterial power, Dictator four times.

suggesting that 'Victricensis' was an addition following the restoration of the colony after the Boudican revolt. Nevertheless, despite all the confusion and difficulty, the careful wording on the Bassus tombstone shows that 'Colonia Victricensis' is the most reliable and accurate name we have at present for the Roman town, and that this is the one that we should use. The name can be translated as 'Colony of the Victorious' or, more loosely, 'City of Victory'.

Colonies were more than simply urban centres. Each colony needed its dependent territory (*territorium*) which was surrounding land which fell within its jurisdiction. These territories were essential since the new settlers needed farm land. Thus the creation of the colony at Camulodunum was not simply the plantation of a foreign town on British soil but also would have involved the settlement of the surrounding countryside on a large scale. Indeed urban and rural settlement would have been so intertwined that it

would be wrong to underestimate the scale and importance of land acquisition in the colonisation process. Sometimes the land for the *territorium* was bought but this was not necessary when the foundation was on conquered land. At Camulodunum the royal estates and other Catuvellaunian land-holdings would have been available for distribution amongst the veteran soldiers.

The army at this time usually gave veteran soldiers either allotments of land or a lump sum as a kind of annuity for their retirement. The normal practice was for the land to be divided up on a grid system (centuriation) and the blocks apportioned accordingly. All the centuriated land would have been within the *territorium* of the colony, although not all of the *territorium* would necessarily have been centuriated.

Founding a town was a well-established ritual, although events at Colchester must have been complicated by the fact that the place already existed as a fortress. However, under normal circumstances the process would have been along the following lines. A three-man commission would have been appointed to supervise the foundation in all its aspects. It was the commissioners' responsibility to decide on the limits of the *territorium*, allot the land to the settlers, set out the constitution for the new community, and appoint its first office-holders and priests. They would also be expected to adjudicate in any disputes which arose with the settlers or the locals. The *territorium* would have been surveyed and divided up into parcels of land ready for distribution among the settlers. Auspices would have been taken and sacrifices made prior to the chief commissioner marking out the position of the intended town wall with a furrow drawn by two white oxen of different sexes. An instrument for surveying called a *groma* would have been set up in the centre of the town and used to strike out the two main streets (*decumanus maximus* and *cardo maximus*). The other streets in the grid would have followed to form square or rectangular blocks of land known as *insulae*. The land in the *territorium* would have been allocated to the settlers by the drawing of lots, and a land register would have been compiled in the form of a plan (*forma*) engraved on a bronze sheet. The colony was officially founded (but far from finished) when the *forma* and a copy of the *lex coloniae* were fixed to a wall in the forum and the *groma* ritually removed from the ground.

Capital punishment

Gruesome heads on poles at the west entrance into Colchester in around AD 50 would have acted as public reminders of the harsh rule of law. Brutality of the most extreme kind is implied by six human skulls in the legionary ditch at Balkerne Lane. Two of the skulls (pictured here) show severe wounds inflicted shortly before death.

Above right: a compressed fracture caused by a blow to the top of the head with a blunt instrument.
Below: a wide cut caused by a poorly-aimed blow with a sword or axe which was presumably meant to sever the neck vertebrae and detach the head.

It is unclear if these executions belong to the military period or the first years of the new town. Equally it is not possible to tell if the victims were Romans or natives. Other evidence shows an arm which was chopped off above the elbow.

As might be expected, centuriation was a very precise and methodical process. The land was divided up into blocks, each equivalent in area to 100 plots of two *iugera* (about twelve and a half acres), which was the traditional size of a Roman land-holding. Generally centuriated land was divided up into squares separated by baulks or roads, with a major road occurring at every fifth square.

The *groma* consisted of two wooden rods fixed at right angles to each other. Plumb-bobs were suspended from the ends of the rods allowing the surveyor to set out lines at right-angles to each other by sighting along opposing plumb-lines. Although this was a very simple tool, grids could be (and were) laid out with great accuracy, although success was dependent on there being little or no wind.

There has been a great deal of archaeological research in and around the Roman town (because of redevelopment pressures), but there has been little opportunity for much work in the surrounding countryside. Consequently there is very little hard evidence about the scale and nature of land colonisation around the town, and indeed there is a question over whether or not the land was centuriated at all. Tacitus tells us that the process of land acquisition in Colchester was not as it should have been. '*The settlers drove the Trinobantes from their homes and land, and called them prisoners and slaves. The troops encouraged the settlers' outrages, since their own way of behaving was the same and they looked forward to similar licence for themselves*'. None of this has as yet been recognised in the archaeological record, but we can assume that this was no minor event but wholesale land grabbing on a large scale. Land could be a highly desirable commodity no matter where it was—witness the thousands of Europeans who were prepared to trek across America in the 19th century and risk everything in the hope of land. The *territorium* of a colony could extend for many miles from the settlement. Clearly any displacement of people on such a scale must have been an extremely unpleasant process.

On the other hand, there is some evidence of a more compassionate (and thus ultimately more pragmatic) treatment of at least some members of the indigenous population. As mentioned on pages 44 and 45, the topographical relationships of the fortress and the Gosbecks fort to the occupied areas of the native settlement hint that the Roman army made some attempts to live with the local population in as unabrasive a manner as the circumstances would allow. Similarly, tolerance of native rights and traditions resulted in the survival of the Gosbecks site throughout the Roman period (it was clearly never confiscated for Roman settlement) and extended to permitting the subsequent developments of the native sanctuary. Thus rather than court conflict in the way described by Tacitus, the Romans may at first have acted diplomatically by not taking the most contentious native lands, in which case Tacitus must be referring to a later phase of undisciplined land appropriation. Alternatively—and perhaps more likely—the absence of archaeological evidence for centuriation could be taken at its face value and we should accept that the land was never centuriated. This would mean that the free-for-all described by Tacitus was probably the way that all the veterans acquired their land. In that case, small wonder that a serious revolt was soon to follow.

One of the important aspects of the excavations at Colchester in the 1970s is that a new way of founding towns was recognised. The process had not involved the laying out of a town on a virgin site in the way just described, but the reuse and adaptation of the former legionary fortress. Reuse of the sites of fortresses had been recognised before (at Gloucester, Lincoln, and Exeter) where Roman towns were found to be on top of the sites of legionary fortresses. What was new and important in Colchester is that the reuse included not just land but streets and buildings too. The fact that this happened at Colchester flags up the likelihood that such a process could have occurred at Gloucester, Lincoln, Exeter, and Wroxeter, where the alignments of fortress and town at each place are the same. It seems that the practice of converting disused fortresses into towns was prevalent between around AD 40 to 110 as the Roman empire expanded to its maximum extent. No examples have been recognised for certain outside Britain but there are a handful of likely candidates on the peripheries of the empire including Cologne in Germany, Ammaedara and Theveste in Africa, and Sarmizegetusa in Dacia (now Romania).

The one factor which marks Colchester out from the others and makes its

Part of a broken military diploma belonging to Saturninus of Gloucester. Diplomas were awarded to auxiliary soldiers on their discharge. They gave the owner's service record and proved he was a Roman citizen. From the site of St Mary's hospital in Colchester.

contribution so special is that archaeological remains show that some military buildings were in use well after the foundation of the colony. There can be little doubt about the identification of the reused military buildings, because the colony was burnt to the ground about a decade after it was founded, and the layer of debris left by the fire shows that many of the buildings which were standing at that time had originally been parts of the fortress.

Building works in the new town

The legionary defences were filled in and a new street grid laid out on a slightly different alignment so that it covered the area of the legionary annexe and the eastern half of the fortress. The grid of streets had the effect of dividing the town into rectangular blocks of land ('insulae'). The main north-south street (via principalis) and the north-south streets to the west were retained for the colony. The street along the inside of the defences (via sagularis) was also kept, except on the east side where it was replaced by a new street built over the levelled legionary defences. The area of the annexe seems to have been given over partly, if not entirely, to public buildings including a great temple dedicated to Claudius and probably a theatre. About two-thirds of the eighteen or so military buildings so far excavated in Colchester were destroyed in the fire of AD 60/1. This fact combined with the reuse of so many streets shows that a substantial proportion of the military buildings must have survived the transition from fortress to town.

In many cases, only parts of the barracks were reused in the new colony. The centurions' quarters of the barrack blocks were ideally suited for use as houses because they

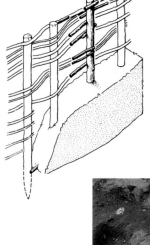

Collapsed wattle-and-daub wall at the Balkerne Lane site (below right). This is a rare example of where traces of the wood still survive, despite the wood not having been burned. Wall construction was very basic in this instance and involved hammering sharpened posts into the ground and then weaving longitudinal wattles between them.

fronted on to a principal street and were divided up internally into small rooms. But the men's quarters were not so readily converted, being in effect a series of small independent compartments. They were also less desirable because they fronted on to minor streets. Thus all of the northern barrack at Lion Walk was converted into houses as well as the centurions' quarters of the two adjacent blocks. The rest were knocked down and their sites used for cultivation.

It is harder to tell what happened to the barrack at the Gilberd School site. A new east-west street was laid out to the north of the barrack as part of the works for the new town. This shared the alignment of the eastern street grid and was set back a little distance from the barrack. Small houses were built along the southern frontage of the new street, one being terraced into the natural slope (rising to the south) so that it cut into the central area of the former barrack, thereby partially destroying it. Parts of the barrack seem to have been reused but perhaps only because it was marginally easier to do this than knock it down. Part of the north wall at the western end appears to have been incorporated in the south wall of the civilian house to the north. There were indications that the eastern end of the building may have seen some reuse but this may also have been as a secondary process associated with new houses to the north. In contrast, all of the barracks of the First Cohort at Culver Street seem to have been made into houses, including (as far as can be judged) all the men's quarters. These were probably more desirable as residences because of their more central position, being just off the main north-south street of the former fortress.

Probably there would not have been enough space within the former fortress for all the large civic buildings which the colonists needed. Accordingly the military defences were levelled so that the area of the annexe could be given over to buildings of this type. This explains the otherwise puzzling statement by Tacitus: 'It seemed easy to destroy the settlement; for it had no walls. That was a matter which the Roman commanders thinking of amenities rather than needs, had neglected.'

The 'amenities' must be the group of public buildings which, as already explained, would only have been laid out after the defences had been levelled. Excavations at Balkerne Lane have confirmed Tacitus' statement that the colony was unprotected in AD 60/1, because it was found that houses burnt in the revolt had been constructed over the levelled military defences and that these defences were not replaced until after the fire.

Public buildings

A key indicator of the status of a Roman settlement was its public buildings. Despite the way the colony was formed, the Roman town is likely to have been well endowed with public buildings, even before the Boudican fire of AD 60/1. We know about some of them as a result of archaeological investigations. Tacitus mentions some of them too, and others can be expected by analogy with other places.

The headquarters building (*principia*) of the fortress would very likely have been reused as a basilica-forum complex for the new town. There is no hard evidence to prove that this happened but buildings of this kind are seen generally as having an evolutionary link with military *principia*. The basilica-forum was the Roman equivalent of the modern town hall. They resembled military *principia* in appearance and to an extent in function, so that it would be surprising if the military headquarters building in Colchester was not reused in this way.

However the site of the former annexe seems to be the place where most of the public buildings were to be found, there being at least four of them known so far: the Temple of Claudius, the theatre, and at least two others, one in Insula 29 and one or more in Insula 30. (The *insula* numbers are parts of a modern reference system; see plan on page 114.) All these buildings have been recognised as a result of archaeological investigations.

Interestingly, Tacitus appears to provide independent evidence of three public buildings when he mentions the Temple of Claudius, the theatre, and the council

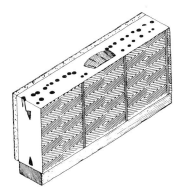

Timber-framed walls (burnt in the Boudican revolt) from the Culver Street and Lion Walk sites. These were well-built, fully framed walls with wattle-and-daub filling the gap between closely-set upright timbers, morticed top and bottom in wall- and ground-plates. The surfaces of the walls were keyed, plastered and painted.

Below right: side view of wall to show the voids left by burnt wattles. To the left is a diagram showing what this section of wall would have looked like when new. (The plaster on the facing side of the wall has been omitted for clarity.)

Below left: the charcoal at the base of the photograph is the remains of the timber which rested on the floor and formed the base of the wall.

57

The Roman theatre

The site of the Roman theatre was confirmed by excavation in 1982. It stood next to the Temple of Claudius, facing northwards down the slope towards the river. (See illustration on page 102.) It was built entirely of stone and tile, and it would have been large enough to accommodate a seated audience of at least 3,000.

Right: part of the D-shaped outer wall forming the auditorium.

Left: continuation of the D-shaped outer wall as revealed in Maidenburgh Street in 1984. The position of this wall is now indicated in the street surface by coloured bricks.

chamber (see page 74 for one of the passages). He also mentions a statue of Victory, which he says fell face down for no apparent reason as if fleeing the enemy. The theatre, the council chamber, and the statue of Victory are essential parts of his description of the bad omens which were to portend the Boudican onslaught. The relevant passage is obviously written for effect and can hardly be true. It is possible that Tacitus simply assumed that the town possessed a theatre, a council chamber and a statue of Victory, because these are the sorts of things that he would have expected to find in a colony such as this. On the other hand, the Temple of Claudius was sufficiently unusual and distinctive to suggest that he really did draw on authoritative local knowledge. (His father-in-law Agricola was in Britain in AD 60/1.)

The Temple of Claudius has been identified and we will examine the building in some detail shortly. Remains of a theatre in an *insula* next to the temple were uncovered during exploratory excavations in 1981. If, as is possible, this building proves to be too late in date to have been the theatre referred to by Tacitus, then it is very likely that the remains of his theatre lie underneath it (assuming of course that it existed in the first place). Nothing is known of the council chamber. However if the colony did possess such a thing, then it is likely to have been a square or rectangular building in the form of a small covered theatre (otherwise known as an *odeon*), near either the Temple of Claudius or the former headquarters building of the fortress. As regards other public buildings, not much is known about the buildings in Insulae 29 and 30 except that they were clearly too large to have been private, and the building in Insula 30 probably contained large columns covered with fluted plaster.

To the Romans, a visit to the public bathhouse was as much a pleasure and a sign of civilised living as a hygienic necessity. Thus the colony would undoubtedly have possessed at least one set of public baths. As yet, none have been recognised in the town but there is evidence pointing to several possible locations. Easily the most likely of these is the northern half of Insula 38a where a 19th-century antiquarian (William Wire) recorded seeing two complete hypocaust flues and three arched 'fireplaces' under the north end of Long Wyre Street. The flue-tiles still exist in Colchester Museum. These have been examined by Ernest Black who has made a special study of such objects and he thinks that they came from a 1st-century bath-house. Another possible site is the western half of Insula 30 where part of what appears to have been the base of a massive suspended floor was observed in 1983—the sort of thing that would be found in a public bath-house. Yet another site still is the eastern half of Insula 20 where excavations in 1990 revealed part of a large public building with very large foundations. There is nothing as yet to show that this was a bath-house except the presence of a large drain and its plan, which (though little is known of it) appears to rule out other possible explanations for the building.

The Temple of Claudius, the god

The Temple of Claudius is the largest classical temple known in Britain, and is of a scale that would have been at home in Rome itself. It was the meeting place and the base of the imperial cult in Britain, where Roman emperors were worshipped with the goddess Roma (the spirit of Rome).

The existence of a temple in Colchester erected in honour of Claudius is known from the Roman writers Tacitus and Suetonius. Around 1920, Dr R.E.M. (later Sir Mortimer) Wheeler and Dr Henry Laver (a local archaeologist) realised that the 'vaults' under Colchester Castle were really part of a large classical-style temple and suggested that this was the Temple of Claudius.

The 'vaults' are not really vaults at all but are formed by the underside and foundations of the podium on which the temple stood. The base of the podium was made by pouring stones and mortar into massive trenches shuttered with timbers to prevent the soft sandy edges collapsing. The timbers were left in position while the mortar hardened and, as a result, their imprints can still be seen today in the walls of the vaults.

Although nothing of the superstructure of the temple podium survives, the positions of the foundations of the podium make it possible to reconstruct its plan. This is because they were the load-bearing parts of the podium, and the principle was that all the walls and columns had to have foundations directly underneath. Unfortunately the absence of a good, accurate plan of the podium prevents really confident reconstruction, but we are helped in a more general way by the ten books on architecture written by a Roman architect called Vitruvius.

The main room in the temple was called the *cella*. This conformed to Vitruvian principles in that its length was one and a quarter times its width. The space (like a porch) in front of the *cella* was known as the *pronaos*. Rows of columns down the sides formed aisles which appear to have been stopped off at the ends by continuations of the rear wall of the *cella*. The aisles were thus not continued around the rear of the temple (like some

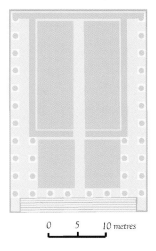

0   5   10 metres

Above: south elevation and plan of the Temple of Claudius. Note the positions of the columns and walls around the four 'vaults' which are indicated as differently tinted areas.

One of the 'vaults' of the Temple of Claudius. This is really the underside of the massive foundations which formed the great platform on which the temple was raised.

A letter 'V' from a monumental inscription. Made of copper alloy. Found near the site of the Temple of Claudius.

others) thereby making it 'peripteral'. As far as can be gauged, the temple was also of 'Eustyle' which meant that the space between each column was two and a quarter times the diameter of the columns apart from the two central columns at the front which were three diameters apart.

There would have been no windows, the only access being through bronze double doors in the front of the *cella*. The building would have been over 20 m high, including the exposed part of the podium. This makes it substantially higher than the castle is today. By analogy with temples elsewhere, it is apparent that the Temple of Claudius had a façade formed of eight columns (octastyle).

The building would have been built of stone with a tile roof. The stone was a mixture of large flints and septaria. The flints would have come from local quarries where the excavated material would have been graded (as is done today) into sand and stone of different sizes ranging up to the large flints like those used in the Temple. The septaria would probably have come from somewhere on the Essex coast like Walton where even today the material occurs in large quantities on the beaches. The core of each column was made of curved bricks. The shafts of the

columns were rendered with plaster whereas their decorative capitals (tops) and bases were probably formed with moulded plaster. The flint and septaria cannot be worked to provide faces so that the finished work had to be plastered and either painted or covered with sheets of polished stone and marble.

There is good evidence that a large altar stood immediately in front of the temple. One theory is that the construction of the temple could not have started until Claudius had died and that the altar was the initial focus of the imperial cult. The model for such an arrangement is to be found at Lyon in Gaul where an altar and later a temple were dedicated to Augustus and Roma.

The statue of Victory

The statue of Victory mentioned by Tacitus is certainly the kind of image that the colony would have possessed. Victory was the Roman version of the Greek goddess Nike. She is sometimes shown as being winged and holding a wreath or a palm of victory. The statue could have been on top of a building like the Temple of Claudius, on the apex at the front for example, or on top of the monumental arch at the west entrance into the town. A prime site for it would have been on the top of a column overlooking the altar in front of the Temple of Claudius.

Simplified drawing of the monumental arch on the site of the later Balkerne gate.

Monumental arch

A major public structure would have been the great monumental arch built on the site of the west gate into the fortress. This would have been the main entrance (*porta decumana*) into the colony from the west, in other words from London and Verulamium. The arch is almost certainly 1st century in date and most likely belongs to the AD 50s. Knowledge of the arch's existence and date relies on excavation. It was discovered during excavations in 1913 and 1919 by R.E.M. Wheeler and others when it was misinterpreted as being rebuilt parts of the later gate.

Although referred to here as an arch, rather confusingly it actually incorporated two arches. Across the front of it there would have been an inscription probably recording the foundation of the town and possibly Claudius' role in the conquest of Britain. Most unusually, the arch was faced with tufa which is a material which can easily be cut to produce clean faces and sharp edges. The tufa was probably brought by sea from quarries near the Hampshire coast.

Making the fortress into a town

Converting the fortress into a town may have taken several years. The evidence for this statement comes from three places: (i) the Temple of Claudius; (ii) the backfilling of the legionary ditch; and (iii) the theatre. It has been argued that the Temple of Claudius could not have been started until after the death of Claudius in AD 54. Since the *insula* containing the temple is apparently the dominant feature of the eastern grid and is an integral part of its layout, then either the grid was set out no earlier than AD 54 or before this date the main feature of the *insula* was the altar (dedicated to Augustus and Roma) mentioned on the previous page. Tacitus of course tells us that during the Boudican revolt a last stand was made by the veterans in the temple. The legionary defences at Balkerne Lane had been much neglected before being levelled. Debris was tipped into the butt ends of the ditch, pits were dug on its western side, and at least one building, probably a workshop, was built up against the southern butt end so that it encroached on to the main street. Since no military commander would have tolerated such treatment of his defences, parts of the bank and ditch must have been intact for some time after the evacuation of the garrison.

The western side of the theatre appears to have overlain the levelled defences of the fortress. Moreover, it was not on the alignment of the eastern grid as might be expected, but shared the same alignment as the fortress. These two factors seem to indicate that, between the destruction of these defences and the laying out of the eastern grid, there was a hiatus long enough for the construction of the theatre to begin.

Taken together the various strands of evidence indicate that the eastern grid may not have been laid out until the mid 50s. The process could have been quite complex, with various stretches of the defences being levelled independently over a period of years.

Fortress into town
Plans of the fortress (above) and the early town (below), showing how many of the streets and buildings survived the transition from military base to the City of Victory.

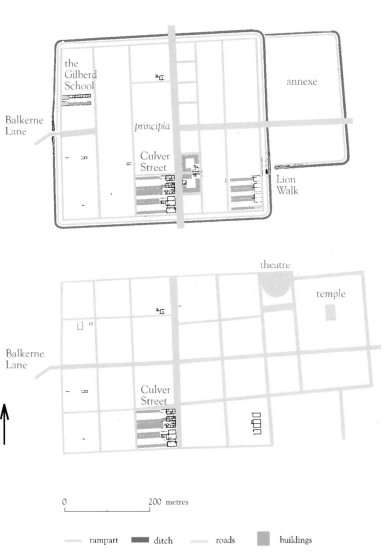

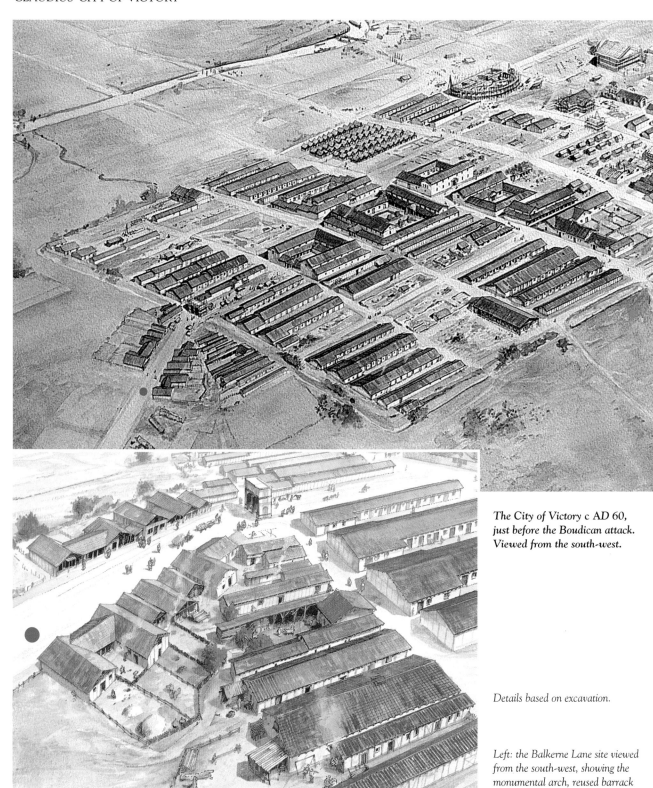

The City of Victory c AD 60, just before the Boudican attack. Viewed from the south-west.

Details based on excavation.

Left: the Balkerne Lane site viewed from the south-west, showing the monumental arch, reused barrack blocks, and buildings on either side of the road into the new town.

Above right: the Lion Walk site viewed from the south-east, showing the partly backfilled legionary ditch, partly reused barracks and a new north-south street on the site of the eastern defences of the fortress.

Right: the Culver Street site viewed from the south-west, showing the site of the demolished legionary gate, the partly backfilled legionary ditch, reused barracks (left) and new houses (right).

Population size

It is almost impossible to estimate how many people lived in the Roman town and its *territorium*. It would not be much help if we knew how many houses existed inside the colony. We could get some idea of the size of the population if we knew the area covered by the *territorium* and the average area of the allotments. But this would only be a maximum since, as we have mentioned, not all of the *territorium* would have been centuriated. Unfortunately there was no standard size of allotment, and nor of course do we know the size of the *territorium* at Colchester. And more to the point, it is not at all clear if any of the land was centuriated in the first place. However we can at least base our calculations on the fact that by the 1st century AD, military settlers were typically allotted 50 or even 66.67 *iugera* (31 or 41 acres) which was a quarter or a third of a centuriated square (a *centuria*) respectively. Thus if the *territorium* had extended on average 10 kilometres out from the colony, then, on the basis of landholdings in centuriated land elsewhere, this would have provided enough land for 1,850 colonists and their families. If the *territorium* extended an average of 15 kilometres from the town, this would have increased the potential number to about 4,000, which would have been large by standards of the time.

Estimating the actual population involves other factors. The settlers would have had families and servants and they would have needed workers to help on their farms, since obviously farms of 30 or 40 acres would be too large to work on their own. Presumably the natives who were dispossessed of their lands would have provided a pool of suitable labour.

They would have lived close by their places of work and would of course have had families of their own.

The Domesday Survey gives us an idea of what the relative sizes of the rural and urban populations at Colchester might have been. At the time of Domesday (AD 1086), about three times as many people lived within a 10-kilometre radius of the town as lived inside it. (The combined total was around 8,000, but that is not very useful since the figure was always changing with time.) If nothing else, these figures underline the fact that the rural population is very likely to have substantially outnumbered that of the town. Of course ultimately we can only make a wild guess, but a population of at least 15,000 for the Roman colony and its *territorium* would seem a modest estimate on the basis of a core of say two thousand settlers.

The redundant military buildings

It is not known how the veterans acquired the redundant buildings. It might be that, as maybe with land allotments, they were distributed via a lottery. Acquisition of these buildings would have been of greatest interest to settlers who acquired land close to the town. Thus the buildings might have been bundled in with allotments of this kind and distributed as part of the lottery. However the distribution of the reused barrack blocks suggests otherwise. The pattern of reuse is not random as might be expected in a lottery, but seems to be related to such factors as the location and the adaptability of the building. Hence the most southerly barracks at Lion Walk were less favoured and, of those that were reused, only the centurions' quarters were kept. On the other hand at Culver Street, where the barracks were of a larger, more complicated plan, the reuse seems to have been total. Various conclusions can be drawn from this. Firstly, the highly selective nature of the pattern of reuse

Three clay figurines from the extraordinary 'child's grave' found in the 19th century. The complete grave group drawn by J. Parish is shown opposite. The grave is famous for its richness, and the number of pipeclay figurines which include people reclining on couches and seated old men who appear to be teachers. It dates to the AD 50s or early 60s. The presence of a 'feeding bottle' and the small size of the pots suggest that it was for a child (page 108).

suggests that the buildings were not distributed randomly via a lottery but were sold or disposed of in some other way which reflected their desirability. Secondly, the barracks in general were not much sought after by the settlers, since only some were adapted for reuse in the colony. Thirdly, the limited survival of the barracks suggests that the Romans were more interested in reusing the main buildings of the fortress as public buildings for the new town.

The inhabitants of the new town

In addition to the veteran soldiers and their families, the new settlement and the fortress before it would have attracted tradesmen, merchants, and other businessmen of various sorts who would have attended the local markets or resided permanently in the area. Figuring prominently among this group would have been immigrants, especially those from Gaul. They would have come to Colchester in the hope of making a good living, attracted by the enormous purchasing power of the army and later of the new frontier town. Those fortunate enough to hold Roman citizenship would probably have lived and worked in the town, while others would have set up shop along the approach streets. For the latter, the Balkerne Lane site was perhaps the predominant area, where small buildings huddled along both frontages of the road leading from Colchester to London and the west. In this area too were likely to be living at least some of the native members (*incolae*) whom Tacitus tells us were present in the town at the time of the Boudican revolt.

In summary, the early colony would have been markedly agricultural in character and, as in immediate pre-conquest days, would have served as the main market place in the region for agricultural produce of all kinds. Opportunities would have abounded in what must have been a fast-developing commercial and industrial boom town. The expanding civilian population, the port, the large native population in the area, and the prospect of lucrative military contracts to help supply a large campaigning army would all have combined to act like a magnet for the skilled craftsman and the determined entrepreneur alike, regardless of whether or not he was a veteran soldier. The extent of the early town and the density of its occupation demonstrate the success of the venture: the ubiquity of the famous 'Boudican layer' testifies to the abruptness with which it all but ended.

Pot showing blacksmith's tools in relief.

J Parish delt

C Benn x

**The Stanway
'warrior' grave**

*Sketch reconstruction plan of the layout of the
Stanway 'warrior' grave and its burial goods.*

*Glass bowl
from the 'warrior'
grave. Imported from Italy.*

British collaborators

While Caratacus and his men were fighting the Roman army in the west, some of his compatriots had stayed at home in Camulodunum and were collaborating with their new foreign overlords. This is not as unlikely as it may seem and indeed, we have the identity of one possible candidate. A few years before the invasion, Caratacus' brother Adminius had fled the country to appeal to the Romans for protection after a quarrel with his father Cunobelin. There is no evidence to prove that Adminius had subsequently been installed as a puppet leader but his lineage would have made him an ideal person for the role. Maintaining a large army in Britain was an expensive business, and so too was the building of Colonia Victricensis. The Britons had to pay for all this, and they could only do so if they were kept working in the fields producing food and other supplies in the way they had before the invasion. Members of the local nobility predisposed towards the Romans were best placed to promote the right atmosphere and help secure the collection of the required taxes. They

Key

1 *amphora from the Pompeii region*
2-7 *pottery vessels (terra nigra from
      northern Gaul)*
8 *terra rubra pottery bowl from
   northern Gaul*
9 *copper-alloy flat pan*
10 *terra sigillata from southern France*
11 *pottery beaker*
12 *pottery bowl*
13 *pottery flagon*
14 *blue glass phial*
15 *white and blue glass game counters*
16 *gaming board*
17 *cremated bones in ?bag*
18 *clear glass phial*
19 and 28 *brooch with ?cloak*
20 *wooden box*
21 *the amber glass bowl from Italy
    (pictured above)*
22 *iron spearhead*
23 *pottery cup*
24 *slip-coated pottery jug*
25 *?shield*
26 *wooden object*
27 *?grid-iron*
29 *copper-alloy jug*
30-31 *copper-alloy armlet and glass
       bead.*

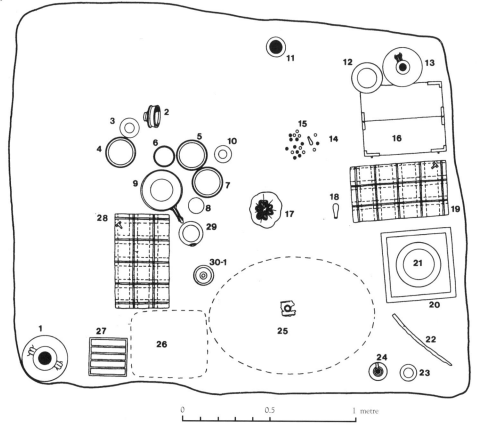

could call on past loyalties and they were aware of local customs and practices.

We shall discuss Gosbecks at greater length later (page 102), but we shall note here that the site is likely to have remained the focal point for the British community for many years to come, until the distinction between Romans and Britons (or at least citizen and non-citizen) ceased to be meaningful in administrative and social terms.

The funerary site at Stanway (page 23) provides us with evidence of collaboration in exchange for privileges. The latest of the chambers dates to around AD 60, showing that the site continued to be used as a burial place for British nobility for about 20 years or so after the Roman invasion. Thus despite Caratacus' exploits elsewhere, not only did elements of the ruling class continue to live in Camulodunum in the shadow of the Romans, but they were also able to bury their dead in a prominent site which had been similarly used by their immediate forebears.

Another sign of privilege comes from some of the remarkable secondary burials which were inserted into the funerary enclosures. At least four of these post-date the arrival of the Roman army, and these are of great interest because the people concerned do not seem to have been relatives of the dead in the chambers but members of the class in Celtic society of learned men who were socially on a par with the landowning/warrior class. These included druids, bards, seers and physicians. One grave contained an ink-pot suggesting that the dead person had been literate. (Illiteracy was normal among the Britons although less so within the upper classes.) Another grave (the 'warrior' grave) contained a spear and perhaps a shield and may thus have been for a member of the nobility or an armour-bearer. Britons would not normally have been allowed to carry arms, and Dio said specifically that Claudius had disarmed the defeated tribes in AD 43. (Armour-bearers could move in high circles. Cartimandua, the contemporary queen of the Brigantes, divorced her husband and replaced him with her armour-bearer.) A third grave contained the basic elements of what is believed to be a small surgical kit, showing that the deceased had been a physician. This extraordinary grave is also remarkable for its 'strainer bowl', its strange collection of rods and rings (which may have been used for divination), and its gaming board with the pieces set out as if in play.

Impression of the graveside ceremony for the 'warrior' grave.

The Stanway 'game' grave

The gaming board lies to the right of the large vessel (amphora) in the top corner. The surgical instruments and the dead person's cremated remains lie on the board. The rods, which may have been for divination (perhaps to check if the time was right for an operation), are in the right-hand corner.

The copper-alloy strainer bowl. It has been crushed by the weight of soil above it. The spout is to the top and the handle is to the bottom. The strainer plate lies just below the spout, inside the vessel.

The gaming board

The gaming board is an extraordinary discovery which caused much media interest throughout Britain and even beyond. Many Roman game boards have been found before, and gaming counters in various materials commonly occur on Roman sites. But this is the first recorded time that a board has been found with the pieces in position.

There are various snippets of information about Roman games in the ancient literature, but there is no list of games and nor is there a complete set of rules for any single game. The Colchester game provides a new, vivid type of evidence, since it is a game set out by somebody who knew how to play it. In a way, this is the most direct and intimate sort of evidence that you can get.

The board was made of two pieces of wood, hinged so that it folded inwards lengthways. Its corners were strengthened with right-angled strips of copper alloy. The pieces lay on the board as if at an early stage in a game. The counters are of opaque glass in the shape of thick chocolate drops. There are twenty-six in all, thirteen white and thirteen dark blue. Each player seems to have had twelve standard pieces, plus a thirteenth which was of different rank. White's thirteenth piece was much smaller than the others, whereas blue's differed solely by being placed upside down on the board.

The wood of the board had rotted away completely apart from where it was in contact with the metal corner pieces and hinges. The overall proportions of the board (3:2) and the positions of the pieces suggest that it was marked out as a grid to form 12 by 8 squares.

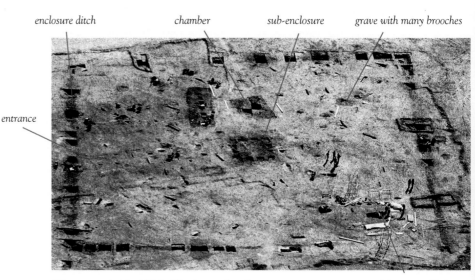

enclosure ditch — *chamber* — *sub-enclosure* — *grave with many brooches*

entrance

rich grave with the gaming board

The excavation in 1996 of Enclosure 5 at Stanway. (*Photograph by Nicky Lewin, East Anglian Daily Times.*)

Right: *the gaming board and counters in situ. On the right are the cremated remains of bone; on the left are some of the possible medical instruments. At this stage in the excavation, not all the counters had been found and so are not in the photograph.*

Below: *close-up of the remains of one corner of the gaming board, showing the blue counter which was upside-down, in position. (The upside-down counter was uncovered after the photograph on the right was taken.)*

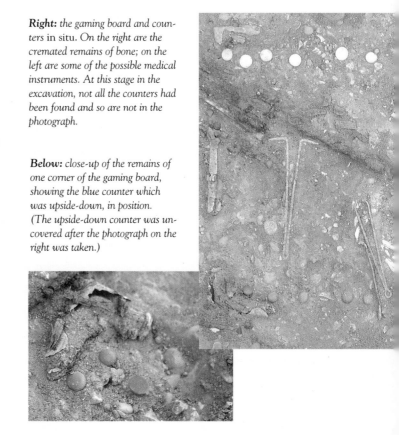

Right: the counters and remains of the board *in situ*, being excavated. Note the instruments and the cremated human bone which had been placed on top of the board.

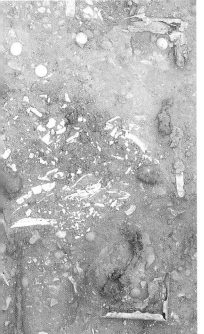

(Photograph by Andrew Cook.)

Below: reconstruction of the game.

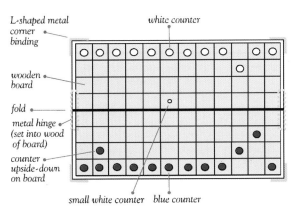

The game

The absence of dice shows that it was a game of pure skill. The most obvious candidate for the game from those that are known is '*ludus latrunculorum*', meaning 'game of little bandits (or robbers)'. The aim of this game was to remove your opponent's pieces one at a time by sandwiching one between two of your own. The pieces could move forwards, backwards and sideways, like rooks in chess, and there were superior pieces which could move in more flexible ways.

Regardless of whether or not the game was actually *ludus latrunculorum*, the play represented by the pieces on the Stanway board might have been along the following lines. Each player sets out his twelve standard pieces in a line down one side of the board. Each then places his thirteenth piece on a vacant square of his choice. Blue decides to play defensively and places his extra piece close to the left-hand corner of the board (as he sees it). White is bolder and puts his extra piece in the middle but in his half of the board. Play starts in earnest with blue advancing his third piece in from the right by one square. White responds by doing the same with his facing piece. Blue then advances his piece second in from the right by two squares. The game, which had barely begun, then goes no further. The dead person's cremated remains are placed on the board (perhaps in a bag). The ?surgical instruments are also put on the board (or maybe on a shelf in the box). Other items are placed in the box and its lid is shut, thereby protecting the contents from the soil that was then shovelled into the grave.

Board games were popular in the Roman world among adults and children alike. The grave with the game was of a British person so the game may not necessarily be Roman, although the pieces are certainly of a standard Roman type. Information about the games favoured by Celts is even sparser than for the Romans. However it seems, in later Celtic legends from Ireland, that skill in board games among the Britons could have been a highly-regarded accomplishment, and that even important matters among the nobility might occasionally have turned on the outcome of a game. Of the eight most important graves found at the Stanway site, three contained gaming pieces, which clearly indicates the popularity of board games among these high-ranking Britons. Moreover, burial practice was itself very ritualised and the Stanway game may have been part of an elaborate graveside ceremony full of meaning for the living participants.

L-shaped metal corner binding

white counter

wooden board

fold

metal hinge (set into wood of board)

counter upside-down on board

small white counter   blue counter

Handle in the shape of a ram's head. Part of the copper-alloy pan found in the Stanway 'warrior' grave.

Evidence such as this for specialists is quite extraordinary and underlines yet again the privileged position enjoyed by a small section of the British community in Camulodunum at this time.

The making of the new province

The colony is likely to have been intended as the centre of the provincial government—what we would describe today as the capital city. The provincial council would have met in the Temple of Claudius, and in the very early years, the provincial procurator and maybe even the governor may each have been based in the colony too (more of these shortly). With the foundation of the City of Victory, the south-east of Britain began to look more like a regular province of Rome than just occupied territory.

Two other major towns were founded in the province at around the same time as Colonia Victricensis. One of them, Verulamium, was located on the site of the tribal centre of the Catuvellauni and was to serve as the tribe's capital town. It was thus similar in many respects to Colonia Victricensis in context and purpose. However, Verulamium was a *municipium* rather than a colony. The legal status of such places is hard to understand, but they were not as privileged as colonies and its members did not all have to hold Roman citizenship, but only the holders of magistracies and members of the city council. Verulamium was protected by dykes, but the system was a good deal smaller and simpler than that at Camulodunum, although it too had been a mint for the manufacture of coins. The coins provide various abbreviations of the name of the original settlement (VER, VERL, VERO, VERLAMIO, and VIR) showing that the Roman town (unlike Colonia Victricensis) was given a Romanised form of its name. Just as its name reflected its British origin, a few of its important later buildings betrayed stronger non-Roman influences than could be detected at Colonia Victricensis. Its principal temple was of the Romano-Celtic type as opposed to the classical design at Colchester, and its theatre (some argue) showed Celtic influences in its plan. There is no evidence that the town was based on a redundant military base, although its street is irregular in its dimensions and makes *insulae* of various sizes, suggesting that its origin is not yet properly understood.

The second of the two major towns was Londinium. London was not a political foundation like Colonia Victricensis or Verulamium: there was no major pre-existing settlement there. Instead it was simply a port which proved so well-placed that well before the century was out it had become the dominant commercial and administrative centre in the province.

Londinium was sited on the north bank of the Thames where there was a ferry crossing place over the river. The river was still wide at this point and it could be reached by large ships without the need for high tides. Londinium was not a colony and neither does it appear to have been a *municipium* although later it was to achieve greater status. It might be expected that Londinium started off in the AD 40s as a military base. Although there is some evidence of early military occupation on the opposite bank at Southwark, most London archaeologists agree that there was no military forerunner to Londinium itself and that the latter was founded on an empty site around AD 50. Overwhelming commercial success based on waterborne trade was to create a major cultural and economic force where there was none before and which was to dominate to this day. London was to prove one of the greatest legacies of the Roman conquest of Britain.

As was normal, the provincial administration would have been divided between two figures: the governor and the procurator. The governor would have been of senatorial rank and in command of the army. The provincial procurator was the Roman equivalent of the chancellor of the exchequer and was responsible for financial matters such as the collection of taxes and the payment of the troops. Provincial procurators were of lower political rank than governors since they were drawn from the equestrian class and were not members of the senate. They answered directly to the emperor and could act as a check on the activities of the governor. It is possible that the governor and his staff would have been based in the new colony at Colchester, at any rate during the winters of the early years. The governor himself may not have been present very often but there would presumably have been a substantial staff requiring a lot of office accommodation. The usual view is that the procurator was in Colchester for a few years before transferring to London perhaps just after the Boudican revolt. The most powerful piece of evidence for his presence in London

Map showing the relationship of the City of Victory to the surrounding countryside, rivers and sea. It illustrates the difficulties in providing the Roman town with good harbour facilities. The extent and locations of woodland and settlements is largely speculative. The wooded areas have been reduced compared with the Iron Age map (page 12) on the assumption that the Roman farmers would have cleared some land and that there would also have been much demand for wood from the new fortress and Roman town.

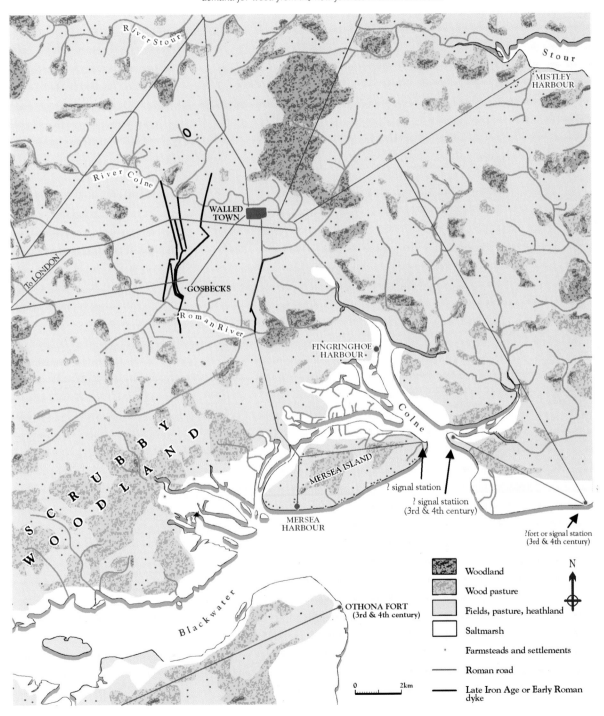

River Stour

Stour

MISTLEY HARBOUR

River Colne

WALLED TOWN

To LONDON

GOSBECKS

Roman River

FINGRINGHOE HARBOUR

Colne

S C R U B B Y   W O O D L A N D

MERSEA ISLAND

? signal station

? signal statiion (3rd & 4th century)

MERSEA HARBOUR

?fort or signal station (3rd & 4th century)

Blackwater

OTHONA FORT (3rd & 4th century)

N

Woodland

Wood pasture

Fields, pasture, heathland

Saltmarsh

· Farmsteads and settlements

— Roman road

— Late Iron Age or Early Roman dyke

0   2km

is the remarkable tombstone of Julius Classicianus who was appointed as procurator immediately following the revolt. However, implicit in Tacitus' account of the revolt is the fact that Classicianus' predecessor (Catus Decianus) was not in Colchester in AD 60 either (see page 74), so that it seems possible that the office of procurator had been in London from its beginning.

The provincial council was made up of delegates from the administrative regions (*civitates*) which made up the province. It served the imperial cult and met in the Temple of Claudius. The running costs of the cult had to be met by the high priest who was elected annually by the council from among its members. The financial burden that the office imposed was said to be one of the causes of the Boudican revolt.

Colonia Victricensis versus Londinium

Colchester, rather than London, would be the capital of Britain today had the Colne been like the Thames. Colchester would have had a population of millions rather than the current 100,000, and the whole of northeast Essex would be a great suburban sprawl. The fact that Colchester was not located on the site of a good natural harbour meant that a more suitable place had to be found elsewhere. London grew out of default. With the commercial stimulation provided by the presence of the procurator, the place flourished and grew with such effect that the port itself became a major city.

We have already looked at the landing facilities at Camulodunum at the time of the Roman military occupation. The problems still remained. Large ships would not have been able to penetrate up the Colne much beyond Fingringhoe except on exceptional tides. The mouth of the Colne is lined with salt marsh and mud flats and is unsuitable for a harbour. Upriver, where conditions are better, the Colne is much shallower and narrower. Large ships needed deep-water wharves like those found in London. Here great vertical-sided quays were built along the north river bank. The side of the river was pushed back to form vertical-sided docks that ships could moor against. Cargoes bound for Colonia Victricensis may have been off-loaded on to smaller ships for transportation upriver.

Alternative facilities were to be found elsewhere but they were even further away. The best harbour may have been ten miles away at Mistley. No evidence of a Roman port has been found there but the present port lies exactly on the spot where the projected line of known Roman road meets the river. The present river channel there would allow the construction of timber wharves as at Roman London. The road is traceable as cropmarks for over 3 miles and has been confirmed by excavation. It points so exactly to Mistley harbour that it can hardly be a coincidence.

Harbour facilities presumably also existed at West Mersea more or less where the present harbour is today. Mosaics and other remains of Roman buildings have been recorded around West Mersea church. They seem rather too dispersed for a large villa and may be explicable as a collection of buildings concentrated on a small harbour. Another source for goods in and out of Colonia Victricensis may have been Heybridge at Maldon via the mouth of the Blackwater.

But all of these places were poorly sited in terms of the Roman town. Mistley meant a land link of 10 miles, and Fingringhoe, West Mersea and Heybridge would have meant land journeys of at least 5, 8, and 13 miles respectively. West Mersea, moreover, had the added problem that it was probably cut off regularly at high tide (although admittedly much less so than today because the sea level was lower then). All in all, the port facilities at Colchester must have been very unsatisfactory and inefficient compared with the purpose-built operation on the Thames. It is easy to see how Londinium was to become so successful at the expense of Colonia Victricensis.

Right: picture lamp showing a Roman galley (the nozzle of the lamp has been broken off). Made in the 1st century AD. From the Culver Street site. 65 mm in diameter.

Below: part of a slave chain from Sheepen, found in the 1930s.

Below right: pillar-moulded glass bowl. Mid 1st century. From the Sheepen site.

THE
BRITISH REVENGE

The Boudican revolt

Claudius died unexpectedly in AD 54, only four years after the foundation of Colonia Victricensis. It is said that he was poisoned by his fourth wife Agrippina so that her son Nero could take his place. As emperor, Claudius had been a huge improvement on his predecessor Caligula, but things were to take a downwards turn with his unbalanced stepson Nero. In Britain, the next six years saw the situation developing to a point where a great native uprising under Boudica, the queen of the Iceni, led to massive loss of life and destruction of property and nearly resulted in the Romans being driven out of the country. The Boudican revolt and its immediate aftermath must have been one of the worst catastrophes ever seen in this country.

There are three main sources which allow us to chart these horrific events: archaeology and the accounts of Tacitus and Cassius Dio. Neither Tacitus nor Dio were present so they both had to rely on secondary sources (although Tacitus would have been alive at the time), and in fact Dio, being later, drew to an extent on Tacitus. As we shall see, the archaeological evidence is of a quite different sort. It concerns inanimate objects and thus is dispassionate; but it is nevertheless extraordinarily telling.

The statue of queen Boudica and her daughters in a chariot. On the Embankment in London. Erected in 1902.

73

There is some uncertainty over the precise date of the revolt. Tacitus makes it clear that it was AD 61 but there are reasons to suppose it was in AD 60. The governor at the time was Suetonius Paullinus. He was anxious for a spectacular conquest and so had crossed over to the island of Anglesey off Wales and was in the process of crushing the Druid centre there. His absence from the mainland provided the opportunity for the revolt. The reasons for it were various. The actual trigger was the Roman army's treatment of the Iceni following the death of their king Prasutagus. He had made the emperor co-heir with his two daughters in the hope that this would ensure the safety of his family and the Iceni. However it was not to be. Under the influence of the provincial procurator Decianus Catus, the Romans not only treated the whole kingdom as if it were theirs but plundered it as if it had been acquired by conquest. Icenian chiefs were driven off their estates and some of the king's relatives were made slaves. Nobody was exempt. Even Prasutagus' widow, Boudica, was flogged, and her daughters were raped. Boudica must have had no difficulty in assembling an army which at this stage, according to Dio, was about 120,000 strong. She and her followers moved south where other tribes joined in. Only one of these is named and that is the Trinovantes who, we are told, had good reason to hate the Romans. The building of Colonia Victricensis had caused widespread misery and resentment. The Trinovantes had been deprived of their land so that it could be given to the new settlers, and some had been imprisoned and enslaved. The Temple of Claudius was cited by Tacitus as a particularly sore point with the Trinovantes: he says that its observances were a pretext to make the natives appointed as its high priests drain the whole country dry.

Unlike Tacitus, Dio cites the abrupt and harsh calling in of loans as a major contributory factor in provoking the revolt. Claudius had lent senior Britons large sums of money and Decianus Catus decreed at short notice that these must be recovered, by force if necessary. Seneca, a close aide of the emperor Nero, had also lent the Britons money and he now wanted it all back, including the interest. Dio says Seneca lent them forty million *sesterces* which was equivalent at the time to the annual pay of about 45,000 legionary soldiers. On this basis, the sum might be equivalent very roughly to around £50 million today. To make the injustice the greater, the loans were not sought by the Britons in the first place. They may have been needed to pay taxes which the Romans demanded or to provide British nobles with the necessary property to qualify for a place on their local council.

The initial target for the Britons was the despised Colonia Victricensis—the Roman show-case and source of so much of their misery. The settlers had some notice of the impending disaster but took few steps to avert it. No hasty defences were thrown up (or so it seems) and there was no evacuation of the women, children and elderly. Instead they sent for help to the procurator who presumably was based in Londinium. According to Tacitus, he sent about 200 poorly armed men to supplement a small garrison in or around the colony. If this refers to the fort at Gosbecks, then in total there would have been around 700 troops. In addition, there would have been the several thousand retired veteran soldiers who had settled in the colony. These men would have been battle-hardened and most of them still quite fit since they would have been out of the army for ten years at most. Nevertheless Tacitus records that '*It seemed easy to destroy the settlement; for it had no walls. That was a matter which Roman commanders, thinking of amenities rather than needs, had neglected.*' Archaeological excavations at the Lion Walk and Balkerne Lane sites confirmed all this vividly. They proved that the colony had no defences at the time, because the legionary defences had been filled

It seemed easy to destroy the settlement; for it had no walls. That was a matter which Roman commanders, thinking of amenities rather than needs, had neglected. At this juncture, for no visible reason, the statue of Victory at Camulodunum fell down—with its back turned as if it were fleeing the enemy. Delirious women chanted of destruction at hand. They cried that in the local senate-house outlandish yells had been heard; the theatre had echoed with shrieks; at the mouth of the Thames a phantom settlement had been seen in ruins. A blood-red colour in the sea, too, and shapes like human corpses left by the ebb tide, were interpreted hopefully by the Britons—and with terror by the settlers...

Tacitus, The Annals of Imperial Rome, xiv.30.

in to allow the construction of the public buildings over the east side of the colony—no doubt the very amenities referred to by Tacitus. The Britons attacked the town and its people, slaughtering, wrecking, looting and burning.

Tacitus paints a heroic picture: when all else was on fire or destroyed, the Roman troops made a last stand in the Temple of Claudius, but after two days' siege, the Britons stormed the building and the Roman resistance was over. The truth is probably a little different. The walls of the temple were of stone, its roof was of tile, it had no windows, and it probably had a great bronze double-door. In other words, the inner room (*cella*) of the temple would have been an ideal place in which to take refuge rather than mount some kind of resistance. There would have been few other stone buildings in the colony, and none would have matched the security provided by the Temple of Claudius. Moreover the temple *cella* was quite large (about 285 sq m in area) and could hold a thousand or more people at a squeeze. Thus it was an obvious choice. Once the bronze double-door was barred shut, it would have been very hard to break into the building or set it on fire. The Britons would probably have had to enter through the roof and this in itself would have

Impression of the Britons trying to drive the Romans out of the Temple of Claudius where they were taking refuge.

been no easy matter since it was over 15 m above ground.

Thus rather than a party of brave soldiers battling to the last, the temple is more likely to have had many hundreds of men, women and children crammed behind its firmly shut door waiting in terror for relief that never came. At first, there would have been some light from lamps and candles but soon these would have been exhausted, and the beleaguered group would have sat in the dark listening to the commotion made by thousands of bloodthirsty Britons outside. Eventually they would hear scraping and banging on the roof as the first of the tiles were levered off, and then suddenly there would be the shaft of light through a gaping hole in the ceiling that was to spell the end.

The Ninth Legion attempted to relieve the town but was routed and lost its entire infantry force while the commander escaped with his cavalry. The procurator fled to Gaul, horrified at the loss of the colony and apparently shocked at the effects of his harsh treatment of the Britons. Paullinus marched to Londinium but decided it was a hopeless cause and withdrew. The inhabitants were allowed to go with him. All who stayed behind were killed, including women and children, as the town was razed to the ground in turn. A third town, Verulamium, was the scene of similar destruction and massacre.

According to Tacitus and Dio, the Britons thought of nothing but plundering, and killed the Romans and their allies without compassion in the most barbaric of ways. He says that they took no prisoners and could not wait to cut throats, hang, burn, and crucify. Dio claims that all sorts of atrocious acts were committed, and gives horrific details.

Paullinus assembled an army of around 10,000 men, which was as many men as he could get at short notice, and decided to fight without further delay. He was heavily outnumbered so he chose the site of the battle carefully. The plan was to present the enemy with a narrow front and prevent them from encircling his troops. Tacitus gives us a few details but not enough to identify the site. The Romans took up their positions in a narrow valley overlooking an open plain. The legionaries were in close ranks in the centre, the auxiliaries to either side, and the cavalry on the flanks. Behind them, thick woodland provided vital rear protection. The Britons were massed on the plain below. They were on foot, on horseback and in chariots. There was a huge number of them. Dio claims a staggering 230,000. The edge of the battlefield was lined with hundreds—possibly thousands—of carts filled with the families of the Britons who had come to watch the spectacle. Boudica in her chariot dashed about among her troops issuing last-minute instructions.

Britons setting fire to buildings in the Roman town. These buildings were redundant barracks which had been converted into houses.

Then the Britons attacked. They raced up towards the Romans, being funnelled as they went by the narrowing mouth of the valley. As one, the infantry launched their javelins. Then, on the appropriate command, they burst forward in wedge formation. With lances extended, the cavalry then shot forward and overwhelmed all serious resistance. The Britons turned and fled but had difficulty escaping because of the carts which encircled the battlefield. Large numbers of Britons were killed. Not even the women were spared, and baggage animals were slaughtered and added to the heaps of dead. Tacitus describes a sickening massacre but calls it a 'glorious victory'. He says with some satisfaction that there was even one report which claimed almost 80,000 dead–clearly the greater the number the greater the perceived glory. He says that there were only 400 Roman soldiers killed with only a slightly greater number wounded. His account of the battle is obviously condensed, and Dio's version is slightly different. According to him, the battle lasts the day. Fortunes initially are more balanced and British chariots figure prominently in the action. However the outcome is the same, although Dio does claim that many Britons were taken alive.

It is all rather reminiscent of Caratacus' last stand in Wales a decade earlier. The lesson for the British was still the same: pitched battle suited the professionalism of the Roman army. All the Britons could really offer in such circumstances was large numbers and big hearts. And, just as in Wales, that proved to be not enough on the day.

Paullinus had to go into battle without any troops from the II Augusta which at that time seems to have been based in Exeter. He had

The Roman town ablaze. Impression of the town viewed from the south-west in AD 60/1. Colonia Victricensis was razed to the ground.

sent for as many men as could be spared but the man in charge, Poenius Postumus, failed to obey the order. When Postumus later received news of Paullinus' victory, he felt he had no choice but to fall on his own sword. Tacitus claims that after the battle Boudica similarly committed suicide, in her case with poison. But this sounds too neat and would be a very Roman response to defeat. There was no dishonour for Boudica in losing the battle. Why would she want to kill herself when she could fight another day? Dio is likely to be closer to the truth when he tells us that Boudica simply took ill and died. He says that it happened as the Britons were making preparations to continue the fight, but they gave her a lavish funeral and then dispersed in the belief that they were finally defeated.

Certainly the British defeat was not the end of the matter. Dio's statement on how the rebellion petered out is too glib: it was all a good deal messier than that. About 7,000 reinforcements were sent from Germany which gives us some idea of the losses sustained by the army. Paullinus was harsh in his retribution, using the sword and fire not only against tribes who continued to resist, but also against those who had showed some sympathy with the British cause. But the worst of the Britons' problems was famine. Tacitus says that the natives had not sown any crops because they expected to seize the army's supplies. This will not do. Apart from the fact that the army would never have held enough stores to feed such a large native population, it seems inconceivable that the British would be so foolish when they were so dependent on their crops. The truth is almost certainly much more grim. It is far more likely that Paullinus and his men were destroying the crops themselves and thereby effectively perpetrating a form of genocide. Famines are usually accompanied by the spread of deadly contagious diseases and no doubt starvation would not have been the only danger that the poor Britons had to contend with. Thus the destruction of their crops would have been a very effective and cruel form of vengeance. Tacitus, apart from a brief mention of famine, provides no details of its effects on the native population. But there was a new provincial procurator—Gaius Julius Alpinus Classicianus—and he was alarmed at what was going on. Humanitarian reasons aside, he could see that the havoc was reducing the value of his future revenues. Indeed his concern was so great that in his despatches to Rome he said that the war in Britain would only end with the replacement of Paullinus, and he even told the Britons to hang on until a more amenable man was in post. A commission of inquiry was sent from Rome and, within a year or so after the start of the revolt, Paullinus had been replaced. Classicianus had his wish: the new man brought a new, conciliatory policy and the difficult situation in Britain subsided.

It is almost impossible to judge the true magnitude of the disaster although clearly losses on both sides must have been horrendous. Tacitus tells us that 70,000 Roman citizens and their allies died in Colonia Victricensis, Londinium and Verulamium alone, and, as we saw above, we can also infer that the death toll must have included up to 7,000 Roman troops. On the face of it, 70,000 seems far too many from the three sacked towns, especially when the populations of two of them were apparently able to flee. Most historians think that this figure must be grossly exaggerated, and it probably is. However we have already discussed how difficult it is to gauge the populations of those towns, and that it would not be surprising if the population of Colchester was as much as 15,000. Of course this figure allows for a substantial native element and presumably many of these people would have joined the Boudican cause. Nevertheless while 70,000 must be an impossibly high estimate, a death toll in the towns running into many tens of thousands is quite plausible on the Roman side.

As for the Britons, the ancient writers had little interest in the numbers of their dead, but, the circumstances being what they were, it would be surprising if in the end their losses did not far outstrip those of their enemy. Dio's claim that Boudica had an army 230,000 strong looks like an absurd exaggeration, but the magnitude of his estimate does at least suggest that the army had been of a quite exceptional size. Losses on the battlefield could have easily run into tens of thousands, given the likely size of Boudica's forces and their treatment in defeat by the Romans. And this was all before the punitive campaign by Paullinus and the famine which he seems to have caused.

Nobody will ever know even approximately how many people lost their lives in the crisis, but there are sufficient clues to suggest that this was one of the most tragic episodes ever to have occurred in Britain.

Broken fragment of a picture lamp from the Boudican destruction layer at the Culver street site. The face is of Sol, god of the sun.

The evidence in the ground

History is punctuated with momentous events but it is rare for any of them to be recognised in the ground. The Boudican revolt is special in this respect. In some ways, it is like a mini version of the volcanic eruption which smothered the Roman cities of Pompeii and Herculaneum less than ten years later. In its wake the revolt left the semi-fossilised remains of Colonia Victricensis as it was at the time of the disaster; it produced a kind of three-dimensional snapshot for posterity.

The effect of the revolt in Colchester (just as in London and St Albans) takes the form of a layer of burnt material underlying practically all of the modern town centre. There are thousands of other layers of archaeological material under the town, but this one is so distinctive that it is easily recognised. Indeed sometimes the layer is so thick that on some sites it represents half of all the Roman material which survives.

Most of the buildings had tiled roofs and clay walls so that unlike the Great Fire of London, once started it would not necessarily have spread very easily. To keep things going, the Britons may have had to set the buildings alight one by one. The destruction layer varies in thickness from just a few centimetres to half a metre depending on how much was cleared away in the rebuilding operations which followed the fire. It takes its colour from the clay material used in wall construction; in its normal state, this material is yellow but it was easily reddened or blackened in the heat. In amongst the debris is charcoal from burnt timbers, fragments of painted wall plaster from the internal wall surfaces, and fragments of tile from destroyed roofs. Often the material lies in sheets where walls collapsed in the heat of the fire, but sometimes it is very mixed, showing that it was shovelled up and moved around as part of the groundworks for the buildings which followed the fire. The layer of burnt debris cloaks the floors and the bases of walls of many of the buildings, and in this way can preserve the stumps of walls in remarkable detail. The wattles and timbers in the walls are reduced to charcoal or burnt away entirely to leave voids in the heat-hardened clay which perfectly preserves their shapes. These extraordinary stumps of wall reveal a surprising diversity of building techniques in the Roman town. Floors are often perfectly preserved under the collapsed debris. They can look

A section through part of the 'Boudican destruction layer' which is to be found under Colchester town centre. The layer is mostly made up of the debris from burnt, demolished 'clay' walls.

Below: A–part of a wooden board floor, burnt in AD 60/1. It was in a room of a house excavated at the Culver Street site.

B–removal of the Boudican destruction layer often reveals well-preserved burnt floors and stumps of timber-framed walls. This is an example from the Culver Street site of the floors and wall-bases of a house burnt in AD 60/1.

very colourful, with great red and chocolate brown patches showing where the fire burnt the most intensely.

You might expect that, as at Pompeii and Herculaneum, bodies would be found in the debris, but interestingly, human remains are rare here. None were found in the extensive areas of burnt remains excavated at the Lion Walk, Balkerne Lane, Culver Street, and Gilberd School sites. In fact there is only one place known in Colchester where there might have been a victim, and that was on a site excavated on North Hill in 1965 where charred bones from a much disturbed human skeleton lay on a clay surface. At London and St Albans, the situation is even more clear cut, with there being no human skeletons found in the Boudican deposits in either place. This suggests that there was no large-scale fighting in or around the buildings prior to their being burnt, although of course any townsfolk in these places could have surrendered or been captured alive before being taken elsewhere. (Dio rather chillingly says that many were taken to sacred groves for slaughter.)

A remarkable effect of the fire is that it preserved organic materials which would not otherwise have survived. The conditions had to be right: the objects must burn enough to char but not enough to turn to ash. This suits grain and as a result there are many instances in the Boudican debris of charred material of this kind. Charred wheat grain is especially common, there being piles of it on the floors in buildings at Balkerne Lane, Culver Street, and the Cups Hotel sites, as well as elsewhere in Colchester. The wheat grain contains comparatively few contaminants, showing

that it had been efficiently processed by winnowing and perhaps sieving to separate out the unwanted parts of the wheat and other plants. The grain from these sites had been stored well since there were no signs of fungus or insect infestation and very few of the grains had germinated. However there was one exception and that was a store of grain at Culver Street which seems to have been deliberately germinated to make malt for brewing. About 10 per cent of the cereal in this sample was barley as if to produce a specific blend.

A more unusual find is a substantial quantity of flax seeds from the Cups Hotel site in the High Street. Like the wheat grain, contamination is very low and thus indicates efficient processing prior to storage. Flax was used to make linseed oil and cloth.

Fruits, as opposed to cereals, also occur occasionally in the Boudican debris. Some figs were found in 1972 under a shop on the High Street. They were accompanied by coriander, cones of stone-pine, spelt, barley, and lentils. But even more interesting is the discovery of dates. These lay on the floor of a reused barrack block on the Lion Walk site, and seem to have been in a bag which was destroyed in the fire. There were 23 dates in all, plus a single plum. The dates were slightly wrinkled on the outside and looked just like what they were—partly-dried, unpressed dates. Being now of charcoal, they are brittle and some have split to reveal the perfectly-preserved shapes of stones inside.

Lion Walk yielded another remarkable find in 1972. This time it was a couch or a bed in the corner of a room in a house. Measuring 1.9 m (6 ft 4 in) by 1.0 m (3 ft 2 in), it was just the right size for a single bed in the modern sense although we cannot tell whether it was a bed or a couch. In terms of Roman measurements, the object was almost exactly 6 feet 6 inches by 3 feet 3 inches and was in the proportion of 2:1. The couch or bed had two mattresses, each made of a casing woven in two-over-two twill. The stuffing appeared to be wool. The presence of a wooden frame is problematic and the evidence appears at first sight to be contradictory. There were no obvious remains of a frame although there was a single piece of burnt timber on the floor lying parallel to the object's long side. Rope had been pressed into the floor under the mattresses along one side, suggesting that they were supported by a rope web, which would of course have needed a frame. On

Burnt dates (and one plum) on the floor of a building destroyed in AD 60/1. Found at the Lion Walk site.

the other hand, the fact that the rope was pressed into the floor at all suggests that there was no frame and that the mattresses lay directly on the floor. The explanation might be as complicated as the following. The rope shows the area of greatest use, and this being the edge rather than the middle suggests that the object was in fact a couch rather than a bed (in which case we should more properly describe the mattresses as upholstery). The couch did indeed have a frame but the webbing had snapped where the couch had been used the most, and the upholstery in this area collapsed so as to rest directly on the floor. The sagging upholstery could not have been too uncomfortable since people continued to use the couch despite its decrepit state. The couch must have been quite low to start with since otherwise the subsequent sag in the upholstery would have left it useless.

In turbulent times, people sometimes buried their savings for safe-keeping. We thus might expect to find lots of hoards dating to AD 60/1 in and around Colchester, especially since the high death toll means that many would never have been retrieved. Strangely none have been found. However various small collections of coins have been recovered from the Boudican debris and thus must have been in the buildings at the time of the fire. The largest of these is the 27 burnt coins of Claudius and Agrippa found in a pot on a site in West Stockwell Street in 1926. Culver Street produced six similar coins which appear to have been kept in a wooden casket with bronze fittings, the remains of which lay nearby. In Balkerne Gardens, four coins lay together on a site

The remains of the remarkable burnt couch or bed found at the Lion Walk site.

Left:
A–remains of rope pressed into the floor because part of the wooden frame had collapsed in use.

Below:
B–the couch or bed (in the background) stood in the corner of a room (wall just this side of it in the photograph). A large section of collapsed wall lay face down on the floor in the next room.

C–closer view of the burnt upholstery or mattress.

D–close-up of the fabric of the burnt upholstery or mattress, showing that its cover was woven in diamond two-over-two twill.

Grid-iron used for cooking over an open fire. Found in place on the Gilberd School site. The last meal to be cooked on this grill was probably on the eve of the Boudican attack on the town.

Lamps were made by copying existing examples using a two-part mould, as pictured here. They are of the type known as 'picture lamps' because of the variety of relief patterns which were used to decorate the discus forming the top.

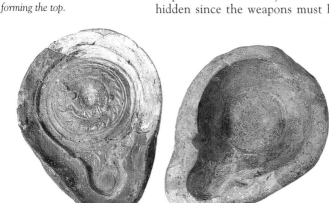

broken and made useless so that they would fit in the oven.

Despite all this, the evidence for furniture, personal belongings and loose items in and around the buildings is not as common as might be imagined. As we have seen, there certainly are such finds but many of the rooms appear to have been empty when set on fire. Did the inhabitants take many of their belongings with them? Would they really have tried to cart off heavy items of furniture such as beds, couches, and tables? Probably not. Instead various factors are likely to be at work here. Firstly many objects must have been burnt so thoroughly that they left no recognisable traces, as with wooden doors for example. There must have been many doors in the buildings and yet no remains have been recognised in the burnt debris. Secondly, many of the rooms would have been fairly empty anyway—certainly by modern standards. And thirdly, there is likely to have been some looting of the buildings by the Britons before they set them alight. For years before the Claudian invasion, the Britons (at least in the south-east) increasingly sought out imported Roman goods. Roman or not, the contents of the abandoned buildings in Colchester and elsewhere would have been too desirable to waste.

If the houses seem to have been disappointingly empty, that was not so with at least some of the shops. Maybe there was just too much material to carry off at short notice. Two shops are known to have existed in the area now occupied by the High Street. In 1927, workmen on the former Cups Hotel site discovered part of the burnt and smashed stock of a Roman shop which dealt in pottery and glass. The vessels had been stored in stacks, the pottery being below the glass in piles on the floor or on a shelf. The intense heat of the fire left much of the glass as shapeless fused lumps and the pottery below covered in drips of melted glass. The fragments were so loose in the ground that when touched, they fell out in a 'tinkling shower'. When collected, the pieces were thought to be only a hundredth part of what survived of the stock. The bulk of the pottery is red-glazed samian and much of the glass is thin-walled and delicately coloured. The entire stock probably ran to thousands of vessels, most (if not all) of which was imported. Another shop, also destroyed in AD 60/1,

excavated in 1965; they had presumably been kept in a bag or purse.

An iron grate (grid-iron) lay on the floor of a house on the Gilberd School site. Rather than the normal square shape, the grate was of an elegant semicircular design. Objects of this kind were used for cooking. Balances for weighing seem to have been common items in these early households as shown by fragments on the floors of several burnt houses. A collection of lamps and lamp moulds was found in a building on the north side of town. This is particularly interesting as an example of a manufacturing trade apparently being carried out inside the built-up area of the town, although the finished lamps would probably have been fired in kilns which were well away from the houses. Strangely, a shield and a spear or javelin had been stuffed inside an oven in a house on the Balkerne Lane. It is questionable if they were deliberately hidden since the weapons must have been stocked pottery (but as far as is known only samian) as well as various foodstuffs already mentioned including the figs. The shops were on opposite sides of what had been one of the main streets in the fortress–the *via praetoria*. This had led from the east gate to the centre of the headquarters building (*principia*), and was now clearly an important commercial thoroughfare.

Large quantities of new pots were stored in part of a building in Insula 10. The stock might have been kept here for a shop either at the front of the building or elsewhere in the town, or it might have been part of an official store of some kind. The rooms were small and clearly they must have been full to overflowing with pottery. One room contained large quantities of carbonised wheat grain, another at least 30 unused and almost identical mortaria (vessels for grinding food), another room and an adjacent corridor over 80 flagons, again of almost identical type, and in another room 20 amphoras of various types. The pots had all been smashed, as if the Britons went on the rampage before finally setting the buildings alight. They recall familiar images of today where city rioters loot, smash, and burn.

In terms of other archaeological remains of the revolt, there is the question of whether there are traces of any defences which the settlers might have built on the eve of the attack. They must have had at least a few days' warning of the impending disaster since there was enough time for them not only to appeal to the procurator (who was presumably in Londinium) for armed assistance but also for the troops which he sent to reach Colonia Victricensis. The settlers probably felt that the countryside was too dangerous and that their best chance of survival would be to stay put and wait for help. Some may

have escaped by sea but presumably there would not have been enough ships to go round. Although, as we have seen, the legionary defences had been dismantled to allow expansion of the new town, it would surely be odd if the settlers did not make some last-minute preparations in the few days that they had available to them. Being largely retired soldiers, digging defensive ditches at speed would have been second nature to them. However no evidence of such last-minute arrangements have as yet been recognised, although this is not proof of their absence. Certainly enough investigation has been done on the line of the main defences around the town to indicate that there was no attempt to re-establish these at the last minute. A much smaller area such as around the Temple of Claudius may have been defended with a bank and ditch.

Broken fragments of burnt samian pottery from the Boudican destruction layer.

Left: the burnt raised area is the base of two ovens excavated at the Balkerne Lane site in 1972. The oven in the foreground is keyhole-shaped and would originally have been completely enclosed apart from a small opening at the front. It contained the remains of a shield and javelin which had both been broken up prior to being put in the oven.

Little work has been done in the countryside but no doubt the devastation was equally bad in the *territorium* of the colony. Whether or not Gosbecks suffered the same fate is unknown but, being tainted with Roman influence, it is likely that it did.

Wherever it is found, the Boudican layer is of great archaeological interest and value. But when studying its contents and marvelling at the quality of preservation that it sometimes offers, we need to be mindful of the terrible human tragedy that accounts for its existence.

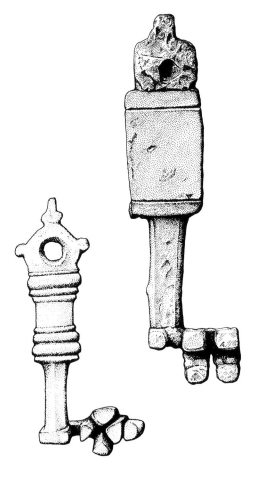

Occasionally the stumps of buildings burnt during the Boudican revolt survive to over a metre in height. Here is the base of a wall of a barrack-block at the Culver Street site. The building had been reused as a house in the new town and was then destroyed in AD 60/1.

Above: two slide keys from the Boudican destruction debris at the Culver Street site.

REBIRTH AND MATURITY

The new City of Victory

The years immediately following the Boudican revolt must have been characterised by bitter hatred and mistrust on both sides and the worry that things were not over. The Romans would have loathed the Britons for their ruthless treatment of their civilian population, while the Britons' natural resentment of their foreign oppressors would have been whipped up to unparalleled levels by Paullinus' campaign of retribution and the famine which he seems to have caused. Hostilities continued, albeit on a much smaller scale, so fears that the situation could flare up again with further disastrous results must have seemed quite justifiable. It is against the background of this tense hothouse atmosphere that we need to view the rebuilding of the colony.

As far as can be judged, the town was completely destroyed. All that remained standing were the few public buildings which had stone walls, and even those were roofless, gutted shells. The task facing the Romans was much greater than in AD 49 when the colony was originally founded. Then they had a head start in the form of the redundant fortress: now there was practically nothing—only tons and tons of burnt debris everywhere. The destruction was so comprehensive that the colony may have been refounded. Indeed some archaeologists speculate that 'Victricensis' in its name belongs to this period and refers to the re-establishment of Roman rule following the revolt.

The restoration was not done in a methodical way. The streets were cleared of collapsed walls and other debris, and the new buildings were constructed on a piecemeal basis. There was no major replanning of the town: few if any new streets were built, and many of the houses were erected on plots of land which had existed in the pre-Boudican town. The re-establishment of pre-Boudican plots is shown by the survival after AD 60/1 of many property boundaries on the Culver Street and Balkerne Lane sites. Stone buildings like the Temple of Claudius were renovated.

It is difficult to know what to make of the reinstatement of many of the pre-fire property boundaries. Some certainly survived the fire, but others seem to have been superseded by completely different arrangements. The most likely explanation is that a substantial part of the original population survived to rebuild their properties, and that those plots with boundaries of pre-fire origin indicate the presence of occupants who returned to reclaim their land. Such a situation makes us recall London after the Great Fire of 1666, when Christopher Wren redesigned the town, but the townsfolk returned and starting re-building their houses before the scheme could be implemented. Alternatively it could be simply that property boundaries which survived

Painted wall plaster. This is from the decoration of one of the first houses to be built after the Boudican revolt, excavated at the Balkerne Lane site. It is a fragment of a panel from a series showing a gladiatorial contest. The gladiator is defeated. He has dropped his shield, blood pours from a leg wound, and he raises his hand in a gesture of submission. His shield and sword, and the fish crest on his helmet, show that he is a 'mirmillo'.

Glass sports cup showing a chariot race in a circus. From the Sheepen site.

Plan of the town, showing the town wall and gates, streets, and with some of the buildings referred to in this chapter.

were used as a basis for reparcelling the land for allocation to the new generation of colonists.

It has been suggested that at Verulamium there was an interval of fifteen years or more between the fire and the start of the rebuilding of the centre of the city, but it is hard to detect any such delay in Colonia Victricensis. The restored street system was the same as before the fire, perhaps with an additional north-south street to the east of the Temple of Claudius. The new houses were modest, much the same in scale and plan as those built by the colonists in the 50s (as opposed to reused barrack blocks), although, not surprisingly, their number was much reduced from the pre-fire level, with areas of the town being left vacant. There had been gaps in the street frontages in the pre-Boudican town. The new town was no different, except that the gaps were now much bigger, reflecting a much diminished population.

Punishment and control

There seems to have been a change of attitude towards the native population after the Boudican revolt. The Gosbecks site continued as the British centre but other sites seemed to suffer irreversible change at this time, suggesting harsh treatment of the natives. This affected those who had previously collaborated with the Romans and who now had presumably sided with their own kin in the native uprising. The Stanway site,

where the evidence of collaboration is clearest, was no longer used as a burial ground after c AD 60, and the Sheepen site changed radically in character from an industrial area to a sanctuary. Excavations in 1994 and 1996 not far north of the central core of Gosbecks again revealed the now-familiar pattern of major change around AD 60, in this case with occupation ominously ceasing at this time. The Romans were to take no more chances and the natives had to be punished.

The town wall

Tacitus had chastised the Roman authorities for not providing the town with a wall. In the light of what happened in AD 60/1, the absence of defences must have been regarded as a scandal, and from then on it became increasingly common to provide major settlements with defences. Generally these took the form of a bank and ditch, but Colonia Victricensis, the premier settlement in the province, was to get what it should have had in the first place—a town wall. In fact this was not only to be the first town wall in Britain, but (as far as we are aware) the only one for many years to come. Fortresses which were to follow the Colchester model and be converted into towns (such as Lincoln and Exeter) were from now on to retain their military defences, regardless of what space might be needed for new buildings. All new developments in these places were, initially at least, to be confined within the circuits of the military defences that they inherited.

Dating town walls is not easy, for various technical reasons, and it is a source of some embarrassment that the wall in Colchester has been given different dates over the years. The most prolific dating evidence is to be found in the rampart which was piled up behind the wall. Pottery and other finds in this material make it certain that the rampart was made somewhere within the period AD 150-200. It was thought that the rampart and the wall were raised as one and that therefore the wall belonged to the same period. However in the 1960s, an excavation by Rosalind Dunnett showed that the wall had been free-standing

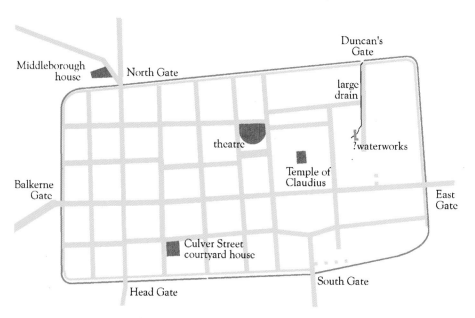

Middleborough house

North Gate

Duncan's Gate

large drain

?waterworks

theatre

Temple of Claudius

Balkerne Gate

East Gate

Culver Street courtyard house

Head Gate

South Gate

Section through the town wall showing its method of construction.

Left: *close-up of the town wall near the Balkerne gate, showing the courses of tile and septaria. The modern ground level here corresponds with the Roman ground level when the wall was built.*

The town wall

The method of building the wall is well understood. During the excavations at Lion Walk and Culver Street, vivid evidence was found of the activities of its builders. At Lion Walk, the base of what had been a large stockpile of unused building stone lay a few metres from the inner face of the wall. And at Culver Street layers of small chips of septaria showed that the masons worked the septaria on the spot rather than at the quarry or in a yard, and patches of abandoned mortar laying on wooden boards indicated how this mortar was mixed on site.

To build the wall, the Romans first dug a trench about 10 feet wide and about 4 feet deep. This was filled with layers of mortar and septaria which were simply poured or thrown in alternately until the top of the trench was reached. By this means the foundation was formed which, considering the height and weight of the structure it was to support, is surprisingly slight.

The wall itself is of ashlar construction. In other words the inner and outer faces were constructed independently of the core. The faces were raised, presumably a few courses at a time, and then the space between the two faces was filled with layers of septaria and mortar laid alternately just as in the foundation. The faces were made of neatly-coursed septaria and tile, usually four courses of tile being followed by four courses of septaria. A small offset was formed at the base of the wall by making the lowest one or two courses slightly wider that the rest.

The purpose of the tile courses is not clear. The courses on the inner and outer faces match each other in terms of height above ground but do not connect up across the thickness of the wall. They are therefore not bonding courses intended to strengthen the wall. They may have been intended as a decorative feature. They may also have had a practical value during the construction work by providing a means of keeping the coursing even and on the same plane.

Of the six gates, parts of two (the Balkerne Gate and Duncan's Gate) are still visible above ground, while the remains of the other four are under modern streets (ie at the top of East Hill, at the south end of Head Gate, and at the foot of North Hill and of Queen Street). Between the gates there were rectangular towers set against the inside of the wall. There seems to have been one in each of the angles of the wall circuit plus one at most of the places where the streets met the wall. As was customary, a deep V-shaped ditch was dug along the foot of the wall to improve its defensive capabilities.

e town wall it is today near the Balkerne gate.

Above: a wide trench dug across the backfilled defensive ditch of the legionary fortress (rear of the picture) and the equivalent ditch for the town wall (front).

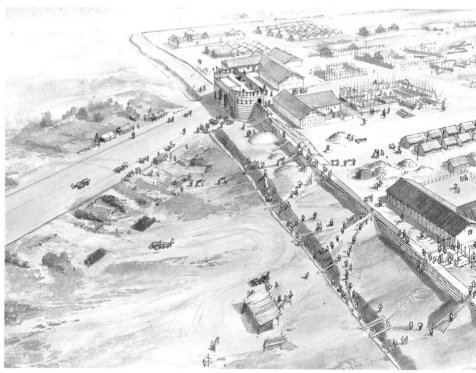

Above right: the west side of the City of Victory shortly after the Boudican revolt in AD 60/1, viewed from the south-west. It shows the building of the town wall and new houses being erected elsewhere. The reconstruction left of the wall is based on the Balkerne Lane excavation.

Right: the same view as above after the completion of the wall, c AD 80-100. It shows the possible aqueduct, evidence for which was found during the Balkerne Lane excavations.

for some considerable time before the rampart was built. Not only was this interpretation confirmed at Lion Walk and Culver Street, but also the evidence from both these sites strongly suggests that the wall was remarkably early and dates to c AD 65-80.

Archaeologists tend to regard most town walls in Britain as belonging to the end of the 2nd century AD when there were various problems both here and on the Continent. For many years the wall at Colchester was reckoned to be of mid 2nd-century date, so it was still seen as unusual. However, the suggestion that the wall at Colchester is as early as c AD 65-80 is not something which is accepted by everyone. Yet not only does the excavated evidence (such as pottery and coins) point to such an early date, but the Boudican revolt provides an obvious and compelling corroborative context for subsequent construction.

The wall at Colonia Victricensis was a major engineering work which would have cost a great deal of money and taken years to complete. It was 2,800 m long and 8 Roman feet (2.4 m) thick. The original height is uncertain but enough is left to show that it must have been at least 6 m high including the battlements. The wall incorporated 6 gates and between 12 and 24 towers. In terms of finished masonry, the stone defences would have represented over 45,000 cubic metres of stone, tile, and mortar. It would

have been built in sections. Given the scale of the Boudican disaster, we must wonder where the money came from to pay for it.

The area enclosed by the wall included the former annexe of the legionary fortress and a strip of land to the north. On the western and southern sides, the wall circuit corresponded to the position of the backfilled legionary defences. But there was a problem. The recently-finished monumental gateway on the west side of town was now in the way. A compromise was reached whereby, rather than demolish the monument, it was incorporated in the new gate. However, although this meant that the monument could now be preserved, it could only be done at the expense of the defensive capabilities of the new gate. The new structure did not have the flanking towers which would normally have overlooked its gates, and it may not even have had an overhead gallery across the front. Regardless of the precise arrangement, it was not very satisfactory and was, as we shall see, to lead to the gate being blocked up and no longer used.

More defensive improvements

The earthwork defences of the Iron Age settlement had been neglected since the arrival of the Romans. However, the situation was to change as a result of the Boudican uprising, and the dyke system was not only to become a significant part of the

Impression of the Balkerne gate in c AD 100, showing how the monumental arch was incorporated in the new gate.

Above:
gold finger-ring
with intaglio of the goddess
Roma. From Colchester.

Below: Roman Britain
c AD 200.

• Town

■ Legionary
  fortress

0 _____ 150 km

Antonine Wall

Hadrian's Wall

Carlisle · Corbridge

Aldborough · Malton

· York

Brough-on-Humber

Chester ■   Lincoln·

Wroxeter·

Leicester·   Caistor-by-·Norwich

Gloucester·   Colchester·

Carmarthen·   Cirencester·

· Caerwent·   Verulamium·

Caerleon■

Silchester·   London·

Winchester·   Canterbury·

Chichester·

Exeter·   Dorchester·

colony's defensive arrangements but it was also to be improved. This was done by adding a new outer element to the system to make what we now refer to as Gryme's Dyke.

It used to be supposed that Gryme's Dyke was pre-Roman (ie pre AD 43) in origin. However dating evidence which proved otherwise came from an excavation across the bank of the dyke in 1977. Coins and pottery which could not date to before *c* AD 55 lay under the centre of its rampart showing clearly that the dyke must have been built after this date. Although we cannot be certain how much later, the years immediately following the revolt seem the most likely. In other words, the dyke seems to have been built at the same time as the town walls and presumably as part of the same scheme of defensive improvements.

Something similar can be detected at the industrial and commercial centre at Sheepen which, like the town, was destroyed by fire in AD 60 or 61. The site had been protected by the Sheepen Dyke but, just as happened in the town, its defences were given little regard in the AD 50s, and the earthwork had largely been filled in by AD 60. Interestingly, the site was refortified with a ditch and wooden palisade which followed the line of the Sheepen Dyke for most of its length. The new work was not as substantial as the Sheepen Dyke, but nevertheless it was significant enough not to have been a hasty last-minute measure. Its excavators, C.F.C. Hawkes and M.R. Hull, thought that the earthwork was post-Boudican (certainly it contained no evidence of destruction by fire) and that it was built either by Boudica or the victorious Romans. It makes little sense to attribute the earthwork to Boudica, but its construction by the Romans after AD 60/1 would certainly fit a scheme of defensive measures which included the building of the town walls and Gryme's Dyke.

The conquest of Britain resumes

Colchester's status as the premier town in Britain probably began to slip immediately after the Boudican revolt. The imperial cult based on the Temple of Claudius was maintained but the fate is uncertain of two other indicators of status: the offices of the governor and procurator. The former is likely to have preferred a base either in London or closer to the frontier, so the opportunity may have been taken to relocate to a more convenient base rather than rebuild in Colchester. As we have seen in the last chapter, the new procurator in Britain immediately following Boudica was Julius Alpinus Classicianus. The presence of his grand monument in London (recovered in two pieces in 1852 and 1935) suggests that he was based in that town at the time of his death. Thus the offices of the procurator must have been shifted to London shortly after AD 60 unless, as has been argued already (page 72), they were there already and had been so since the foundation of London *c* AD 50. With the foundations of colonies at Lincoln in *c* 90 and Gloucester in *c* 96-8 (both reused fortresses), Colonia Victricensis was to face competition from similarly ranked towns. Moreover other towns were springing up, some from redundant fortresses (like Exeter and Wroxeter) and others apparently as new foundations on or near existing British settlement sites (such as Silchester and Winchester). This network of new towns across the country was to provide centres for a system of regional local government based to a large extent on existing tribal boundaries.

In the 60s, Roman Britain still consisted of not much more than the south-east of what was later to become England. Wales remained untamed and northern England was for the most part controlled by the friendly Brigantes under queen Cartimandua with whom the Romans had formed a mutually beneficial alliance. However the 70s and 80s was a period of rapid military expansion, such that by the mid 80s there was the prospect that the whole of mainland Britain could be conquered. The trigger for the change was the overthrow of Cartimandua by her former husband Venutius and the resultant appearance on its northern frontier of an actively hostile enemy. It was Cartimandua who had handed over Caratacus to the Romans and for twenty years or so provided them with a safe buffer state along their northern border. With Cartimandua gone, all that had to change. After a few years of war, the Brigantes were finally defeated and the Romans turned their attention to Wales where, after a few years, the Welsh tribes were crushed and the conquest of the west completed with the capture of Anglesey. The Roman army under Agricola, governor in Britain between AD 78 and 84, then pushed northwards into Scotland. His series of annual campaigns culminated in a battle at Mons Graupius somewhere in north-east Scotland, where the Roman army defeated the massed men of the remaining Caledonian tribes. The conquest of the whole of mainland Britain was in their grasp. Agricola was there to stay and began to build a network of military bases to consolidate his gains. This included the legionary fortress at Inchtuthil in Perthshire which was begun in AD 84 and was to be the home of the Twentieth Legion, the same unit that had probably been based in Colchester forty years earlier. But problems abroad demanded reinforcements from Britain with the result that the new military gains in Scotland could not be sustained. Inchtuthil was abandoned before it could be finished and within a few years all the military sites north of the Clyde and the Forth had been given up.

Most of Scotland was never brought under Roman rule and as a result a strong military garrison was always needed along its border. The shape, position, and nature of the border changed as the years went by with the building of Hadrian's Wall, the Antonine Wall, and various networks of forts, signal stations, and look-out towers, all linked by a road system. The history of the northernmost part of Britannia was punctuated by violent episodes. The south however enjoyed stable conditions for most of the time—at least until the latter part of the 3rd century—and as a result town life was able to flourish there.

City of Victory prospers

Despite being comparatively sheltered from the stormy north, the defences of Colonia Victricensis were not only maintained, but actually saw some major improvement with the addition of a bank along its inner side. Most towns in Britain were given wholly earthen defences which consisted of a ditch and bank made of the excavated material from the ditch. Sometimes a wall was later inserted along the front of the bank. However Colonia Victricensis was unusual in that it had a ditch with a free-standing wall

behind. This meant that when they came to build the bank, there was a problem: where was the material to come from, since they already had a ditch? Various sections through the bank suggest that it was made up largely of sandy clay of the sort used to make clay walls, and that therefore the bank had been made mainly from the remains of demolished buildings and waste materials from building sites. At Lion Walk, in particular, it was possible to see how cart-loads of this debris had been used to build up the bank gradually to the desired height. Had it been made from the upcast of a ditch, the bank would have been predominantly sand. The dating evidence for the bank is plentiful and points to a date of AD 150-200. This makes sense, since many of the small, modest houses were being demolished in the 2nd century to make way for the land-greedy mansions which came to characterise Colonia Victricensis in its middle years.

The building of the bank would not have been undertaken lightly. Although not on the scale of the wall itself, it nevertheless was still a major civic project which would have been carefully planned and closely monitored. The question naturally arises as to why it was done. Was there some external

Top: two copper-alloy lamps from Colchester.

Above and left: two mosaic pavements uncovered in 1906. From a house at the foot of North Hill.

91

Water supply

The town was provided with a pressurised water supply from the very beginning. Water was conducted underground in water-tight wooden mains. Each main consisted of a series of straight pipes held together by thin flat circular bands of iron (loosely referred to as 'collars') hammered into the thickness of the wall of the main. Each pipe in the main had to be straight because the hole along its centre was bored out. A series of four water-mains (**right**) was found on the Balkerne Lane site. The mains were curved to pass through the Balkerne gate. (Note how each main is made up of straight sections of pipe.)

Below right: a 'collar' in position at Balkerne Lane. The brown band of soil in front of it is all that remains of the wooden pipe. Pressure would have been achieved by means of a tank in a water tower. Water was probably brought into the town in an aqueduct. The remains of a possible timber aqueduct were found at Balkerne Lane (see picture on page 88) but it does not seem to have lasted more than fifty years or so. Water would have been supplied to houses, public fountains (for drinking water), and public baths.

*Below: the principal room in the so-called 'mithraeum' excavated in 1927-8 (and also in 1954). The site of the building is in the Castle park, near the children's playground. This room would fill with water, suggesting that the building was probably some kind of waterworks and that the slots in the floor held timbers supporting gear such as a water wheel which would have lifted water into a header tank. It had a large arched drain (**right**) which took surplus water into the town ditch.*

circumstance which made the operation seem worthwhile? It is hard to imagine that the bank was added to the wall simply to make it more difficult to push over. A more likely explanation is that its presence allowed easier movement of soldiers and equipment along the top of the wall. Advances in weaponry and siege tactics may have been behind the timing of its construction, or it may have been a response to a more volatile period when towns in the south were under threat. The most obvious historical context is the late 2nd century when Albinus, the governor in Britain, started a civil war by declaring himself emperor. Although no fighting is recorded in Britain (he was subsequently defeated in Gaul), the incident and the uncertainty during its aftermath have prompted archaeologists to argue that many towns in Britain were equipped with defences at this time. Clearly, this could be the context for the building of the bank at Colonia Victricensis although it is possibly a little late according to the dating evidence, and the apparent slow pace of its construction suggests a less dramatic explanation.

Although Colonia Victricensis never quite regained its pre-Boudican vigour, it did gradually recover from the disaster of AD 60/1, so much so that by the 2nd century a substantial group of wealthy citizens had emerged who could afford large, well-appointed town houses. These buildings are a compelling sign (visible in all the towns of Roman Britain) of a maturing social structure where success in politics and business led to the emergence of a class of wealthy families. These people would have included successful merchants or businessmen and well-to-do farmers who had large estates beyond the walls. They would also have included men of equestrian class (knights) and perhaps even one or two of senatorial rank (as in the senate of Rome). As such they might have previously held high office in government somewhere abroad within the Roman empire. Compared with what went before—and indeed compared with today—these grand houses were almost palatial in scale. They were better built than their predecessors, with foundations, footings, and sometimes walls of stone. They were usually constructed around three or four sides of a square or rectangular courtyard. Rooms were large and accessed off generously-proportioned passages which extended around the yard. Painted walls, tiled roofs, a pressurised water-supply, and drainage systems are all present in these buildings just as they were before. But hypocausted heating systems and mosaic and tessellated floors, very few of which have as yet been recognised in the 1st-century town, become the norm in these large houses. Stone-lined cellars also appear at this time, presumably providing cooler storage conditions than were previously available.

Some of the houses could occupy as much as a quarter of an *insula*. The Lion Walk and Culver Street sites both included the remains of a square courtyard house which was 40 m (130 ft) across and contained at least thirty rooms. As many as four mosaics were found in the house at Culver Street, and there was still half of the building which could not be excavated. The house contained at least two basements: one was a stone-lined cellar and the other was a large room which contained a mosaic and may have been a shrine. The quality of the building is underlined by the discovery in the cellar of part of a table leg in the form of a panther head. This belonged to a three- or four-legged table carved out of expensive Italian marble.

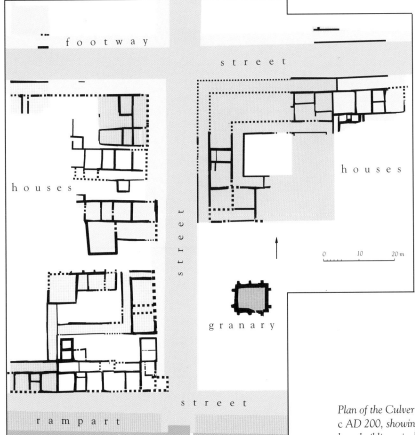

Above: private baths in a house excavated at the Middleborough site with remains of a hypocausted heating system. The stacks of tiles supported the floors and allowed hot air to circulate underneath them and rise up ducts in the walls.

Above: tessellated pavement at the Culver Street site.

Plan of the Culver Street site c AD 200, showing some of the later buildings, including the large courtyard house (grey).

Left: the remains of the steps leading down from the kitchen (Room 10) into the stone-lined cellar (Room 9).

Left: plan showing the excavated areas of the house, and its room and passage numbers.

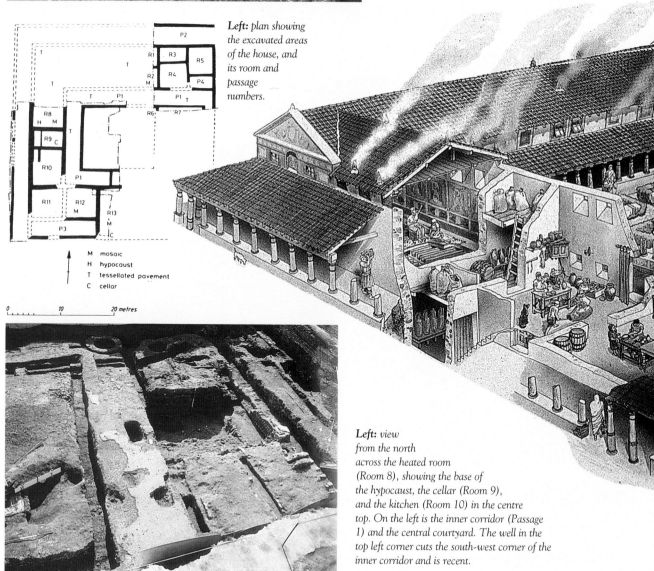

Left: view from the north across the heated room (Room 8), showing the base of the hypocaust, the cellar (Room 9), and the kitchen (Room 10) in the centre top. On the left is the inner corridor (Passage 1) and the central courtyard. The well in the top left corner cuts the south-west corner of the inner corridor and is recent.

The large courtyard house at Culver Street

Palatial house at the Culver Street site. The details in the cutaway part (picture below) are based on the excavation in the 1980s.

Reconstruction painting of the house viewed from the south-west corner.

Right: upper part of a table leg carved in the form of a panther head, made of Italian marble. Found in the backfill of the cellar (Room 9).

Painting of one of the mosaics from the house (right) and in situ (above right).

The remains of the large house at Middleborough during the excavation in 1979.

Below: a plan of the house.

Below right: the Middleborough mosaic on site.

Large palatial houses were even built outside the walled part of the town, with one at Middleborough being 45 m (150 ft) long. This is the building which contained the well-known mosaic pavement which includes pictures of sea-beasts, birds, and a central panel with two wrestling cupids.

Remarkable collapsed gable walls at Meonstoke (Hampshire) and Redlands Farm (Northamptonshire) show that villas could be two-storeyed. Such clear evidence has not been found in Colchester. However, there is no reason why many of the buildings could not have been similarly designed, and if so, then the accommodation which they provided would be even more impressive.

Similarly, the smaller houses which appear in the colony in the 2nd century indicate greater opulence and higher living standards, at least for some. The quality of build seems to have improved because many of the new houses, large as well as small, were to last for up to two hundred years and consequently were the last Roman structures to be built on their sites. Plain red tessellated pavements became the norm for most domestic floors, and mosaics and heated rooms were widespread. Some of the heated rooms seem to have been parts of private bath suites, again pointing to improved living standards.

Left: impression of Middleborough c AD 200, viewed from the south. The large building in the centre is the house with the 'Middleborough mosaic'. The site of the Roman gate in the top left-hand corner is at the foot of modern North Hill.

Mistakes in the Middleborough mosaic

The Middleborough mosaic is a beautifully designed and executed piece of work, yet despite all the effort and skill which went into its manufacture, the pavement contains some surprising mistakes. They make us wonder if the person who commissioned the mosaic realised what had happened and what his reaction was. These mistakes suggest that the mosaicists responsible for laying out the pavement did not understand the principles of its design and that they relied on somebody else's pattern-book. The mistakes are all to be found in the foliate scroll which forms a border around the work. It contains four different motives, based on lotus flowers and ivy leaves. They ought to be duplicated around the panel in logical fashion so that each motif occurs only twice in each side, but the mosaicists became muddled, with the result that one side is almost completely wrong. They even made a mistake with a corner motif (bottom left; detail shown **below**) by not pointing it in towards the centre like the other three corner motifs.

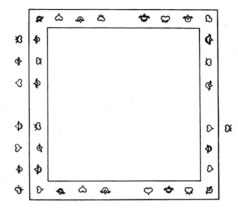

Diagram of mistakes in the mosaic
The inner square shows the border motives as they occur on the pavement. The motives in their correct alignments are shown on the outside where the mosaicist positioned them wrongly.

Part of an antefix decorated with a Medusa head, from the Gilberd School site.

Decorative tiles like this were fitted along the eaves of elaborate tiled roofs.

Jugs from the City of Victory.
Below: a jug made of copper alloy.
Below right: three glass jugs.
Facing page: pottery jug.

The City of Victory in c AD 250, viewed from the south-west.

Public buildings

It might be expected that the increase in the personal wealth of many of the colony's inhabitants evident in the houses of the 2nd century would be reflected in the provision of some new and grander public buildings, particularly since it was the custom for the burden of the cost of such buildings to be borne by private individuals when holding public office. No increase in works of this kind has been detected, but then our knowledge of public buildings and other structures such as aqueducts is very limited.

The only possible exception is the remodelling on a grand scale of the southern side of the precinct of the Temple of Claudius. This is usually thought to have happened around AD 100, although the dating evidence is rather thin and the work could have been done in three stages, spanning a considerable

period of time. The courtyard was entered via a centrally-placed monumental arch which was flanked on either side by a large arcaded screen extending the full width of the frontage. Not much is known about the arch but it would have been a grand structure. It seems to have been about 8 m wide, which would make it about 2 m wider than the arch on the site of the later Balkerne Gate. Also, like the latter, it was faced with tufa. This material was rarely used in Colchester and its appearance in the arch in front of the Temple raises the possibility that it too was Claudian. Indeed, the entrance into the temple precinct would have been a much better site for an arch recording Claudius'

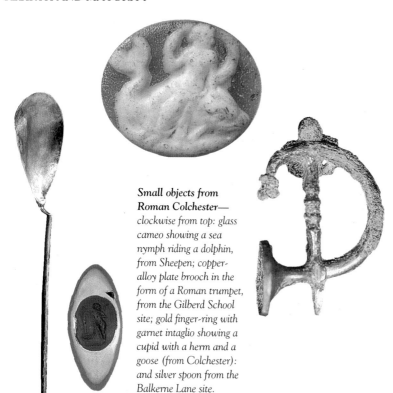

Small objects from Roman Colchester—clockwise from top: glass cameo showing a sea nymph riding a dolphin, from Sheepen; copper-alloy plate brooch in the form of a Roman trumpet, from the Gilberd School site; gold finger-ring with garnet intaglio showing a cupid with a herm and a goose (from Colchester): and silver spoon from the Balkerne Lane site.

conquest of Britain than the arch at the Balkerne Gate (see picture on front cover).

The screen to either side of the arch in front of the Temple of Claudius consisted of a series of arches with half-engaged columns to the front and rear of the piers. Each column was 0.9 m in diameter, suggesting an overall height for the screen (including the moulded part along the top) of at least 8 m and probably much more.

There are likely to have been many public buildings in the colony but our knowledge of them is still extremely limited. Public baths, a forum, and an amphitheatre are all major amenities which we would expect to find in an important town such as Colonia Victricensis. (A forum was an open space of assembly, often with temples and other monumental structures.) The 'Colchester Vase' (see below) and many other locally-found images of gladiators are vivid testaments to the popularity of gladiatorial combat in the colony. There might have been a suitable arena for activities of this kind in the vicinity. Generally contests such as these

The Balkerne Lane site in c AD 275, viewed from the south-west.

The cultivation beds are shown at the centre of the very bottom of the picture. They have been partly covered by the outer bank which was made by widening the town ditch.

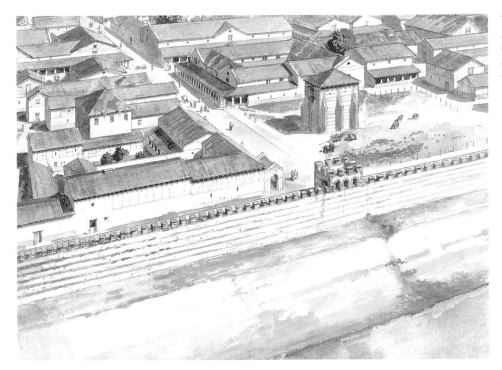

The Culver Street site in c AD 275, showing the granary (right) with the large courtyard house behind. Viewed from the south-west.

The Lion Walk site in c AD 275, viewed from the south-east.

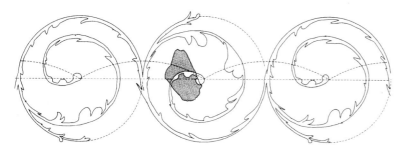

Decorative plant scroll on wall-plaster from a house at Culver Street.

Left: the figure of a gladiator (a mirmillo), made of bone. From Lexden. (Compare with page 85.)

Left: hairpin made of bone, carved in the shape of the bust of a woman. From the Gilberd School site.

Right: impression of the temple and precinct, and the adjacent theatre (semicircular) at Colchester in c AD 275. Viewed from the north-west.

would have been staged in an amphitheatre, although a suitably modified theatre could do. No amphitheatre has yet been identified in Colchester, although there was of course a theatre next to the Temple of Claudius and, as we shall see, a much larger one at Gosbecks.

Gosbecks

In Roman times, Gosbecks was a market, a religious centre, and (probably) an administrative centre all rolled into one—just as it had been before the arrival of Claudius and the Roman army. In terms of broad public functions, nothing much seems to have changed. Physically, though, the site looked very different with the addition of major buildings which in plan, scale, and appearance were rooted in an alien Mediterranean-centred world. What had been the focus of the British stronghold before the Roman invasion became a showpiece for Roman culture afterwards.

There has not been enough archaeological excavation to tell what happened to the site during the Boudican revolt. However, the chances are that it suffered in the same way as the Sheepen site, although there are no cropmarks or other evidence at Gosbecks to indicate that the site was defended immediately after the revolt in the same way as seems to have happened at Sheepen.

The Roman period saw the construction of two major public buildings—a large Roman theatre and a massive 'portico' or covered walkway—and a road leading to the Roman town two miles to the north-east.

The theatre at Gosbecks could hold up to 5,000 people seated. It is the largest of the

Roman theatres known in Britain, and it could accommodate almost half as many people again as the theatre inside the walled area of Colonia Victricensis. The theatre at Gosbecks was discovered by Rex Hull around 1950, and was the subject of a substantial excavation by Rosalind Dunnett in 1967. It is unusual in plan and in its method of construction. The auditorium was set on a solid mound of layered turf and soil, which was contained within a mortar and stone D-shaped outer wall. Most of the seating was accessed via four external staircases placed evenly around the outer wall. The only passages inside the theatre were an axial north-south one at ground level and four shorter passages half way up the auditorium which connected the external staircases with a landing around the midway of the auditorium. Another unusual feature of the theatre is the apparent absence of any rooms behind or to the side of the stage. Indeed the stage itself seems to have been unorthodox in design and modest in size and finish. These factors suggest that the building was not intended primarily for the performing arts, but rather it was also a place of assembly and a place for ritual and ceremony.

The semicircular area in the middle of the theatre was known as the 'orchestra'. It was at ground level and, in theatres everywhere, was where seating was provided for local dignitaries, rather than musicians as might be thought from the name.

The layouts and alignments of the Gosbecks theatre and portico suggest that they were probably linked functionally. Indeed, in general, theatres and temples were often built in close proximity to each other (as with the Temple of Claudius and the theatre in Colchester itself). We can imagine therefore that the Gosbecks theatre was where the local British council met, and maybe afterwards the members processed to the portico and temple to participate in various rituals that were regarded as important for the success of their activities. In other

Left: aerial view from the north-west of the cropmarks at Gosbecks, showing the square ditch within the portico, and the site of the theatre (background).

Below: impression of the Gosbecks site in c AD 200. Viewed from the north-west, showing the temple and portico, the theatre, and the site of Cunobelin's farmstead (right).

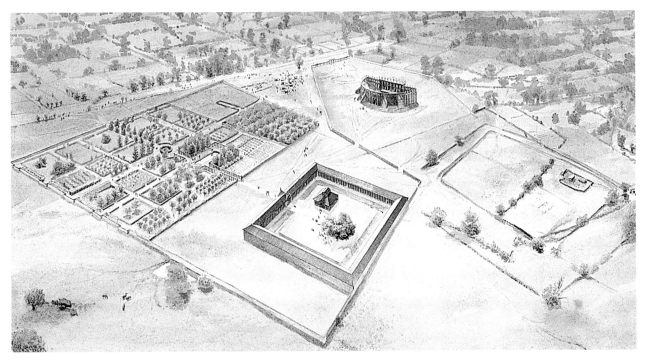

words, we can see in the theatre at Gosbecks signs of possible continuity between pre-Roman and Roman times in terms of the administration and the social and political hierarchies of the native population. We have already discussed how important it would be for the Romans to enlist the co-operation of sympathetic members of the local nobility (page 66). Gosbecks is likely to have been the focal point of whatever minor notions of self-determination and authority the Romans allowed them to have.

Most of the major features of the pre-Roman settlement were retained after the Roman conquest and enhanced in various ways. Rather than being parts of an overall plan, the alterations are likely to have been a series of unconnected developments over many years. The farmstead, where Cunobelin

and his family had lived, continued in use but in a remodelled form, and the deep defensive ditch which formed its core (the so-called 'trapezoidal enclosure') was replaced by a less substantial boundary in the form of a wall or narrow ditch. The square sacred area, which was demarcated on the ground by the deep ditch (page 27), was lavishly treated. A Roman temple was placed in one corner and a classical-style walkway, known as a portico, was built around all four sides of the ditch. Roman temples normally stood inside a precinct defined by a boundary wall or, in some more elaborate examples, a portico. The resulting arrangement meant that the temple at Gosbecks conformed to the grander type, with the sacred area becoming the temple precinct. The ditch does not seem to have had a bank, the spoil having been removed, if not when it was dug in the Iron Age, then certainly later when the portico was built.

The temple portico was a covered walkway built on a magnificent scale and no doubt at considerable cost. It consisted of a solid, presumably windowless, outer wall and two lines of columns, all supporting a tiled pitched roof. The outer wall was almost a quarter of a mile in length, measured around all four sides. There would probably have been about 260 columns. Each seems to have been about 5 m high, giving a headroom (including the moulded architrave above) of around 6 m or 20 Roman feet. The columns were placed in two lines at just under 2 m intervals along two continuous foundations. These extended around all four sides of the building except in the centre of the east side, where there was

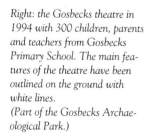

Impression of the theatre at Gosbecks. Viewed from the north-west. It is unclear whether the building had a rear wall behind the stage.

Right: the Gosbecks theatre in 1994 with 300 children, parents and teachers from Gosbecks Primary School. The main features of the theatre have been outlined on the ground with white lines.
(Part of the Gosbecks Archaeological Park.)

an entrance vestibule. One line of columns formed the innermost side of the portico and the other line ran along the centre of it. This arrangement meant that people in the portico could look into the sacred area, but they were prevented from entering it by the deep ditch.

In plan, the temple took the form of two squares, one placed centrally within the other so as to make an inner sanctum (*cella*) and a surrounding corridor or ambulatory. Temples of this type are referred to as 'Romano-Celtic' because they occur in quite large numbers in the north-west part of the Roman empire.

The fact that the temple was not placed centrally in the sacred area means that there may have been at least one other important feature in the enclosure which we do not know about, such as a large altar, a mausoleum, or even the burial place of Cunobelin (see page 27). Certainly, the area is likely to have contained such things as statuary, smaller altars, and Jupiter columns (which were giant columns each with a statue on top).

The plan of the temple and its portico is known mainly from aerial photographs which show the positions of the various walls making up the complex. However the photographs are of limited value when it comes to exact dimensions. The first excavations took place in 1842 when the Reverend Henry Jenkins thought he was digging a Roman villa. In 1936 Rex Hull cut a trench diagonally across the whole complex, but did not recognise any foundation trenches. A trench across the portico in 1977 provided

measurements for the width of the portico and its foundations. Most informative of all was a trench dug across the temple in 1995. This not only provided some plan-measurements for the temple, but also building debris in the adjacent section of ditch revealed much about the temple super-structure.

When it comes to reconstructing buildings, we are lucky that copies of a Roman

Above: the temple, portico and square ditch as marks in a ripening crop.

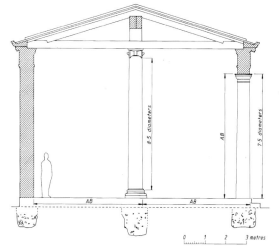

A reconstructed cross-section through the portico at Gosbecks according to the rules of the Roman architect Vitruvius.

Right: a trench being dug in 1995 across the site of the temple at Gosbecks.

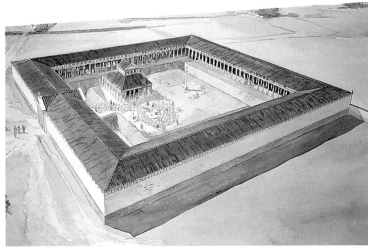

Left: impression of the temple, portico and square ditch at Gosbecks. Viewed from the north-east.

Mercury was the Roman god of trade and communication. The bronze statuette is about 30 cm high. It was ploughed up at Gosbecks by Mr A. Beales in the 1940s.

Inset: Mars, the Roman war god. The figure is 12 mm high. It is engraved on a red semi-precious gemstone which was set in an iron finger-ring. It was used to make impressions in wax seals. Found in 1995 on the site of the Gosbecks temple.

architect's treatise still survive. Vitruvius seems to have written his ten books on architecture about half a century or so before the Claudian invasion of Britain. In this work, he explains that the various elements making up a building should be in proportion with each other so that the building is satisfactorily designed regardless of its actual size. He gives what he considers are the appropriate proportions of one element to another, and uses the column diameter as the unit around which the building should be designed. Thus armed with Vitruvius' rules, it should be possible to reconstruct a building knowing only its ground plan and the diameter of its columns. Although few

surviving classical buildings conform exactly to the rules set out by Vitruvius, nevertheless his principles can give us a good approximation of what the buildings looked like. Unfortunately Vitruvius does not describe Romano-Celtic temples (probably because this type of building was not common in his day), but he does give details for porticos, and these rules can be applied, not only to the main temple portico, but also to the portico or ambulatory forming the outer part of the Romano-Celtic temple.

Reconstructing the temple portico should be quite simple. All we need to know is its width, and this will provide such details as the height and diameter of the columns and the spacing between them. The 1977 excavation across the portico did just that. If the portico had been built according to Vitruvian principles, then floor to ceiling it would have measured 19.25 Roman feet (5.7 m) with external Doric columns around 2.25 Roman feet (0.67 m) in diameter at the base, internal Ionic columns around 2 Roman feet (0.59 m) at the base, all spaced at 6.2 Roman feet (1.83 m) between. Regardless of how closely it followed Vitruvian principles, it is clear that the building must have been very impressive.

The 1995 excavation across the Romano-Celtic temple not only provided some measurements for the ground plan, but also various pieces of building material, including pieces of column, were found in the backfill of the adjacent section of ditch. These remarkable column fragments are large enough to show that the shafts were 2.25 m (or more) in diameter, which is far larger than would be expected if the temple was of what is regarded as the conventional form, ie a relatively low colonnaded corridor around a central, tall *cella*. The diameter of the columns suggests a building with a tall ambulatory and either a single pitched roof or a very tall tower-like *cella*. If true, the resulting temple would have had a very conventional, classical appearance, with a ceiling height in the ambulatory of almost 20 Roman feet (0.67 m)—just like the colonnade. This is surprising. If fact, the size of the columns suggests that the temple and colonnade were really parts of the same design and architecturally were much more mainstream classical than hitherto supposed. Of course the obvious explanation for all this is that the columns really come from the portico rather than the temple, in which case their size is really no surprise at all. However the relationship between the building remains in the ground and the temple gives the impression that this was not the case. Further excavation is needed to resolve the matter.

The building materials in the ditch and over the site of the temple also showed that the lower parts of some of the walls had been sheathed in purbeck marble and that the columns had been plastered and painted with stippling to give a marble effect. The floors seem to have been of plain black and white mosaic, and the roof was of red tile.

The discovery in the 1940s of the statuette of Mercury at Gosbecks suggested that he was the god who was worshipped in the temple. However a fragment of an iron finger-ring found on the site of the temple in 1995 suggests otherwise. The ring incorporates a semi-precious gemstone which has the figure of Mars engraved on it. You will recall that Camulodunum took its name from Camulos who was the Celtic god of war. Mars was his Roman equivalent so it would be fitting if he was the principal deity worshipped in what would have been the centre of the British settlement.

Temples

The Romano-Celtic temple at Gosbecks was not the only temple of this kind in Colonia Victricensis. In fact seven of them are known, and there must have been many more. Their distribution is interesting because it reveals the areas of greatest British and Roman influence. The Romano-Celtic temples occur widely across the former Iron Age settlement but are absent within the walled part of the colony, where instead we find the only known classical temple in the town (the Temple of Claudius).

There were at least four Romano-Celtic temples on the Sheepen site. This had been a major industrial and commercial site in the Iron Age and early Roman periods; the presence of the temples indicates that it continued after the Boudican revolt as a native sanctuary. A bronze plaque from the precinct of the largest of the four shows that it had been dedicated to a god appropriate to its size, namely Jupiter, who was the most powerful of them all.

Another Romano-Celtic temple was built in a very prominent site—outside the Balkerne Gate—where it would have been very obvious to everybody passing through the gate. On the opposite side of the road lay a square building, three sides of which were built on piers to create a series of seven continuous arches. The foundations and floor of the building had been destroyed in recent times, but it is clear that the foundations were built on wooden piles driven into the natural sand below. Constructions of this kind are unusual in situations which were not water-logged, and the use of piles suggests that the building was rather top heavy, perhaps because of the presence of an upper storey. Given the Romano-Celtic temple directly opposite, the building might have been a shrine of some kind although, in view of the arches, it may have been something which was open to the public like a shop or mini covered market. A great bank of oyster shell lay nearby (shown to the right of the water-mains on page 92), although slightly earlier in date, suggests the possibility that the building housed a stall or shop selling shellfish.

An interesting temple was found in the Royal Grammar School playing-field. It was detected as cropmarks in 1938 and excavated just after the war by Mr A.F. Hall, a classics teacher at the school, and the headmaster, Mr J.F. Elam. The temple stood in the heart of Camulodunum, in wooded or open countryside some distance away from the areas of major occupation. This is clear from two votive plaques and the figurine of a stag which were all found during the excavation. The dedications on the plaques show that the temple was erected in honour of Silvanus, god of woodland and hunting. The stag suggests that deer were hunted in the vicinity.

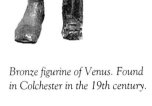

Bronze figurine of Venus. Found in Colchester in the 19th century.

One of several copper-alloy votive plaques from temples in Colchester. This one was found in 1976 on the site of the temple at St Helena's School in Sheepen Road. It reads:

P ORANIVS
FACILLIS IOVI
SIGILLUM EX
TESTA

(Publius Oranius Facilis gave a statuette to Jove under the terms of his will.)

Above: the 'Colchester sphinx' was found on the site of the Essex County Hospital in 1821. Part of an elaborate tomb. The sphinx is the classical symbol of death. She holds a head symbolising the soul of the deceased.

The 'Colchester Vase'

The Colchester Vase is decorated with three scenes showing gladiatorial contests and blood sports. One scene shows two armed men (*bestiarii*) cruelly baiting a bear. One of the men is whipping the animal; the other hits it with a club as he menacingly carries a sword in his other hand. The next scene shows the end of a gladiatorial combat. The victor on the left is a type of gladiator known as a *secutor* (themselves divided into Thracians, Samites, and Gauls), who were each armed with a sword, a shield, and body armour. The other man is a *retiarius*, a kind of gladiator equipped with a shoulder guard, net, and trident. He raises his finger as a gesture of submission, having dropped his trident and lost his net. The third scene shows two stags being chased by two hunting dogs.

Below: the Colchester Vase was found in 1848 during one of the earliest known archaeological excavations in the town, when John Taylor, a keen antiquarian, uncovered 170 or more pots in the grounds of his house off Lexden Road. The pot was part of a burial group which included three other vessels.

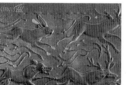

Burial practice

For the first two hundred years or so of Roman Britain, the normal way to dispose of the dead was by cremation, with the ashes being buried in a pot. However in the 3rd century, inhumation became the norm with the bodies usually being buried in heavy plank coffins. Sometimes some of the dead person's belongings such as pottery and personal jewellery were buried with the remains, and in some cases there may have been food and drink. Burial was not usually allowed in the built-up areas of Roman towns, which is why at places like Colonia Victricensis the dead were buried outside the walled area of town.

In the 1st and 2nd centuries, the most prestigious place to be buried was alongside the main road leading from the west side of town to London and St Albans. It must have been so extensively lined with grand graves and tombs that it could have been called the 'Street of Tombs' like the similar street in Pompeii. The monuments included the two military tombstones of Facilis (page 39) and Longinus (page 50), and what appears to have been a small open-air walled cemetery in the grounds of what is now the Royal Grammar School in Lexden Road. Important burial areas developed behind the tomb- and monument-lined front-ages, especially to the south. Most of the town's richest burials come from these areas. They include the famous so-called 'child's grave' from near the junction of Creffield Road and Cambridge Road, the grave near West Lodge Road with the Colchester Vase, and the 'tile tomb' from Beverley Road. The wealth of many of the burials suggests that this was predominantly the final resting place of many of those who lived in the colony. Elsewhere cremation cemeteries such as those in the vicinity of the Abbey Field and North Station were distinctly less well endowed, and thus may have been for the dead of the British.

The law against burial within the walled areas of towns did not apply to babies of less than a few weeks of age. Over two dozen examples have been recognised in Colonia Victricensis of babies who were buried under or close by what were presumably their parents' houses. One ancient source said that young babies had to be inhumed because their bones were too small to recover after cremation, while another said that their lives were not of sufficient value to warrant a proper grave.

Pottery manufacture

An important industry in the colony for practically the whole of its life was the manufacture of pottery. The industry seems to have been at its technical and commercial peak between the mid 2nd and the 3rd centuries when contracts with the army meant that Colchester products were being exported as far afield as forts on Hadrian's Wall and beyond. Mortaria, which were thick grit-lined bowls used for grinding foodstuffs, were in demand by the army, and over half of the Colchester output of the mid 2nd century is thought to have been exported to the northern frontier, especially to forts on the Antonine Wall in Scotland.

Some of the Colchester potters, such as Miccio and Minuso, came from East Gaul which explains why, for a while at least (between c AD 160 and 200), the colony had its own factories for the production of the high-quality red-slipped ware known as samian. Pottery of this type was made in vast quantities in factories in various parts of Gaul until the 3rd century. It was in great demand and was shipped throughout the whole of the Roman empire and beyond.

Samian was technically much more demanding to make than ordinary pottery and it needed elaborate and specialised kilns. Much of it was decorated on the outside with patterns in relief and stamped on the base with the maker's name. Decorated vessels were made in moulds using a fast wheel, their rims and base-rings being added later. Over 400 fragments of moulds have been found in Colchester, and they can be attributed stylistically to three different potters. Unfortunately, these men did not stamp their wares so we do not know their names, although one of them (now referred to simply as 'Potter C') has been identified as having worked earlier in the potteries at Sinzig in East Gaul. Plain samian (in the form of cups, plates, and bowls) was usually stamped, and as a result we now have the names of at least fourteen potters who worked in Colchester.

A lucrative British market beckoned, and the successful production of samian in Colchester promised considerable commercial success. Until then, the demand in the country for samian could only be satisfied by imported wares surcharged with heavy transport costs. The Colchester factories did manage to produce high-quality products to a standard comparable with their Gaulish competitors, but as an industry it had little impact, even in Colchester where negligible transport costs should have given it the overwhelming edge over samian from elsewhere. The figures speak for themselves. Out of 1288 pieces of decorated samian excavated in the town in recent years, only five—a meagre total—seem to be Colchester products. The manufacture of plain vessels appears to have been more successful, but only marginally so. Even in Colchester, during its peak of production, not much more than one in twenty plain samian vessels in the average household are likely to have been produced locally. It is still unclear why samian production in Colchester never really flourished as it should have done. There is some evidence for the making of samian at other sites in Britain but these centres had much less impact even than the Colchester factories.

Other types of pottery made in the colony include wares decorated with trails of slip (barbotine) and moulded figures applied to the surface. The end result was decoration in relief, just like decorated samian, but the visual effect was more fluid and the pots could be marketed more cheaply because they were less complicated to make. The most accomplished pottery of this type was probably made by the same highly-skilled men who made the Colchester samian.

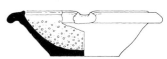

A mortaria (grinding bowl) from Colchester.

Below: pottery kiln found at the Middleborough site in 1979. Pots were stacked on the perforated floor (A). Fuel was burnt in the chamber below (B).

*Samian
mould of Colchester Potter A.*

The Colchester Vase is a superb example of the technique, although it is not certain if this particular vessel was made in Colchester or East Gaul.

Over 40 kilns have been discovered in Colchester, and there would have been many more. The kilns were situated in the open air, well away from the built-up areas of the colony. Most of the kilns which have been found occurred in groups and a few have recognisable compounds. The kilns were generally 2 or 3 m long, round or square in shape, with a stoke hole set below ground level. The pots were stacked on a suspended floor in the upper part of the kiln over a fire which was lit in the lower part. Large, rectangular kilns, of which two are known in Colchester, were used for the manufacture of tile and brick.

Rex Hull discovered and excavated in 1933 a kiln used for the manufacture of samian. Not only was samian technically more demanding to make than normal pottery, but it also needed kilns where the temperature could be carefully controlled and spoilage minimised. Hence the kiln contained lots of pieces of unusual 'kiln furniture' in the form of hollow pipes, spacers, and supports of various kinds. A uniform temperature throughout the firing chamber was maintained by means of a complicated series of vertical flues lining the walls of the kiln and placed through its floor, and a whole array of different supports and spacers was used to support the stacks of pots during firing to prevent them from buckling and spoiling adjacent stacks of vessels.

Animals and food

Unfortunately animal and plant remains recovered from archaeological excavation in Colchester are very limited, and represent only the tiniest fraction of the material which must have passed through the sites. Also the pattern of survival is distorted. Soft animal tissue normally decays without trace and we have to be content with bones. And as for plants, only their seeds have much chance of survival unless the material has been charred. Nevertheless bones can provide a lot of information about diet, farming methods, and animal products, and even limited plant remains can reveal much about food and the environment of the time.

Animals were kept for various reasons. Dead animals were a source of meat, horn, bone, hide, fur, down, feathers, sinew, and gut—in fact very little was wasted. Live animals provided milk, wool, manure, eggs, sport, and, of course, power for traction and transport. And just as today, some animals were kept as household pets.

Cattle bones are the commonest, testifying to the popularity of beef. Horse remains are rare, and there is little evidence that they were eaten in the Roman colony. Both horses and oxen would have been important providers of muscle power for traction and transport. Pork and mutton were popular as well as beef. However the colonists liked tender young meat and this preference became more marked with the passage of time. Most sheep were slaughtered between the age of six and twelve months but later a clear preference emerged for young lambs. This change would have had the effect of releasing large quantities of sheep's milk, and thus may show an increased demand for the milk for human consumption. Something similar can be detected with pigs and cattle. At first pigs were slaughtered when they were young adults, but later six-month old piglets were preferred. Cattle were eaten when they were about three years old but, as with pigs and sheep, it was later the custom to slaughter them a little younger.

Animal figurines from Colchester: cockerel and lion (above), and boar (right).

Left: the largest of the houses excavated at the Lion Walk site contained a number of mosaics. This one included a walking lion with a basket of ?fruit and leaves to the right of his head. Although the mosaic lay under part of a street called Lion Walk, this is a coincidence (it was previously known as 'Cat Lane').

Caesar writing a hundred years before the Claudian invasion said that the Britons would not eat fowl, geese, or hare. The Romans certainly had different ideas. Chicken was extremely popular in Colonia Victricensis—maybe more so than red meat. Hen birds were only slightly more common than cocks. The male birds would have provided more meat than the females, and they could have been used for cock-fighting. Geese and duck were also eaten in significant numbers, but hare rarely so.

Dogs were much more common than cats. Many would have been working animals, although most seem to have been kept as pets. A 1st-century pit on the Balkerne Lane site contained the remains of eight dogs ranging in size from short squat animals to tall slender ones. The Roman occupation of Britain saw the appearance of a greater range in the size and shape of dog skulls, suggesting that they introduced many new breeds into the country.

Just as today, farming was a highly organised industry which fed the population, whereas hunting made only a minor contribution to the food supply. This is evident from the comparatively low incidence of the bones of wild animals. The commonest of these are of roe and red deer, and in fact these animals may have been exploited for their antlers as much as their meat. Antler was a strong, useful material, used for making articles such as needles, hairpins, combs, dice, tool-handles, and weaving implements. Interestingly, the bones of deer are at their commonest in deposits belonging to the traumatic years of the mid to late 40s, and this may point to a brief period when the volume of meat needed by the new population could

not be sourced entirely from domestic stock.

Bones of various medium to large birds have been found in the colony showing that game could be on the menu. Many of the birds would have been caught on the mudflats and meadows around the coast. They include black-tailed godwit, mallard, whimbrel, widgeon, lapwing, tufted duck, teal, woodcock, swan, and curlew. The common crane and the corncrake are two of the species which the Roman population ate, but which no longer inhabit the region.

Bones of foxes and ravens show the presence of scavengers in and around urban areas. Single bones of two bears were found at Balkerne Lane and Butt Road. The animals could have been trophies from some hunting expedition or they might have been used in bear-baiting. Bears inhabited the remoter parts of Scotland and Wales, and the Roman poet Martial tells how bears from Britain were taken to Rome to be used in shows.

The river Colne and its estuarine waters provided important marine foodstuffs for the local population. Oysters were dredged from the muddy silts in their millions and were a major staple of the diet. Oyster shells occur in large numbers on all sites in and around Colchester, proving their importance in the diet in Roman (and later) times. At the Balkerne Lane site, just outside the Roman gate, impressive banks of almost nothing but discarded oyster shells lined both sides of the road. These suggest that there was a shellfish shop nearby, and vividly underline the popularity of the oyster. Mussels were also eaten in large numbers, and so too (but to a lesser extent) were winkles, whelks, cockles, carpet shells, and possibly scallops.

Objects carved out of bone show how little was wasted from animal carcasses.

Bone die from Lion Walk.

Below: unfinished objects from a bone-working industry. Found on the Butt Road site where they predated the first cemetery.

Fragment of the shoulder of an amphora with the painted inscription FAL LOLL, which tells us that the vessel contained Falernian wine made by Lollius in Italy.

Below: an almost complete amphora from Culver Street. A similar vessel from the Thames was filled with olive stones, showing that it had been used for the transportation of olives.

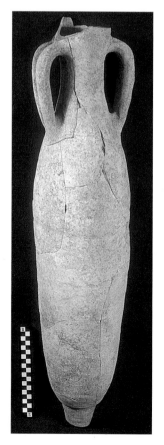

Inshore fishing with nets, traps, and lines provided a range of fish such as cod, haddock, whiting, grey mullet, mackerel, plaice, flounder, and herring. Eel and trout or salmon (the bones are very similar) were caught in the fresh water upriver. Herring, plaice, flounder, and eel were the favourites. Most fish would have been eaten fresh, but out of season it would have been available salted and dried.

Beer was made from malted wheat and barley of the sort found during the excavations at Culver Street. Wine was also popular and was imported in large quantities from Spain, Italy and elsewhere in wooden barrels and in large pottery containers known as amphoras. Falernian wine from Campania in Italy was the most famous and prestigious of the wines, and there is a painted inscription on a fragment of amphora from Colonia Victricensis showing that at least some of its inhabitants could afford to indulge in nothing but the best.

Roman food tended to be richly spiced, so much so that one Roman writer commented, 'Men will eat herbs which the cows leave alone'. Herbs recognised at Colonia

Microscopic evidence

Microscopic examination of extracts from soil samples from pits, hearths and other places is sometimes very informative as these often contain interesting organic remains.

Fragment of carbonised walnut shell (3rd century).

Mineralised grape pip from a latrine pit in the fortress. Microscopic examination of faecal material from the same latrine pit showed human consumption of bran.

Fragment of carbonised olive stone (1st or 2nd century).

Victricensis include dill, coriander, aniseed, celery seed, and poppy seed. Cooking was done with lard or olive oil; the use of butter is more problematic. Cheese was the chief dairy product and cheese moulds have been found in the colony. In the absence of sugar, honey was an important sweetener. As always, salt was an essential ingredient in cooking. In the 1st and 2nd centuries AD at least, it would have been readily available from the salt-making sites along the coast. Vinegar, which was a low-quality wine, was important and used in different ways. It served as an effective preservative, an ingredient in sauces and dressings, and, in diluted form, as a refreshing drink. Most distinctive of all Roman ingredients is a sort of fish sauce, known as *garum* or *liquamen*. It was imported in large quantities in amphoras such as those found in Colonia Victricensis and was rather like an anchovy essence.

A chief everyday food was a sort of porridge made of wheat or barley. Its popularity probably accounts for the frequency with which wheat is found in the Boudican deposits in the colony. Various breads were available, as were vegetables such as cabbages, onions, leeks, and turnips. Pulses were popular. The Romans grew peas and beans and imported lentils: examples of horsebean and lentil have been found in the colony. The Culver Street site produced evidence of various fruits, nuts, and flavourings (elderberry, fig, grape, hazelnut, olive, raspberry, sloe, and walnut), and at Lion Walk there were the extraordinary dates and plum (page 80). All these crops could have been grown locally apart from the olives and dates which were imported.

The main cereals are wheat and six-row hulled barley (this being preferred for animal fodder). Oats and rye are also known in Colonia Victricensis. Fragments of shell confirm the consumption of eggs. The thinness of the shells points to birds like modern domestic fowl rather than birds like the goose, swan, and guinea fowl which lay eggs with thicker shells.

Many of the foods which we eat in large quantities today such as potatoes, tomatoes, and oranges would not have been available, and others such as carrots would have been less palatable fore-runners of the varieties we know today. Nor were there any rabbits, and we have yet to find any bones of the poor dormouse, which the Romans are famous for eating stuffed.

TROUBLED TIMES

Problems at home and abroad

It would be a mistake to claim that the late 3rd century marked the beginning of the end of Roman Britain: there was after all well over a century to go, and good times as well as bad lay ahead. Nevertheless there is a sense that somehow this was a turning point in the fortunes of Roman Britain, and that things were never to be quite the same again. Civil wars, severe inflation, and raiding by hostile peoples from outside the empire combined to make this a particularly difficult and turbulent time for the inhabitants of Britain and Colonia Victricensis. Evidence of this is clear enough in the archaeological record in Colchester but, before we look at this, we must briefly review the political events of the second half of the 3rd century as they affected the north-western part of the empire.

The revolt of AD 259/60 was unusual in that it resulted in the formation of a fully-functioning independent Roman state. Known as the Gallic Empire, this was made up of the provinces of Britain, Germany, Gaul, and Spain. The state survived for thirteen years until Tetricus I, the last of its emperors, surrendered to Aurelian after the battle of Chalons in 274.

The ending of the Gallic Empire was followed by least two revolts in Gaul in the 270s and at least one in Britain. The latter was led by the governor of Britain in 277/9 and was put down by German 'barbarians' (Burgundians and Vandals in this case) who had been settled in Britain a few years earlier. The fact that the newly-settled troops had to be used shows that there was strong support for the governor from at least some of the army in Britain.

The region was still not free from internal troubles and the next revolt met with more success than the last. Carausius, a naval commander charged with dealing with raiders operating along the north coast of Gaul, was accused of malpractice for personal gain, and the emperor Maximian sentenced him to death (as the story goes). Carausius fled to Britain where in 286 or 287 he established himself as emperor. With the support of the British army (or at least a large part of it), naval forces in the Channel, and substantial land forces in Gaul, Carausius successfully resisted attempts by the Roman empire to restore the situation. However in 293, Carausius was defeated in his great naval base at Boulogne by Constantius, the newly-appointed Caesar (second-in-command) to the west. Shortly afterwards Carausius was assassinated by Allectus, a close associate, who then proceeded to rule the breakaway state in his place. After a delay of three years, Constantius crossed the Channel, defeated Allectus, and united Britain once more with the Roman empire.

Behind these difficulties, there were the troubles caused by people whom the Romans referred to as 'barbarians', meaning those who lived outside the empire. Like civil war, conflict and warfare with people beyond the frontiers were recurring features of the Roman world which were particularly acute in the north-western part of the empire during the late 3rd century. In 258, the Alamanni, who for some years had been causing severe problems on the German frontier, broke through in force and were stopped only when they had reached Milan. Much the same happened again in 276, but this time the invaders are reported to have captured 50 to 60 Gallic cities deep in Gaul before the situation could be rectified. Although the British cities like Colonia

A 1st-century brooch found in the late Roman cultivated soil at Balkerne Lane.

Victricensis were protected by the Channel from these land-based incursions, the chilling prospect of hordes of marauding barbarians over-running cities almost at will in Gaul must have made them think very hard about their own defensive arrangements.

As if all that was not bad enough, there were also the barbarians who preyed on the empire from the sea. As far as the British were concerned, they brought the prospect of real trouble much closer to home. The Saxons were a sea-faring Germanic race who lived beyond the Roman empire in what is now Denmark and northern Germany. They indulged not only in raiding and looting along the coast, but also in piracy on the open sea. They were joined in these practices by Franks from what is now northern France and the Low Countries, and raiders from Ireland. Between about 268 and 283, it seems that there was a very real threat of raiders along the east-facing coastline of southern Britain. The numbers of raiders may not have been great and their main target was the Gallic side of the Channel, but their speed and their ability to strike unexpectedly must have caused much anxiety among those living in the coastal margins of Britain.

City of Victory in decline?

In Colchester itself, there were important developments in the late 3rd century which were not to be reversed and which seem to foreshadow the ultimate fate of the town over a century later. We need to examine these changes before considering what they mean in the context of what was happening in Britain and the north-western part of the Roman empire generally.

Around AD 275, the town ditch was

Map of the City of Victory showing the latest arrangement of the town defences. A rampart on the outer side of the town ditch blocked the road out of Duncan's gate, and the butt ends of the town ditch have been joined up by a stretch of ditch across the adjacent road to leave the Balkerne gate inaccessible from the west.

The built-up areas are shown white.

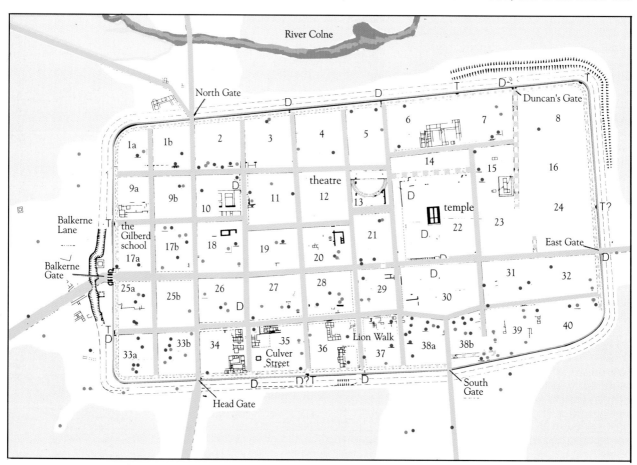

═══ street	• wall	— building remains
┄┄ probable street	• tessellated pavement	D drain
▬▬ town wall	• mosaic	T tower

widened to convert its profile from a deep V-shape to a very wide, truncated U-shape. At Balkerne Lane, the widening had been achieved by digging out the far side of the existing ditch and piling up the excavated material much further out to form an outer (ie 'counterscarp') bank. The excavated soil at Balkerne Lane had been dumped on an allotment in which the soil had been mounded to form cultivation beds (page 100). Fortunately the dumped soil contained many coins—nineteen in all—and these indicate a likely date of c 275 for the ditch-widening.

But these improvements were not enough. In fact the need for more effective defences was so great that the number of gates in the town wall was reduced. The Balkerne Gate was closed, and this was done by cutting off the road leading into it. To do this, the butt ends of the widened town ditch on either side of the road were joined together with a new length of ditch to make a continuous earthwork across the face of the gate. The event cannot be dated as closely as the widening of the town ditch, but it seems to belong to around AD 300.

The incorporation of the monumental arch into the gate in the 1st century, when the town wall was built (page 89), meant that the gate was never very satisfactory as a defensive structure. The arch and part of the rest of the gate were demolished and the rubble this produced was used to block the gap, apart from the south pedestrian footway which seems to have been left open (see picture on page 132). It is not possible to be certain when the blocking wall was built, but it seems likely that it was contemporary with the connecting up of the ends of the town ditch. The blocking of the gate meant that the Head Gate became the main entrance into town (as it was throughout the medieval period).

The Balkerne Gate was not the only gate to be blocked. Duncan's Gate seems to have been treated similarly, because a counter-scarp bank added to the outer side of the town ditch passed unbroken across the front of the gate. This shows that the road through the gate was no longer used and that the gate itself must have been permanently closed.

The changes to the gates and defences were bound up with the decline of the suburbs in the late 3rd century. By c 300, practically all of the houses at Balkerne Lane seem to have been demolished without replacement, and the area was used largely for dumping, pit-digging and quarrying. At Middleborough, the story was much the same. The coins found during the excavations of 1979 make it clear that the site was vacant in the 4th century: there were lots of coins datable up to AD 294 but very few afterwards, suggesting site clearance after 295 and before 335 at the very latest.

Inside the town, similar things were happening, as houses were being demolished without replacement. At Lion Walk, only one house was still standing by the end of the 4th century, the others being removed without replacement in the early and mid 4th century. At Culver Street, the pattern was the same but more extreme. Here, within the space of maybe 50 years or so, at least eight substantial houses were demolished and the area left as open land.

In general, cultivation within the walls must have become more widespread. Part of Culver Street had already been cultivated for many years: some areas had probably been ploughed since the late 1st century (part of a ploughshare was found in Roman cultivated soil at Culver Street), and a granary was built in the cultivated area in about the 2nd century. But now, following the demolitions, even more land was available for agriculture and horticulture. Here, some time between 275 and 325, a massive aisled barn was built which partly encroached on the nearby east-west street. The building seems to have had no proper floor, and there was no evidence of plastered wall surfaces. Its plainness suggests that it served some agricultural function.

At around this time, it seems that forts at Bradwell (known as Othona) and Walton-on-the-Naze were built which would have provided some protection for Colchester from sea-borne raiders. They belong to a defensive system known as the forts of the Saxon Shore, which stretched along the coast from Brancaster in Norfolk to Portchester in Hampshire. The system was developed over a number of years, starting possibly in the first part of the 3rd century. Very little is known about the fort at Walton because the last of it was washed away by the sea in the 18th century, but parts of Othona still survive today. Othona was well placed to overlook the mouth of the Colne, and thus would have been vital for the protection of the Roman town. The limited dating evidence such as there is for its construction suggests a date of around 270 which, if correct, would tie in well with the dates of the

The iron tip of a wooden ploughshare. Found in the cultivated area around the granary at the Culver Street site, this provides evidence for ploughing in the Roman period inside the walled town.

Plan of the Balkerne Lane site c AD 250-400, showing the town ditch, the latest buildings to front the main street, and the raised beds in the allotments to the south.

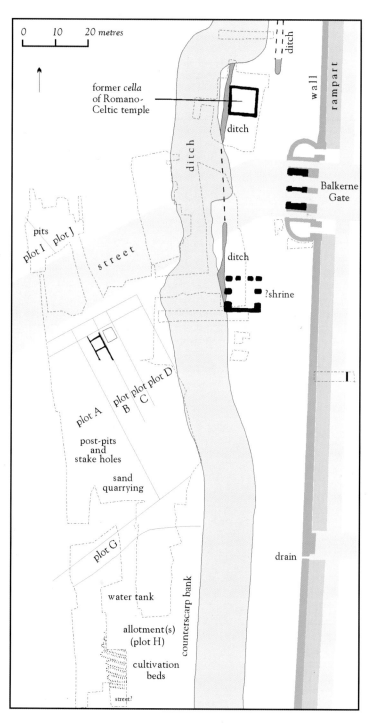

defensive improvements we have noted at Colchester. Being on the south side of the Blackwater, it was some distance by land from Colonia Victricensis, showing that its function was as a base for sea patrols, surveillance and communication rather than for land-based forces, tasked to intercept raiding parties. The system of forts is likely to have been supplemented by signal stations and good inter-connecting roads. There is, for example, the possibility of a small fort or signal station on the east side of the mouth of the Colne. A Roman road known from cropmarks heads straight for the spot now occupied by the Martello Tower at Point Clear, which would have been an ideal place for such a facility. We can imagine something similar on the opposite side of the estuary, at Mersea Stone on Mersea Island (see further map on page 71).

At this point, we need to turn briefly to the subject of coin hoards, because it would seem that they can indicate times of insecurity. There were no banks in Roman times, and so some people would keep their savings in the ground for safe-keeping, particularly in times of unrest. Hoards which are found today only exist because the owner failed to recover the money, presumably because he died or could not find it again. This is not as unlikely as it might seem. In his diary, Samuel Pepys vividly describes his panic when he could not find the gold sovereigns and other items of value which had been buried in his father's garden during a Dutch invasion scare. In the end, he and his family were successful in their search although not everything was recovered. Of the eleven savings hoards of Roman date known from the Colchester area, three were closed at the same time, namely between AD 271 and 274. The biggest of the hoards consists of over 6,000 coins in three vessels (found in 1983 at Gosbecks). Another is made up of over 650 coins from East Mersea (found in 1980), and the third is a group of maybe 84 or so coins from an unrecorded location in the Colchester area (found before 1906). It is remarkable that not only do these hoards share the same closing date, but they also appear to be contemporary with the widening of the defensive ditch at Balkerne Lane. The latest of the coins from the dumped soil there are of the same types as the latest from the three hoards. This suggests that the deposition of the coins and the widening of the ditch took place within a few years of each other, ie between 271 and 274/5.

What does it all mean? First of all we need to consider the widening of the town ditch. This would have been done primarily in response to developments in weaponry and siege tactics. The widened ditch meant that attacking forces could not take shelter in the ditch and were fully exposed to arrows and bolts which could be fired from the walls by hand or machine. The widening of the ditch need not therefore be seen as a response to an historical event or threat but more as a necessary upgrade. Nevertheless the shared date of the coin hoards and the ditch widening strongly suggest that we should search for a cause, if not between 271 and 274, then certainly within a few years later. Saxon and other raiding parties would have found it difficult to capture a walled town. They are unlikely to have had the heavy gear necessary to besiege a town and breach its defences. Thus the town ditch may not have been widened primarily with itinerant raiders in mind. It is more likely that the perceived enemy was sections of the Roman army itself—in other words, the threat of civil war may have made the defensive upgrade imperative. Thus if we need to find a single explanation (and that may be a dubious approach), then the ending of the Gallic Empire in 274 is it. This fits the date perfectly and provides a suitable context for the widening of the ditch and the burying of lots of coin hoards. The period leading up to the battle of Chalons must have been an anxious time within the Gallic Empire, with people wondering what might happen if Tetricus was defeated (as indeed he was). The fact that he was allowed to continue in public life afterwards suggests that if there had been a direct link between the ditch widening and the hoards, then this related to the last days of the Gallic Empire rather than to its immediate aftermath.

What about the closing of the Balkerne Gate and Duncan's Gate? The excavation at Balkerne Lane shows that the blocking of the Balkerne Gate and the widening of the ditch were separated in time by two decades or so. This supports the view that we should not try to attribute historical contexts to these topographical events, but should instead see them simply as improvements which the turbulent climate of the day made prudent. Nevertheless if we are to pursue this route, then just as with the widening of the ditch, the blocking of the gates could be seen as being directed more towards improving the defensive capabilities of the town against the onslaught of Roman soldiers skilled in siege tactics rather than against raiding parties from across the sea. This suggests that maybe the blocking of the gates belongs to the period of Carausius and Allectus, when the fear of civil war in Britain was ultimately realised with the invasion of Constantius in AD 296.

Another issue we need to consider is the cause of the dramatic decline of the suburbs. Was this caused by the defensive improvements, does it indicate a reduction in the population of the town as a whole, or is it to be explained in some other way? The answer is likely to be a complicated one.

It could not have been simply a matter of people moving from the suburbs into the safety of the walled part of the town. People clearly managed to continue to live in undefended villas and settlements in the countryside and anyway, as we have seen, there was no obvious corresponding increase in the numbers of houses in the walled part of the

A Roman allotment where the soil has been mounded to form beds suitable for growing vines or plants such as asparagus. The surface of the allotment (which is fully exposed in the photograph) was perfectly preserved because it had been buried under a thick dump of soil.

Below left: the cultivated beds.

town—in fact quite the reverse. Perhaps safety was a factor in deciding where to build a new house, but it was not sufficiently important to make the inhabitants knock down their existing houses and replace them within the walls.

Obviously the closure of the road through the Balkerne Gate would have made it very inconvenient to live in the Balkerne Lane area, and this must be an important factor in the disappearance of most of the houses there. But this would not explain what happened at Middleborough, where there is no reason to suppose that the nearby gate was closed in the manner of the Balkerne Gate.

It is possible that houses which were near the widened ditch were cleared away as part of the scheme to improve the ability of the town to withstand a siege. Clearly buildings on the far side of the ditch could have been used for shelter by a hostile enemy. The trouble with this idea is that there seems to have been a shrinking generally of all the built-up areas around the town, not just close to it. This is clear if we compare the distribution of cremations with that of inhumations. As we have already mentioned, it was not normal practice to bury the dead in the built-up parts of Roman towns (apart from babies), so the location of burials gives some indication of the occupied areas of a settlement. Broadly speaking, cremations are 1st and 2nd century in date whereas inhumations (bodies which have not been cremated) belong to the 3rd and 4th centuries. When plotted on a plan, it is striking how the inhumations at Colonia Victricensis occur much closer to the walled part of the town than do the cremations. This is powerful evidence of the reduction of the built-up areas around the town walls since it suggests that, in the 3rd and 4th centuries, areas once occupied by buildings were cleared and thus became suitable for burial.

Could the decline in the suburbs reflect, in part at least, a big drop in the population of the town? This is the most obvious conclusion to make, given the vacant areas that were opening up in the walled town. The rate of new building in the late 3rd and 4th centuries seems to support this. There was new work—eg the palatial house at Culver Street dates to the late 3rd century, and the extra rooms added to the largest of the houses at Lion Walk in the 4th century—but the new work was not that common. The point is reinforced when we look at mosaics: the overwhelming majority known from the town

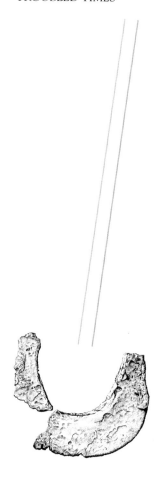

An iron 'shoe' from a wooden spade provides evidence for horticulture within the walls. From the Culver Street site.

are mid 2nd to early 3rd century in date, with very few belonging to the 4th century. In fact the house just referred to at Lion Walk has produced the only certain examples of late mosaics from Colchester.

But the declining suburbs are not necessarily to be explained this easily. Apart from anything else, there clearly was still a significant population in the 4th century—as we shall soon see, the Butt Road cemetery indicates a substantial number of local inhabitants. Part of the explanation for the reduction in the built-up areas may be to do with a change in the size of later Roman houses. The houses of the 2nd and 3rd centuries took up a lot of ground space, yet were each the home of just one family (plus slaves and other servants). It could be that houses in the 4th century tended to be smaller, so that a reduction in the size of the built-up areas would not necessarily mean a reduction in the population. It is relevant here to note that the two sites to have produced the most intensive evidence of late occupation were both on the High Street (the Cups Hotel in 1973 and Angel Yard in the 1980s). They prove the existence of occupation in Colchester in the 4th century and suggest that maybe it had become concentrated along the High Street. The High Street probably always was an important commercial street—remember the two shops which were destroyed during the Boudican revolt in AD 60/1 (page 82)—so presumably the street was still important in this way in the 4th century. It could therefore be that smaller houses were favoured in the later Roman period, and that these were concentrated on both sides of the High Street, in a manner which anticipated the later post-Roman town, as will become clear in the last chapter.

If it seems that we have been overly circumspect in the treatment of the late 3rd-century Colchester, it is because we need to think hard before trying to explain what must have been important changes in the town. Undoubtedly the defences were improved during this time and at some cost to the convenience of the town's inhabitants. Times were difficult and dangerous, and there were many factors at work to make the defensive improvements worth the sacrifices. There are indeed good reasons to suppose that there was some depopulation of the town and that this was a slow, long-term trend which was never to be reversed. But the evidence is not yet sufficient to be sure.

FOURTH-CENTURY CHRISTIANS

St Helena as she is represented on the Colchester Borough charter of 1413.

The triumph over paganism

At times it was dangerous to be a Christian. Churches could be demolished and congregations persecuted according to the hostility of the emperor of the day. The most famous of the Christians in Roman Britain was St Alban who, in the 3rd century, was martyred at Verulamium for his beliefs. All this was to change with the rise to power of the emperor Constantine, who not only ended the persecutions, but positively encouraged the religion by becoming a Christian himself. Constantius, his father, had been lukewarm in his application of the emperor Diocletian's policy of persecution and had restricted himself to the closure or demolition of some churches in the west of the empire where he was Caesar (second-in-command). His mother was Helena, a devout Christian who became famous for her supposedly successful quest for the Holy Cross. In 313, the 'Peace of the Church', marked by the 'Edict of Milan', legalised Christianity and allowed its followers freedom of worship. Churches sprang up all over the empire and Christianity became much more popular, even in far-flung places like Britain. Paganism went out of fashion and many pagan temples were destroyed as Christianity basked in imperial favour.

Evidence of early Christianity in Britain is fairly thin, and it is difficult to tell just how widespread its support turned out to be. However, just one year after the Edict of Milan, we find three British bishops and representatives of a fourth attending a major ecclesiastical gathering in Gaul. At Colonia Victricensis ten to twenty years

St Helena

According to the erroneous medieval 'Colchester Chronicle', Helena was born in Colchester. She was the daughter of a man called Coel, who founded Colchester and was later king of England. Helena married Constantius. supposedly to end his two-year siege of Colchester. Her supposed connection with the town is reinforced in the Chronicle with the claims that their son Constantine (who became the great Christian emperor) was born in the town, and that she founded St Helen's Chapel.

It was widely believed in the medieval world that Helena found the holy cross (by excavation in Jerusalem), which is why she is shown here with a large wooden cross.

The mythical king Coel of Colchester may be the product of the 'Col-' element in the place name and a semi-historical person called Coel who was active in the north of England in the 5th century. (At one time, the Balkerne Gate was known as 'Colkyng's castle'.)

119

later, there was not only a substantial Christian community but one which found no difficulty in building a church in a prominent place in the town. Most of the pagan temples in Colchester are likely to have continued in use for some considerable time after 313, showing that, as elsewhere, the imperial endorsement of Christianity did not mean the end of paganism. Dating evidence is meagre but the largest of the temples at Sheepen may have been in use until the last decade or so of the 4th century (to judge by the coins found there). Although the date of the demolition of the Gosbecks temple can only at present be stated as being some time after 337, the building does at least seem to have been knocked down before the end of the Roman period—an action significant in itself. It is true that the Romano-Celtic temple at Balkerne Lane was still standing for most if not all of the 4th century (page 107), but the building had been altered to such an extent that its function must have changed too. The colonnaded corridor around all four sides was demolished to leave just the central room (*cella*) standing. The building must have been converted for Christian or some other use.

The great Temple of Claudius was clearly not demolished, since, as we shall see, it was still standing over 700 years later when the Normans arrived. Classical temples like this were sometimes converted for Christian use in the late Roman period. There is no evidence that the Temple of Claudius at Colchester was adapted in this way, although a piece of pottery with the Chi-Rho symbol scratched on its surface has been found near the temple. There is a suggestion (by Paul Drury) that the front of the temple was completely redesigned in late Roman times, but a small excavation inside Colchester Castle in 1996 showed that this was not the case.

Rim fragment of a large pot with the Chi-Rho symbol (used by early Christians) scratched on it. Found near the Temple of Claudius.

Butt Road church and cemetery

The Butt Road site is remarkable for its Christian church and cemetery. The church was first examined in 1935 by Rex Hull, but its true nature was not properly appreciated until the building was fully excavated in the 1970s and 1980s prior to the construction nearby of a large police station. We cannot be certain that the building was a church rather than a pagan temple but its date, plan, orientation, and associated cemetery make it very likely that it was Christian. Much of the cemetery was also excavated at the same time (about 660 graves), although the site had been found much earlier when the cemetery was recorded by the Victorian archaeologist William Wire.

The cemetery was really two successive cemeteries. In the first, the graves (59 excavated) were aligned north-south. Many of the graves were accompanied with objects such as personal ornaments and pots containing food and drink. The alignments of the graves and the relatively high proportion of objects suggest that these were probably the graves of pagans.

The second cemetery was laid out on top of the first one during the 4th century. The graves were aligned east-west, with the heads of the bodies to the west. Objects were much rarer than in the first cemetery, and those present were buried mostly with children. The bodies were tightly-packed in ill-defined rows which, as the number of burials grew, crept over and obliterated the graves of the first cemetery. The orientation of the bodies in the second cemetery and the reduced numbers of objects in the graves indicate that the dead had probably been Christians.

Almost all of the bodies had been buried in nailed wooden coffins. Although these had almost completely rotted away, the positions of some of the timbers were shown by rusted nails and thin brown layers of decayed wood. Traces of wood on the nails show some of the planks to have been over two inches thick, indicating that some coffins must have weighed up to four hundredweight. A few of the coffins must have been even heavier because they were lined with lead.

Burial in a coffin as opposed to cremation was done in the hope that the body could be preserved for the after-life. A few of the corpses were covered with gypsum or lime plaster with the aim of achieving better preservation.

The dead were made to look their best,

since a few of the females had hairpins on the skull, showing that their hair had been dressed. However, the dead were not buried in their best clothes, but instead were probably wrapped in shrouds made with different pieces of cloth. The shrouds may have been quite fancy items since one of them incorporated silk, which possibly had been imported from China. Nor were the corpses dressed in personal ornaments such as rings or bracelets. Where objects of this kind did appear in graves, they were usually to one side of the body, close to where they would have been worn. Where present, footwear was either on the feet or, more often, neatly set to one side.

?church

Plan of the cemetery

Simplified plan of the graves excavated at the Butt Road site in 1976-9.

sand pit

0   10 metres

A collection of jet, glass, amber, and copper-alloy beads from a grave at Butt Road; these have been restrung as two necklaces.

Pottery or glass vessels had been deposited in a few of the graves. Although this was a pagan practice, the tradition must have been sufficiently strong for it to appear in the Christian cemetery, albeit less frequently. The vessels presumably contained food or drink for the dead person to consume on their journey to the next world. The vessels were put inside the coffin when there was enough room; otherwise they were placed on the floor of the grave, to one side of the coffin.

An important and unusual aspect of the Butt Road cemetery is the evidence it provides for family groups. The distribution of various finds and the characteristics of some of the more distinctive forms of burial all combine to show a cemetery which was partitioned, at least to a limited degree, in terms of family plots. An indicator of these divisions comes from a study of the bones, especially the skulls. Stephanie Pinter-Bellows examined the bones for a number of variations or defects which are thought to run in families. When plotted, some of these characteristics were found to occur as groups, thus confirming the presence of family plots.

The church stood at the edge of the cemetery. Few Roman churches have been recognised in Britain. Other examples include a small church at Silchester, a possible cemetery church at Verulamium, and another in the Roman fort at Richborough in Kent. The

Left: a glass cup and jug placed inside the coffin at the feet of the deceased. (Included in the picture below.)

Right: four glass vessels from three graves at the Butt Road cemetery. Glass vessels are very rare in the cemetery, yet the graves with glass were clustered together. This seems to provide evidence of family groupings.

church at Butt Road would have been big enough to accommodate over a hundred people, provided they were not seated. As became the norm in churches, it was aligned east-west with the altar at the east end. It had stone-and-tile walls and a tiled roof, and its floor was littered with animal bones and hundreds of coins.

The various finds and other forms of evidence enable us to build up the following picture of what might have happened to the building. It was constructed *c* 330, possibly around the existing grave of an important local Christian such as a bishop. The building was used mainly for memorial services and funerary feasts (as in the modern wake) in which the predominant meat dishes were of chicken and young pig. A timber building was erected just to the west of the church to serve as a cook-house. The apse was added to the east end possibly around 380, and aisles were put in the eastern half. Later, perhaps around 400, the aisles were replaced with new aisles extending the full length of the building. Two graves were dug into the floor of the church at its east end. One of these contained a timber vault for the body, and was placed between two of the columns forming the south aisle. Meanwhile extensive structural repairs were necessary because the northern part of the building started to subside where it had been built on deeply

Impressions of the presumed church at Butt Road. Viewed from the south-west (above) and from the south-east (below).

The remains of the Butt Road church in 1989 after the site was laid out as a public monument.

The human skull and femur (thigh bone) found in a pit inside the Butt Road church in 1935. Possibly holy relics.

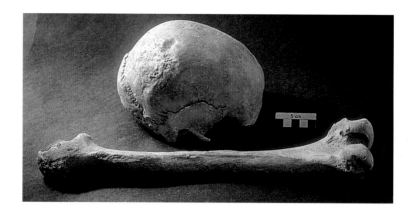

made-up ground. In the 5th century, when the building was in a dilapidated state, a round pit about a metre across was dug inside the church, close to the apse. The skull and a femur of a woman were placed in the bottom of the pit, presumably in the belief that they were holy relics. The woman, who seems to have been middle-aged and fairly short in stature, had survived a depressed fracture of the skull. Two iron vessels and a knife, which were presumably associated with the funerary meals, were put in the pit, which was then backfilled and sealed with a large slab of worked stone. The church was never demolished, but by the end of the Roman period it had become a ruin. At least part of the roof

was missing and some of the aisle posts had been taken down. Materials salvaged from the building included a large sheet of lead. The sheet was cut up for removal off site and parts buried for safe-keeping in a pit which had been dug to remove one of the aisle posts. Whoever buried the lead, never returned to collect it (see page 131).

The Butt Road church is an extraordinary building. The evidence for feasting, the utensils in the pit, the supposed holy relics, the strange burials near the apse, and the cut-up lead sheet are some of the tantalising features which make it quite exceptional, and one of the most important and interesting Roman buildings known in Colchester.

Above: a forensic reconstruction of the head of the woman shown in the timber vault illustrated on the right.

Right: timber vault which contained the coffined bodies of a man (in the picture, below) and a woman (above).

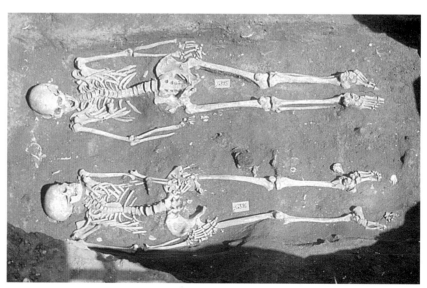

THE END OF THE ROMAN CITY

The last years

It is a common misconception that the end of Roman Britain was marked by the Romans leaving the country. Long before the 5th century, when the end came, the Romans and the Britons had merged to the extent that there was not an identifiable group of Romans who could have left. In fact only a proportion of the original 'Roman' invaders had themselves been Roman since the army was made up of men from all over the empire. The end of Roman Britain was not simply the product of internal factors in Britain alone but was a result of dramatic events being played out across the whole of the western part of the Roman empire. Things might have worked out differently had the army concentrated more on protecting its frontiers against barbarian encroachments. Instead power struggles between rival elements of the army meant that too much effort was expended on civil war. Roman Britain was an early casualty in what was turning out to be the break-up of the Roman empire. As we shall see, civil war, barbarian invasions and attacks, and too great a reliance on barbarian mercenaries, all played their part in bringing about the end in Britain of almost 400 years of Roman rule.

It is impossible to know exactly how Britain found itself outside the Roman empire and what the events were which led up to its separation. Even more difficult is the linked question of when and how eastern England came to be dominated by settlements of Saxons at the expense of the existing Romano-British population. Although there is quite a lot of evidence for all this, the sources are patchy in their coverage and in places appear to conflict with one another, with the result that archaeologists and historians are continually reassessing their interpretations in the light of new discoveries.

The Roman empire had over the years become increasingly reliant on barbarian mercenaries for their support. Military services could be obtained by offering barbarian peoples cash or land for settlement. We have already mentioned the Vandals and Burgundians (both Germanic tribes) who had been settled in Britain in the late 3rd century in this way. The trouble was that the barbarian mercenaries could be fickle with their loyalty and therefore dangerous military forces. Alaric, with his Goths (another Germanic tribe), proved the point and more, when in AD 410 he did the unthinkable and sacked Rome.

As far as Britain is concerned, the break with the Roman empire seems to have occurred around 409, although the Roman way of life continued for some years afterwards. In the run-up to this event, there had been important victories over the Saxons, Picts, and Irish Scots. Then in 406-407, there were three successive mutinies in Britain with three usurpers assuming power in quick succession. The last and most successful of these men was Constantine III. Soon after taking power, Constantine entered Gaul to tackle Germans who had crossed the Rhine and were threatening to occupy the Channel coast. By the end of 408, Constantine had based himself in the city of Arles, having taken control of Gaul and Spain. In the meantime, forces in Britain turned against Constantine and declared their

Late Roman military buckle made of copper alloy. Probably from Colchester.

The City of Victory in c AD 400, viewed from the south-west.

Details based on excavation.

Left: the Balkerne Lane site, viewed from the south-west, where extramural settlement has almost entirely ceased and the Balkerne gate has been cut off.

Right: the Culver Street site, viewed from the south-west, where all the houses have been demolished and the area is now occupied by a large aisled barn, a corn-drying oven, and cultivated fields. (The building seen in the top left-hand corner lies to the north of the excavated area and is conjectural.)

independence. It seems that Constantine must have taken a large part of the British garrison with him and left the army back home badly depleted. A serious attack by barbarian forces apparently brought feelings of discontent to a head, and forced the Britons to deal with the intruders and make new arrangements for their own longer-term defence which did not include the Roman army. The expulsion of key members of the Roman civil service broke relations with the controlling administration abroad, Roman law was no longer recognised, and Britain was never to be part of the Roman empire again.

Meanwhile, back on the Continent, Constantine had other things on his mind. German barbarians were still active in Gaul, and Gerontius, his British general, proclaimed another (called Maximus) as his rival. Constantine invaded northern Italy, but ended up back in Arles under siege by Gerontius. Alaric with his Gothic army destroyed Rome, and an army of the emperor Honorius marched on Arles which led to the suicide of Gerontius and the execution of Constantine.

In 402, the official importation of new bronze coins into Britain ceased and, within a few decades, coinage probably stopped circulating in the country altogether. Bronze coins had no intrinsic value, but silver and gold coinage may have continued to circulate for a little while as bullion. Coinage had been issued largely to pay troops and the civil service. With the end of coins probably came the end of taxation on a national basis with

the result that whatever remained of the standing army could not be paid, and the soldiers presumably simply gave up. The collapse of the money economy must have had a serious, if not terminal, effect on the viability of towns where the exchange of specialist services and goods was so dependent on the use of coinage. Tradesmen such as bakers or blacksmiths would have had great difficulty in making a living if the sale of products and the purchase of materials depended on barter. This must to a degree explain why, for example, the mass production of pottery stopped early in the 5th century.

As we shall see in the next chapter, Britain without the defensive umbrella of the Roman empire was not successful in holding its own against outside forces—at least not in the longer term. However life probably continued much as before for some years immediately after the break in 409. It is recorded that in 429 two bishops from Gaul visited the shrine of St Alban which we now know was at the Roman town of Verulamium. One of the bishops, St Germanus, addressed a large audience of Britons on a religious matter and supposedly led Britons in a war against Picts and Scots. The bishop repeated his visit some years later, perhaps as late as the 440s. (He died c 448.) These two episodes give the impression that, until at least the 440s, the Romano-Britons were still in control of large parts of the country at least as far east as Verulamium.

The political situation immediately after the final break with Rome is obscure. The country may have fragmented into a series of small states, each ruled by a local tyrant. Meanwhile, the Saxons are likely to have continued their raids until, after maybe forty to fifty years, they started to come and settle in large numbers in places where presumably they were not met by any serious opposition. Some archaeologists believe that British resistance collapsed much more quickly and that the migrations started much earlier. Colonia Victricensis, being close to the east coast, would have been in the front line and so exposed to the first waves of immigrants.

In terms of the country as a whole, the numbers of Romano-Britons eventually affected by the Saxon migrations must have been huge: many hundreds of thousands are likely to have been involved. What were they to do? Presumably many relocated themselves in safer areas to the west, some left the country altogether (an exodus of well-off

Fragments of roof tile mixed with topsoil overlying the floor of a derelict house after the end of Roman Colchester. At the Lion Walk site.

Britons to Gaul is recorded for 461), some resisted and were killed (but maybe proportionally not that many), and others stayed put to be subsumed by the new culture. Archaeologists and historians used to favour the idea that large numbers of Britons fled to the west, but now there is growing support for the notion that there was a fusion between the two cultures with the Britons largely staying in place.

The end of Colonia Victricensis

There are a few towns in Britain where archaeologists believe they have detected isolated instances of Roman occupation continuing well into the 5th century. Generally, however, the absence of new coins and pottery after the opening years of the 5th century means that archaeologists are denied their normal dating materials, and the result is that proving the existence of such occupation can be difficult and contentious.

There are no convincing examples of very late occupation from any of the large sites excavated in Colchester, although, from elsewhere in the town, we can point to a contemporary coin hoard and perhaps even the remains of a few of the people who died at this time. The hoard came to light in 1964. The exact find spot of the discovery is not recorded but it seems to have been found in the vicinity of Artillery Folly, which is about 300 m south of the walled town. The hoard consists of at least 15 silver coins and belongs to the reign of Constantine III (407-411) or later. The coins have been heavily clipped which suggests that the hoard post-dates the break with the Roman empire. The clipping of coins (gold certainly and silver presumably) was forbidden and punishable by death. Although lightly clipped coins did occur in Britain before 409, heavy clipping, such as occurs on the coins in the Artillery Folly hoard, suggests that they were still in circulation after this date when, as we have seen, Britain ceased to obey the Roman rule of law.

Another interesting discovery was in the form of two graves in the grounds of East Hill House in 1983. They are of note because they were inside the walled town, and because the bodies had been decapitated after death. As we have already mentioned, burial of human remains (apart from babies) was not allowed in built-up areas of Roman towns (page 109) so their location suggests that, like the heavily clipped coins, they belong to the period immediately after c 409

when Roman law was no longer being adhered to in Britain. One of the graves contained the remains of a middle-aged man and the other an eighteen-month old infant. Their heads had been cut off at a point between the upper neck vertebrae, and placed in the graves between their knees. Decapitated burials occur elsewhere in Roman Britain but they are not particularly common. The decapitations were carefully done with a scalpel after death and seem to have been associated with the Celtic cult of the head. Burials of this kind also occur in the Anglo-Saxon period, so it is possible that these graves could in fact be post-Roman.

There are other burials from inside the walled part of the town which need to be

The hoard of fifteen silver coins found near Artillery Folly in 1964 or earlier. They date to 407-411 or later.

Close-ups of five of the coins show the extent of the clipping.

mentioned here. Two were inside the great 4th-century barn in Culver Street. One of the bodies had been laid in its grave in what is regarded as being a characteristically pagan manner: flexed and on its side. The bodies seem to have been buried when the barn was still standing, rather than after it had been demolished. They appear to be Roman in date but may prove later than AD 409 because they were inside the walled area of the town. The other instance was in the Berry Field where the remains of a body (thought to be that of a girl) were found in 1928 on a mosaic floor. Some people have taken this as being evidence of a dramatic and violent end to Roman Colchester, with the unfortunate girl left dead on the floor of a house. However her remains appear to be extended, suggesting that in fact she lay in a grave. The Berry Field body was found not far from the decapitated burials in East House gardens, so they might belong to the same cemetery. However, the circumstances of the Berry Field grave imply that there must have been a long enough interval between the abandonment of the house and the burial of the girl for a substantial layer of topsoil to develop on the tessellated floor. This favours a much later date for the grave. (The name 'Berry Field' or 'Bury Field' may support the idea that this was a burial area in medieval or later times.)

The idea of a violent end to Colonia Victricensis at the hands of the barbarians has been supported by the interesting discoveries at Duncan's Gate. The gate has been excavated twice, once in 1853 by Dr P.M. Duncan who discovered the gate, and again in 1927-9 by Rex Hull. Both excavators talked of fire. Duncan's account hints at over-coloured interpretation: '... *human bones, horse bones, much charred wood ...large pieces of burned fatty material, in contact with charred wood, of disagreeable import ...weapons, large human bones and lumps of semi-vitrified substances*'. Rex Hull confirmed the presence of burnt remains but was more restrained in his assessment of what he found. Hull felt that he could detect two successive fires, the earlier one sealing a 4th-century coin. He wrote that there were traces of intense heat, including large pieces of burnt oak, some of which were seven inches wide and lay north-south (in other words at right angles to the doorway). Above the planks and charcoal was a layer of brushwood. '*Had brushwood been piled against a gate or a barricade [on the outside], and fired, and the whole mass fallen inwards, the result would be exactly as found.*' Hull found none of the human bone noted by

The remains of a female found in 1928 in the Berry Field, on the tessellated floor on which it was supposed that she had died.

Duncan but he went on to observe, 'This may be the best evidence we shall see of the end of Roman Colchester.'

Clearly this is a most remarkable and dramatic discovery which, if we could be more confident about the details, might have important implications for the later years of Roman Colchester. The gate was in a quiet area of the medieval and later town so that, at least until Duncan and Hull, the archaeological deposits behind the gate were well preserved. The problem now is that the published accounts do not provide anything like enough detail to let us evaluate the dating evidence and Hull's interpretation of the remains. Without further excavation (and there is probably not much left of these precious deposits anyway), we can only rely on the excavators' brief descriptions of their findings.

If indeed there were two fires rather than just one, then clearly these do not have to be associated with the end of Roman Colchester. If the town could survive the incident that led to the first fire, then no doubt the same could apply to the second. As far as dating evidence is concerned, all we have to go on is the coin under the remains of the first fire. Hull's description of the coin indicates that it is unlikely to date to before AD 330. Thus the fires are likely to be later than this date, although how much later, we cannot say.

If we need to find an historical context for the fires, then the 'Barbarian Conspiracy' of 367 is the most obvious. This was the time when the Picts, Attacotti (apparently from Ireland or the Western Isles), and Irish Scots attacked and overran Britain, and Franks and Saxons raided Gaul. Some regular troops in Britain deserted and joined the anarchic free-for-all. A Roman army of relief landed at Richborough and marched to London. It was a nasty situation which took over a year to recover from.

In fact it is not hard to find other occasions after 330 when Colonia Victricensis could have been under siege and Duncan's Gate burnt as a result. But we should remember that there is no reason to suppose that the gate had to have been burnt as a consequence of an assault. Maybe long after the end of the Roman town, somebody simply piled kindling against the wooden construction which blocked the gate and set it alight. (We have already argued that the gate may have been in its blocked state since around 300.)

On balance, it seems doubtful that Colonia Victricensis met its end at the hands of Saxon invaders who stormed its walls and killed its inhabitants. Given how little is known of the period, such a scenario is of course conceivable but the truth is probably a good deal less dramatic. As we have seen, the disappearance by c 420 of bronze coins for everyday transactions must have made living and working in town more difficult. It is possible therefore that Colonia Victricensis continued to be the administrative centre for the region and a place of shelter in times of stress. But for the overwhelming majority of Romano-Britons, life was to be sustained by working in the fields and on the fishing grounds, not in the decaying, emptying streets of Colchester. Of course, the rural population in the territorium had probably always outnumbered those living in the colony itself. But by the time the Saxons came to settle the region in numbers, the numeric difference between the two groups may have been much more marked, and Colonia Victricensis may have already become a run-down monument of the past whose main virtue was its protective walls.

Looking back over almost 400 years of the Roman town, it is interesting to note how the colony did not fulfil its original promise. For the first decade or so, it was the principal town in the province, but the absence of a good natural harbour nearby meant that the provincial administration was to end up in Londinium. The displacement may always have been inevitable but the Boudican revolt probably brought the realignment forward in time. Although always one of the richest and

One possible reconstruction of Duncan's gate.

The last recorded act by an inhabitant of the City of Victory. Fragments of the lead sheeting which was cut up and buried for safe-keeping on the site of the derelict Butt Road church in the 5th century. Some lead was removed but these pieces were never collected (see also page 124).

best endowed towns in the province, there was probably never an administrative role for it on a national basis much after AD 60. Even when the province was divided up into smaller units, first into two around AD 200 and then subdivided further about a century later, Colonia Victricensis was not selected as one of the new capitals, no doubt because it was too close to Londinium geographically. Prominence under the British usurper Carausius and his successor Allectus may be illusory too. The letters 'C' or 'CL' on some of their coins have led to the suggestion that Colchester (CL as in Colonia) was a mint centre in the late 3rd century, but an alternative location such as Clausentium (Southampton) or Gloucester cannot be ruled out. Similarly there is a view that one of the British bishops who went to Gaul in 314 (page 119) came from Colonia Victricensis because, as the senior colony, the town is likely to have had a bishop. However this is far from certain since it depends on re-reading *Colonia Londinensium* in the textual source as something like *Colonia Camulodunensium*.

In fact the City of Victory had peaked on the eve of the Boudican revolt when it was only ten years old, and the colony was never to be the same again. Boudica would have taken some comfort from that, could she have known it. Ironically, the descendants of Boudica and her followers were later to become so well integrated into the Roman empire and the Roman way of life that the eventual demise of the City of Victory was to be mourned, not celebrated. Boudica would have felt betrayed, but then Britain and the British had irreversibly changed and had sensibly left the past behind.

The rebuilt and blocked Balkerne Gate. (Follow the evolution of the Balkerne Gate, from monumental arch on page 60, into gate on page 89, and to this.)

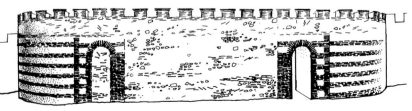

NEW BEGINNINGS

Different peoples, different cultures

Following the end of the Roman period, there were three invasions of Britain which directly affected Colonia Victricensis. In the 5th and 6th centuries, the Saxons came and settled in large numbers and profoundly altered the culture of Britain. In the 9th century the Danes settled large parts of eastern England and the Midlands, but integration rather than change was the long-term effect. The Norman invasion of 1066 was not followed by mass migration—maybe no more than 10,000 Normans came to Britain as a result of it. However the newcomers displaced the existing Anglo-Saxon land-holding gentry and played a key role in the creation of an Anglo-French culture that was to dominate the country for two hundred years. By the time of the Norman invasion, many traces of Roman Colchester had disappeared, and the town had assumed a form which is recognisably that of Colchester today.

The 10th-century poem 'The ruin' conjures up a picture of deserted, derelict towns in a Britain abandoned by the Romans.

'Wondrous is the masonry shattered by fate, the fallen city buildings; the work of giants has decayed. The roofs have caved in, the towers are in ruins, the barred gates destroyed, there is frost on the mortar, the gaping shelters collapsed and torn apart, undermined by age.'

The remains of great Roman towns like Silchester, Wroxeter, and Caistor-by-Norwich, now covered by fields, encourage the idea that towns were left empty and unwanted at the end of the Roman period. However, the situation was far more complicated than that, and many modern towns such as London, Canterbury, and Winchester clearly owe their origins to the Roman towns whose sites they cover. A thorny task for archaeologists is understanding how modern towns such as these developed from their Roman beginnings, and to what extent there was continuity of occupation in them between Roman and medieval times. As we shall see, Colchester never developed into a major city but the town does provide some interesting and useful information about the processes involved. Compared to the Roman town, the archaeological evidence for life in Colchester between the end of the Roman era in the 5th century and the arrival of the Normans over six hundred years later is extremely meagre. However the evidence does exist, and it suggests that Colchester is not likely to have been deserted, even briefly, although the numbers living in the town were probably very low compared to those in Roman times.

The Anglo-Saxons

'Adventus Saxonum' (the coming of the Saxons) are the words used by the 8th-century historian Bede to describe the start of Anglo-Saxon England, an event which he dates variously to around 449. Similarly an anonymous Gallic chronicle datable to 452 tells us that Britain was reduced to subjection by the Saxons in 441-2, and the 6th-century writer Gildas recorded that Britain appealed to the Romans for help against barbarian

Two cruciform brooches found near the Guildford Road estate with the aid of a metal detector in 1971-2. Early 5th century.

attack, the appeal being datable to between 446 and 454. These and other literary references suggest that there was a sudden and overwhelming influx of barbarian settlers into Britain around 440-450. However this conclusion is at odds with the archaeological evidence which points to a gradual and halting spread of Anglo-Saxon occupation which did not extend over most of England until the 6th century.

The Saxons who migrated to Britain in the 5th and 6th centuries were the original English. Just as the Scots actually came from Ireland, the English came from what is now Denmark and north-west Germany. These original English men and women followed an agrarian life-style in extended family groups, living in houses made of timber, turf, and thatch. They were illiterate pagans who spoke what we call Old English, which developed into the English spoken today in many countries around the world.

With the introduction of a new language, Colonia Victricensis would have acquired a new name. The earliest known forms of it belong to the 10th century, when we find the town being referred to as 'Colneceastre' and 'Colenceaster', probably as in 'Colonia camp' rather than 'camp on the river Colne' as is sometimes supposed. Colchester, the modern spelling of this name, can be traced back to the 15th century.

Being near the east coast, Colonia Victricensis would have been ripe for Saxon settlement early on in the migration phase, and, as we shall see, archaeology confirms that this did indeed happen. Anglo-Saxon settlement, some of it possibly early, is indicated in the Colchester area by place names which end with '-ing' such as Tendring, Messing, and Frating.

Evidence for Anglo-Saxons living in Colchester between the end of the Roman period and the 8th century is easy to find. As far as can be judged, the occupation does not seem to have been concentrated in any one area but was scattered throughout the walled town. Those

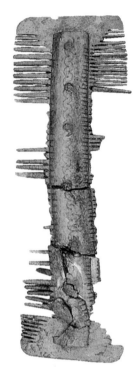

A decorated Anglo-Saxon bone comb of 6th- or 7th-century date. Possibly made of antler.

Right: a pot from the Anglo-Saxon hut discovered at the Culver Street site.

burials which have been recognised were outside the walls, in areas formerly suitable (if not actually used) for burial in Roman times. In other words, the pattern of Anglo-Saxon occupation seems to repeat its Roman predecessor, which seems surprising given the differences between the two cultures. Anglo-Saxon pottery is distinctive and easily recognised, and pieces have been found at various locations throughout the town. Three Anglo-Saxon houses have been discovered so far in Colchester, and there are several other possible examples. The earliest of the houses belongs to the mid 5th century, and the latest to around the 7th century. Burials have also been recorded, including women, and warriors with their weapons and shields. They date from the 5th or 6th centuries to *c* 700. Stray finds include two coins (datable to the 7th and 8th centuries), fragments of loomweights, various brooches ranging in date from the 5th to the early 7th centuries, and some swords of probable 8th-century date. The volume of material is not great, but the dates give a good spread from the mid 5th to the 8th centuries. The result is that significant occupation in Colchester throughout this time can hardly be doubted, even though we struggle to understand its character and its regional significance.

Anglo-Saxon houses are of two types, which archaeologists generally refer to as 'halls' and 'sunken-featured buildings'. Halls were rectangular in plan, with walls incorporating posts set in the ground. 'Sunken-featured buildings' are Anglo-Saxon buildings which were built over a hollow. All the buildings found so far in Colchester are of this last type. There is disagreement over whether the hollows in the floors of these buildings were covered with wooden floors. The cumbersome term 'sunken-featured building' has been invented to avoid any preconception about the nature of these hollows or the function of the buildings in which they occur. As it happens, Colchester can offer good

evidence of both treatments of the hollowed-out floor.

The earliest of the houses was one of two discovered during the Lion Walk excavations in 1972. The pottery associated with the building includes early forms and suggests that the building dates to around the middle of the 5th century. The hut was small. It would have had a ridged roof supported on two stout posts, one in the middle of each of the end walls. The characteristic hollow seems to have been covered with a timber floor at ground level, in the manner that can be seen in the reconstructed huts in the Saxon village of West Stow in Suffolk. The presence of a timber floor was suggested by the irregular shape of the hollow and by the presence of stones which projected into it from the base of Roman tessellated floor through which it was dug.

The other hut at Lion Walk clearly could not have had a wooden floor, because the hollow was peppered with holes caused by driving wooden stakes into it. Not only that, but there was also a very distinctive trampled surface on the base of the hollow which could only have been the result of people walking directly on it. Stake holes around the edge of the hollow must have formed the hut walls. Many of the stake holes inside the hollow occurred in clusters, and shallow slots in the floor looked as if they had been formed by benches or cupboards against some of the walls. Clearly the stake holes could not all have held stakes at the same time or it would have been impossible to move around inside of the hut. The absence of a hearth would seem to point to a utilitarian rather than a domestic function for the building, although it seems likely that it was used for both. A piece of broken loomweight and a spindle-whorl in the backfill of the hollowed out floor combine to suggest that weaving took place in the building, but the pattern of holes is not easily reconcilable with Saxon looms.

A similar hut to this one was found during the Culver Street excavation in the early 1980s. Its floor had a trampled surface, and it had been punctured with a dense scatter of stake holes which, as with the similar example at Lion Walk, would seem to rule out wooden floorboards. The patterning of the stake holes was not quite so distinctive as at Lion Walk, although there were still discernible lines of holes set forward of some of the walls.

An interesting aspect of the last two buildings is their relationships to earlier Roman houses on their sites. When the Anglo-Saxons were digging out the floors for

Two of the three Anglo-Saxon huts excavated in Colchester. The single holes at each end were to hold posts which supported a ridge for the roof.

Below left: at Lion Walk (1972); a 5th-century hut.
Below right: at Culver Street (1981-2); a 7th-century hut.

Left: modern reconstruction of an Anglo-Saxon hut at West Stow in Suffolk.

*Part of an
Anglo-Saxon
cruciform brooch.
Late 6th or early 7th century.
Found near Balkerne Lane in
the mid 19th century.*

*An Anglo-Saxon coin
(a sceatta) from
Colchester.*

these two buildings, they came across the buried foundations of Roman houses. Breaking out the foundations would have been hard going, so instead they simply readjusted the position of the hollowed floor. The result is that the hollows in both buildings butt against and follow Roman foundations. This relationship did originally make us think that the Anglo-Saxon building at Lion Walk had been built against a standing wall of a Roman house rather than just a foundation, but the Culver Street example shows that this could not have been the case.

The existence of a sizeable Anglo-Saxon community at Colchester begs the question as to how much of the surviving Roman remains were reused, and to what extent these shaped the settlement. Anglo-Saxon villages did not have defences but maybe the defensive circuit of the town would have been of some protective value for its inhabitants and those living in the surrounding area. However, few of the Roman houses had mortared walls, most being timber and daub or made with solid blocks of a sandy clay material. They would thus have quickly decayed and collapsed to leave great areas of the town clear of derelict standing remains. Within decades most of the Roman streets would have vanished under vegetation and accumulated soil, with few of the property divisions of the Roman town surviving. Only public buildings, such as the Temple of Claudius and the theatre, which were built with stone and tile, would have survived. It is true that much of the town within the walls had been under cultivation in the Roman period, but now, probably in much less than a century, Colchester would have acquired an overwhelmingly rural appearance. Dozens of little wooden houses, interspersed with grazing animals and cultivated areas, would have been scattered over a landscape sealed off by the town walls and dominated by the towering, crumbling remains of unwanted, stone monuments of the past. Given how little interest the occupants of Colchester seem to have paid to the fabric of their Roman inheritance, we might wonder why there was Anglo-Saxon settlement here at all. Presumably Colchester continued to serve its traditional role as a regional market and focus of administration and justice, and to this end was under the control, if not ownership, of the royal house of the East Saxons.

The Danes

The word Viking, meaning pirate, was coined by their victims. It was applied equally to two races. The Norwegian raiders favoured travelling around the north of Scotland, whereas the Danes usually went southwards to the east and south coasts of England and to Gaul. The Vikings would sow their crops in spring, go off raiding in the summer in search of booty, and return in time for the harvest in the autumn. The first recorded Viking raid in England was in 789, but compared with what was to come, this was a minor event since it involved only three ships. At first, their summer visits were sporadic, and they kept to within ten or fifteen miles of the coast. Monasteries were easy targets—but anywhere with loot would do. From 835, the attacks seem to have been practically every year. Events took an ominous turn in 851 when the Danes overwintered on the isle of Sheppey. Worse still, 350 ships entered the Thames, and London and Canterbury were stormed. Then in 865 things reached crisis point with the landing in East Anglia of a great Danish army of invasion. Within three years, the great Anglo-Saxon kingdoms of Northumbria and East Anglia were no more, and the Danes turned their attention to Wessex, home of the West Saxons. Another Danish army landed, and the outlook for Wessex was bleak. But in the midst of the crisis, Alfred became king. He managed to buy off the Danes, and so instead they attacked and invaded the kingdom of Mercia to the north. The Danish army then split, one half moving north to settle in what is now Yorkshire, and the other launching an attack on Wessex. The Danes withdrew. Sections of the army again split off, this time to settle parts of the Midlands. Yet another attack on Wessex followed, but after a while, Alfred and the Danish leader Guthrum negotiated a settlement which effectively ceded most of eastern England north of the Thames to the Danes. The remainder of the Danish army then began the systematic colonisation of East Anglia. Essex seems largely to have escaped this process apart from the north-east corner around Colchester, where place names such as Kirby and Thorpe show it to lie on the fringe of the East Anglian settlement.

Alfred's success in resisting the Danes is to be explained to a large extent by his practice of building strongholds (boroughs) across his kingdom. Responsibility for the manning of these fortified places lay with local landowners. It is believed that street systems were laid out in some of the strongholds such as Winchester and Wareham with the effect that they were planned, fortified towns.

Alfred died in 899 and was succeeded by his son Edward the Elder. About a decade later, Edward started the reconquest of the Danish-held territories. He was helped by his sister Aethelflaed, who was in control of the adjacent kingdom of Mercia. Guthrum's kingdom had been established by treaty with Alfred in 878, but within about thirty years, East Anglia and the whole of Essex including Colchester were back in English hands. By 920, the English frontier was fixed at the Humber, and six years later Athelstan, brother of Edward and successor to his throne, captured York from the Norsemen to leave him king of the English and the Danes.

Elements of the Danish army attempted to hold out in fortified towns, including former Roman walled settlements such as Lincoln and Leicester. The Anglo-Saxon Chronicle shows the same high drama at Colchester. In 917, 'a great [English] host ...from Kent, from Surrey, from Essex and from the nearest boroughs ...went to Colchester and besieged the borough and attacked it until they took and killed all the people and seized everything that was inside—except the men who fled there over the wall.' The fact that so many Englishmen were needed to drive out the Danes shows that their target must have been part of the Danish army which had occupied Colchester on a tactical basis, rather than any Danish settlers who had moved into the town some years earlier.

There is no trace in the archaeological record of the Danish presence in the town. Some Danish-style weapons have been dredged up from the river Colne but these almost certainly reflect the wider cultural impact of the Danes on England rather than a physical presence in Colchester itself. It is impossible to tell if any Danes settled within the walls between the foundation of Guthrum's kingdom in 878 and the expulsion from the town of the Danish army about thirty years later. We may suspect that, at most, the overlord became Danish but the population remained overwhelmingly English. The Domesday Survey gives 276 names of people who lived in Colchester in 1086. Of those, seven out of eight had names of English origin, the rest being evenly divided between Scandinavian, German and others. Another group of names is to be found on the coins minted in Colchester between the 990s and Domesday (1086). Of the thirty-three names of moneyers which this source provides, one is of Scandinavian origin and the rest are English. Of course, figures of this sort do not give a head count of the various nationalities in Colchester at the time. Various factors combine to prevent a more accurate measure of the ethnic make-up of Colchester's inhabitants. People could change their name for reasons such as fashion or marriage, and sometimes having a Danish name could be dangerous. For example, in 1002 King Aethelred and his council ordered a massacre of all the Danes living in England. None the less, compared with other parts of England, the impression is that the population of Colchester was predominantly English with only a minor Danish element.

Edward continued his father's policy of making fortified towns as a way of consolidating his gains and allowing the local population to resist Danish reconquest. Occupation by a large hostile Danish army is likely to have been damaging enough for any town, but pitched battle would have finished the job off, and left Colchester an empty, burntout shell which, for tactical reasons, Edward would want to restore. This explains a subsequent entry in the Anglo-Saxon Chronicle (also for 917) which states that 'King Edward went with the army of the West Saxons to Colchester and repaired and restored the borough where it had been broken'. From this we can conclude that, at the very least, there was some repair of the town defences, and

The heads of two Viking-type axes. Late Saxon to Norman in date. Found earlier this century in the River Colne.

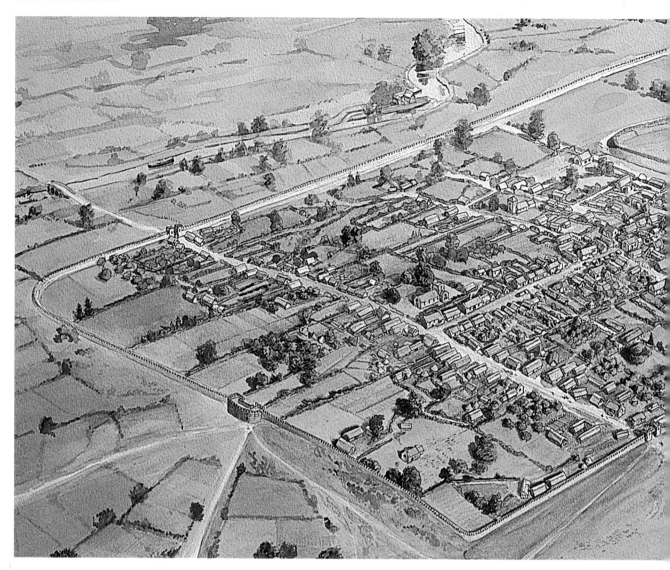

Churches

A.. St Mary's   E.. St Runwald's
B.. St Peter's   F... All Saints'
C.. Holy Trinity G.. St James'
D.. St Martin's   H.. St Nicholas'

I.... Moot Hall
J.... stone house at Lion Walk
K... castle and bailey
L.. St John's Abbey
M.. St Botolph's Priory
N.. St Helen's Chapel

O.. Middle Mill
P... East Mill

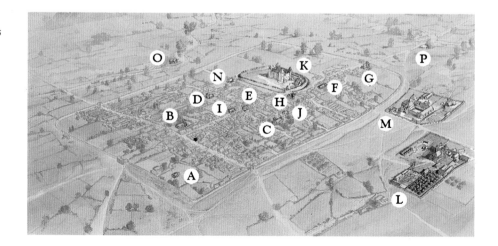

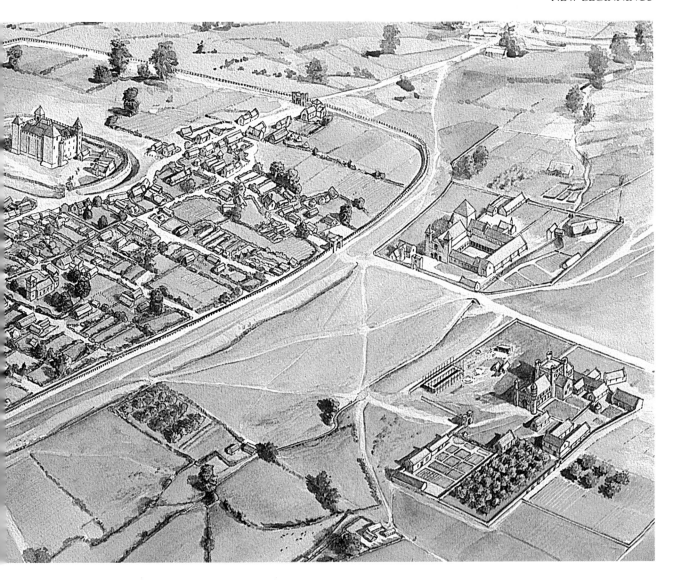

Colchester c AD 1150, viewed from the south-east.

that maybe the restoration extended to the laying out of streets as part of an attempt to repopulate the town. Following his excavations in 1917, Mortimer Wheeler suggested that the wall which blocks the Balkerne Gate was part of repairs to the town defences undertaken by Edward the Elder. The excavations at Balkerne Lane in the 1970s gave indirect evidence that the blocking was actually Roman (pages 115 and 132), but conclusive proof is absent and Mortimer Wheeler may yet be proved right. Otherwise it is not possible to point to any part of the town wall and argue that it is the work of Edward. We will return to the related question of new streets shortly.

The birth of modern Colchester

When it comes to finding the Danes by means of archaeology, there is a wider problem, and that is to do with the apparent dearth of pottery datable to the 9th and 10th centuries. This means that it is hard to detect occupation in this period, not just for the Danish period on its own. This is a problem which affects Essex generally and which has led to the suggestion that pottery was hardly used at this time. 'Thetford-type' ware is a wheel-made pottery which is found all over East Anglia and beyond. Production started in the 9th century, and continued until after 1100. 'Early medieval sandy ware' is another kind of pottery which occurs in Colchester at

139

this time. It is thought to date from around 1000 on the basis of evidence from elsewhere. Most Thetford-type ware in Colchester has been found with pieces of early medieval sandy ware showing that the contexts concerned are likely to be 11th century or later. There are a few pits which have been excavated on some High Street sites which contain only Thetford-type pottery and are therefore possibly 9th or 10th century in date. But these are rare, and overwhelmingly both types of pottery occur together. We have three explanations to choose from: that early medieval sandy ware starts earlier than is generally assumed, or that occupation in 10th-century Colchester was minimal, or that Essex was comparatively free of pottery in late Anglo-Saxon times.

It is hard to believe that there was relatively little occupation in Colchester in the 10th century. As we have already seen, Edward took steps to re-establish the town in the early part of the century. Later, in 931, King Athelstan held a meeting of the royal council in Colchester, which was described (perhaps rather grandly) at the time as a 'town well known to all men'. Athelstan was the first of Edward's sons to be king. From his reign onwards, kings made laws more often and in more detail than before. Laws and charters were issued at meetings of the royal council, or 'witan', which became a bigger and more important assembly than before. These meetings were held at various venues around the kingdom, including relatively minor places. Athelstan's *witan* at Colchester was attended by at least seventy noblemen, senior clergy, and important men of influence. Those present included at least thirteen earls (of whom six were Danes), thirty-seven thanes, three abbots, fifteen bishops, and the archbishop of Canterbury. In 940, yet another royal council was assembled in Colchester, this time under Athelstan's brother Edmund who had succeeded him as king.

Another indicator of urban status is the presence of a coin mint. In around 991, a 'moneyer' called Sweting came from London to start striking coins in Colchester. Soon he was joined by half-a-dozen other moneyers, and it is estimated that between them they produced about half a million coins in the space of about six years. Coins were struck in the town for the next two centuries but never in such prolific numbers as in those early years.

The large output of the mint in the 990s may be linked with the need to pay off the

The first Anglo-Saxon coins struck in Colchester were made by a moneyer called Sweting. This is one of only two examples known of his coins.

Vikings. After a long lapse, the old menace had reappeared, this time more chillingly in a professional form. Vikings were now living military-style in great fortresses in Denmark, and were paid from the tributes they demanded from their victims. The deep ditch found in 1972 in Vineyard Street (during the Lion Walk excavations) may have been dug in an effort to protect the town against Viking raiding parties. Pottery in the bottom of the ditch indicates a date of *c* 1050-1075 for the earthwork, which is consistent with such a possibility. The new ditch was probably the work of the townspeople because we learn from Domesday that they rented from the king the slip of land, 8 *pedes* (132 feet) wide, immediately outside the town wall.

Most of the street system of the Roman town must have disappeared fairly rapidly after the end of the Roman period. Without maintenance or frequent use, the gravel streets would have quickly become overgrown and been lost. The only streets to survive seem to have been those which connected the main gates. Thus Head Street and North Hill led to Head Gate and North Gate, and the High Street linked these two streets with East Gate. Similarly Queen Street connected the High Street with South Gate and to an extent seems to have followed the route of its Roman predecessor. The High Street did not continue west of Head Street/North Hill (as explained on page 115), because the Balkerne Gate had been closed in the late Roman period.

At some stage the High Street seems to have been widened to create a market place. This must have been a radical operation since it would involve the realignments of the frontages along much of the street, and any buildings on these frontages would have to be demolished. Culver Street was laid out as a back street terminating properties on the south High Street frontage. Other separate developments included the creation of Trinity Street, Lion Walk, and Long Wyre Street on the south side of town, and East and West Stockwell Streets and the southern end of Maidenburgh Street on the north side. The two Stockwell Streets may have originated as routes to the Stockwell, which was an important public water supply. The well would have been shallow and thus easy to build since, being downhill from the High Street, the water-table is close to ground-level in this part of town.

None of these developments need have happened at the same time, although we may suspect that the formation of the enlarged market place in the High Street was contemporary with the creation of Culver Street, which in turn was bound up with the laying out of new building plots along the south side of the High Street.

It is noticeable that West Stockwell Street lines up with Trinity Street and that Maidenburgh Street lines up with Long Wyre Street. These alignments may be coincidental since East Stockwell Street does not line up with Lion Walk. On the other hand, they could point to a layout of streets which predates the creation of Culver Street and the laying out of plots along the south frontage of the High Street.

There are some indications of the likely date of these operations. When the castle was built in the late 11th century, the area immediately around it was defended by a deep bank and ditch to form the bailey. Space was tight to the south of where the castle was to be built, so the High Street was diverted southwards in a gentle curve to make more room. This curve is clearly visible in the High Street today. The east end of Culver Street shows no corresponding diversion, thus suggesting that it already existed in the late 11th century when the castle bailey was made. The location of Holy Trinity church indicates that Culver Street is likely to be substantially earlier than this, since it looks as if the street already existed when the church was founded. The church tower is distinctive in its architectural features but is difficult to date closely. However it is generally regarded as being 11th century. The tower is visibly a later addition to the west end of the nave, which makes it likely that the church was founded some years before the Norman conquest.

If we need to associate Edward the Elder and his restoration of the borough with the laying out of streets and plots, then we possibly have two major phases of replanning to choose from, both of which seem equally likely. There is an initial phase which involved the creation of a grid of the minor north streets which have just been mentioned (West Stockwell Street, Trinity Street, etc), and there is the widening of the market in the High Street and the laying out of building plots along the south frontage. This last episode was a replanning of the core of the town which partly obliterated the early work.

Before the first phase of town planning (whatever that actually was), Colchester

The streets of the medieval town

One possible sequence explaining the development of the streets of medieval and later Colchester.

A 8th/9th century

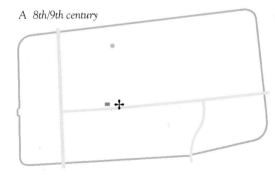

A *Colchester in the 8th and 9th centuries when occupation centred around a church (St Runwald's) and the lord's hall close to the centre of the High Street. The main streets were still essentially Roman.*

B 917

B *Town restored under Edward the Elder in 917. Defences repaired, new streets laid out, new properties created.*

C *Replanning of the south side of the High Street in the mid to late 10th century.*

C late 10th century

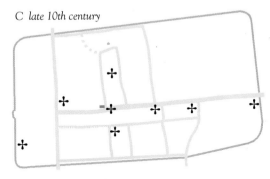

D *The building of the Norman castle bailey and the development of the east end of the High Street in c 1075.*

D 1075

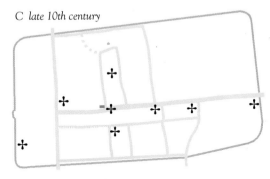

+ church   ■ (moot) hall   · Stockwell

Key to streets
A.. High Street; B.. North Hill; C.. Head Street; D.. Trinity Street; E.. Lion Walk; F.. Long Wyre Street; G.. Queen Street/ St Botolph's Street; H.. Culver Street; I.. East Hill; J.. West Stockwell Street; K.. East Stockwell Street; L.. Maidenburgh Street; M.. Northgate Street; N.. Sir Isaac's Walk/Short Wyre Street.

The tower of Holy Trinity church. Built in the 11th century entirely of reused Roman building materials.

The west doorway of the tower.

would have been little more than a one-street town. In its embryonic state (in the 8th or 9th centuries), it may have taken on the appearance of a small village where the lord's hall and church formed the nucleus. The equivalent at Colchester (and this is all speculative) may have been St Runwald's church and a hall on the site now occupied by the present town hall. This putative Anglo-Saxon hall would have stood on the site of the Moot Hall (which we will examine shortly), and was presumably where the witans of Athelstan and Edmund were held. Other churches (St Peter's, St Nicholas', All Saints', and maybe St James') were built at various points along the High Street as the town began to grow. (St Mary-at-the-Walls was early too but is a special case since it lay within the jurisdiction of the Bishop of London.) The widening of the High Street left St Runwald's stranded in the middle of the improved market.

There were three Runwalds. The last of them died in 1027 although the dedication of our St Runwald's church is usually identified with a child saint from Mercia said to have lived in the 8th century. There is an argument that St Runwald's was a relatively late foundation, which was built in the middle of the market place. However, St Runwald's church seems to have occupied such a central position in the town that it is hard to see the building as a late arrival. Like the evolution of the street system, this is an intractable problem which perhaps only excavation will ever solve.

The Normans

For the first twenty or so years after the Norman conquest in 1066, the people of Colchester seem to have suffered badly under the administration of their new overlords. By the time of Domesday, the sum which had to be collected on the king's behalf to pay rents and other dues had risen to five times its level immediately before the conquest. Only one other town (Rochester) had to suffer a worse increase, and no doubt herein lay the cause of much anguish. However matters much improved when William the Conqueror gave Colchester and 'all its appurtenances' to Eudo Dapifer. From now on, matters were to be handled much more sensitively, so much so that Eudo came to earn the respect and gratitude of the local community (or at least so it is claimed by our medieval sources).

Eudo Dapifer (or Eudes the steward as he is sometimes called) was an important Norman baron who owned at least 64 manors in the eastern counties of England, in addition to his holdings in Normandy. He was a son of Hubert de Rie, lord of the small town of Rie which is about 10 miles from Bayeux in Normandy. He acquired the name Dapifer when William granted him the office of Seneschal (meaning high steward) of Normandy, and as such he ranked as an important member of the courts of William the Conqueror and his sons and successors William II and Henry I.

Eudo dominated the town from the latter part of the 11th century until his death in 1120. As a public benefactor with an eye on the afterlife, he founded St John's Abbey and the leper hospital at St Mary Magdalen, and he restored St Helen's Chapel. The greatest of all his works was Colchester castle, which turned out to be the largest Norman keep in Europe. He seems to have built the castle on behalf of William the Conqueror but later held it in his own right. Eudo is also credited with building the Moot Hall—the equivalent of the town hall—although, as we shall see, this is a dubious claim. Eudo died in the castle at Préaux in Normandy, and was buried in accordance with his wishes in St John's Abbey in Colchester. On his death, the ownership of the castle reverted to the king.

The castle

Perhaps the most remarkable aspect of the castle is that it was built around and over the base of the Temple of Claudius (page 146). The builders of the castle must have cleared away whatever survived of the superstructure of the temple to leave the podium and the remains of the flight of steps which led up to the front of the temple. The four outer walls of the castle, each twelve feet thick, were then raised so that they tightly clasped the sides of the podium except on the south side, where the wall was set back to clear the remains of the steps and allow a fifty-foot well to be dug within the confines of the keep. It would not have been possible to make the castle any smaller and still encapsulate the temple podium. Thus we should not think that the size of the castle was a reflection of the political, economic, or military importance of Colchester in the Norman period; this was, at least to an extent, more an unavoidable consequence of how it was built. From an engineering point of view, it

was a bold decision to build the castle on the temple podium, since this might have led to disastrous cracking and subsidence of the outer walls. Whoever designed the building and oversaw its construction either had great confidence in his engineering skills or was just lucky that it never collapsed.

The building needed at least 25,000 cubic metres of stone and mortar. There is no good natural building stone in the immediate area, there being only sand, gravel, and the London clay. However the remains of the Roman town provided an obvious source of easily accessible building materials. Many of the largest Roman public buildings were probably still standing: the baths, the theatre, and the Temple of Claudius among others. The town wall would have been an easy target but it was too valuable an asset to destroy.

An indication of when building work began is provided by the 'Colchester Chronicle'. This is a brief history of Colchester which was probably written in St John's Abbey in the 13th or early 14th centuries. In the past, the chronicle has been dismissed as being too fanciful to be taken too seriously. Yet, although the Roman part has little historical value (page 119), the section dealing with the medieval period seems to contain elements of truth which are of some interest.

Eudo de Rie or Eudo Dapifer (the statue on the present town hall; c 1900).

This section reads as follows:

1145 *A certain monk of St Edmund's called John, a Roman, carried the head of St Helen from Rome to the monastery of Bury St Edmunds.*

1175 *The castle of Colchester, with 1115 other castles of England, was almost destroyed.*

1071 *Colchester, after the wives of the citizens had been carried off, was burnt by Danish pirates.*

1072 *King William the Conqueror, on account of this, granted Colchester to Eudo Dapifer.*

1076 *Eudo Dapifer built the castle of Colchester on the foundation of the palace of Coel, once King, and restored the chapel of St Helen which she built herself, it is said, and gave it to St John.*

1089 *King William the Younger gave to [Eudo] the town of Colchester with the castle, to possess in perpetuity et cetera.*

1239 *The said chapel was dedicated on St Katherine's day in honour of St Katherine and St Helen, by Roger, Bishop of London, in the presence of William, Abbot of St John.*

The chronicle is likely to be a compilation made from sources of differing reliability. Of course

Norman ship in the invasion fleet of 1066 (taken from the Bayeux tapestry).

143

none of it can be taken at face value but there is much that must be based on fact. The problem is knowing what is true and what is the product of myth, error, and garbling during transcription and 'editing' in antiquity. For example, the entry for 1239 is likely to be reliable since the date fits the known dates for the bishop and the abbot named in it. Indeed the chronicle may have been prepared to mark the dedication of St Helen's Chapel, because the ceremony was a comparatively minor event in the town's history and mention of it here would seem to be out of place otherwise. And it is moreover the subject of the entry with the latest date.

Similarly, the entry under 1175 has some basis in truth, since it clearly refers to the rebellion in 1173-4 which led Henry II to destroy some baronial castles. However the number is wildly exaggerated and it is doubtful if Colchester castle would have been affected.

In terms of the castle, the entry for 1076 is important since it is the only year given for its construction which appears in historical sources. Again the entry clearly has some basis in fact since it talks of the castle being erected on the site of a Roman building. The description of the castle as having been built on the site of the palace of Coel is uncannily near the truth. Even the way that we are told that the castle was built on the 'foundation' echoes the temple podium too much to be other than factually-based. The identification of the temple as the palace of Coel should not put us off since this could presumably have been what the Norman builders believed.

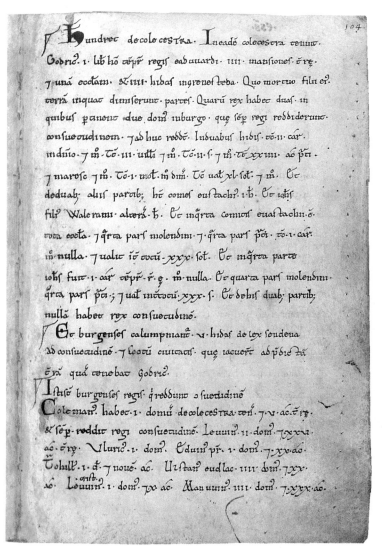

Domesday

The Domesday Book was effectively a detailed tax assessment drawn up in 1086 on the orders of William the Conqueror. He wanted to know what he was owed and by whom, and if his newly-acquired assets could yield even more. The survey describes the state of the country in 1086 and in 1066 (just before the Norman invasion). It was so thorough that one contemporary considered it shameful that not so much as an ox, cow, or pig could escape his surveyors' attention.

Here is one of the pages in the Little Domesday covering Colchester. The first two paragraphs deal with an estate at Greenstead which we learn had been held in 1066 by a nobleman called Godric. Then follows the start of a list of the townsmen (burgesses) who paid rents to the king. There were 276 of them, accounting for 355 houses and 1347 acres of land. Each is named in turn, beginning with Coleman whom we are told held one house and five acres. On subsequent pages the survey lists the holdings of the property holders in the town, including Eudo Dapifer who is said to own five houses, 40 acres, and a fourth part of St Peter's church. In among all the detail, we learn such facts as there were at least seven priests in the town and there was a crier (called Ulwine).

Nevertheless, too much weight should not be put on the 1076 date, and there is in any case ambiguity in what 1076 refers to. While it seems likely that the date indicates when the building was finished, 1076 could refer instead to the start of the work, or even to the completion of the castle in its early temporary form. The chronicle tells us that William the Conqueror gave Colchester to Eudo the year after it was burnt by the Danes, the idea presumably being that Eudo should start building a castle there as soon as possible. In 1069 a large Danish fleet appeared off the Kentish coast and moved northwards, unsuccessfully attacking in turn Dover, Sandwich, Ipswich, and Norwich. Colchester was on the route and therefore may well have suffered in the manner described in the chronicle. This suggests that Colchester was granted to Eudo in 1069 or 1070, and that a start was made on the building of the castle within a year or so of then.

The difficulties we have today in understanding the castle stem from the fact that the upper part is missing. This is the fault of John Wheeley who acquired the castle in 1683 with the intention of demolishing it entirely and selling off the building materials for profit. Fortunately the castle proved to be too well-built and he gave up before the job was done.

The castle now stands to a height of two storeys. Confusingly the ground floor is not at ground level but is raised and is roughly equivalent in level to the floor of the temple podium. Being poorly lit and unheated, the ground floor of the castle would have been used mainly for storage. The south-east corner of the building incorporated a stone vaulted structure consisting of the substructure of the chapel (the sub-crypt) and a vaulted strong room (the so-called 'Lucas vault') which had a narrow doorway and a small window high in the outside wall. The entrance into the castle is on the ground floor which is unusual since, for security reasons, entrances were generally on the first floor. Although early in date, the present entrance is not original and is a replacement for an even earlier one. The first floor was much better equipped as living quarters than the floor below: it had plenty of windows and it contained four wall fireplaces and five latrines. In fact it had as many features crammed in the outer wall as space would allow. This floor also contained the crypt. This was a vaulted room, built in stone like

the sub-crypt below, which was presumably to form the base of the stone chapel above. The floor of the second floor is at the roof level of the castle today. Had the castle been like the Tower of London (it is in any case very similar) then the second floor would have been for the accommodation for the lord or constable of the castle and any guests. It would have contained a great hall, sleeping accommodation, latrines, and a private chapel. Unfortunately Wheeley removed this part of the castle and there are no records of what it was like.

An unusual feature of the castle is the battlements which can be seen on the outside of the building at a level corresponding to the base of the first floor. These show that the construction of the castle was halted, and that the structure as it stood at that time was provided with battlements. There was a threat of invasion from Denmark in the mid 1080s and it is usually argued that this was the most likely reason for the temporary change of plan. However, this is probably far too late if, as seems likely, work on building of the castle began in the early 1070s.

A much more likely occasion is the rebellion of 1075 which was partly centred on East Anglia. It was to be supported by a large Danish fleet although the rebellion was over by the time the ships arrived late in that year. The Danish threat seems to have led to the garrisoning of the English castles as a precaution. If, as seems likely, Colchester castle was being built as a direct consequence of a calamitous Danish raid six years earlier, then it would be no surprise if the work was abruptly stopped and the building garrisoned for the first time.

It seems quite probable that the chapel and great hall were not built as originally intended and that there had been a late change of plan. This is partly shown by the position of a passage in the thickness of the keep wall (passages of this kind normally appear one storey higher) and partly by the absence of any substantial traces of a chapel.

Like the chapel in the Tower of London, the chapel at Colchester was to be entirely of stone and built on two solid vaulted basements, raised one on the other (the crypt and sub-crypt). The site of the chapel was investigated in 1988. Being on the roof of the castle, this was the highest ever excavation to take place in the town. Its floor was of stone, and

Bronze mount found in the castle bailey in 1937. It dates to the 11th or 12th century.

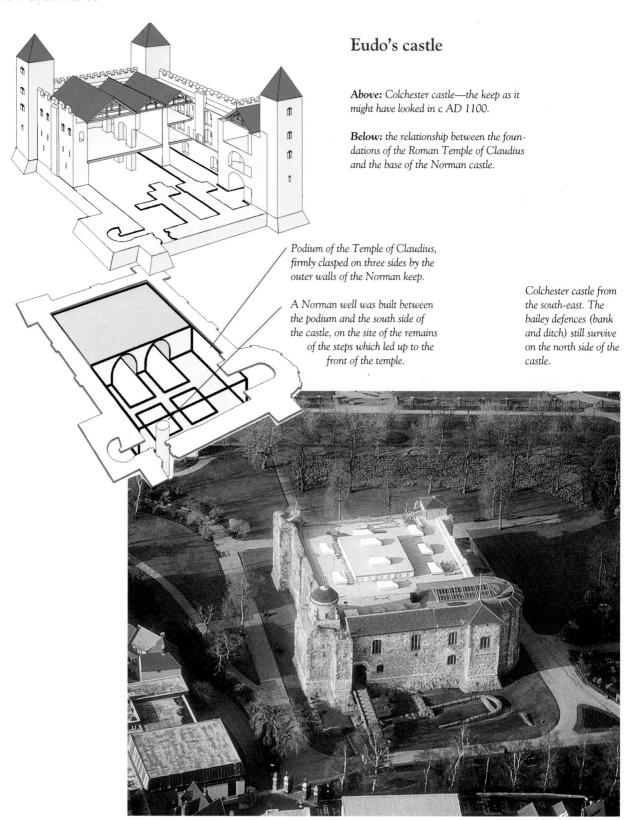

Eudo's castle

Above: *Colchester castle—the keep as it might have looked in c AD 1100.*

Below: *the relationship between the foundations of the Roman Temple of Claudius and the base of the Norman castle.*

Podium of the Temple of Claudius, firmly clasped on three sides by the outer walls of the Norman keep.

A Norman well was built between the podium and the south side of the castle, on the site of the remains of the steps which led up to the front of the temple.

Colchester castle from the south-east. The bailey defences (bank and ditch) still survive on the north side of the castle.

How the castle might have been built

The south front

An east-west section from the centre of the chapel to the south-west tower.

A. It was to be four stages high with entrances at first-floor level on the north and south sides. The upper two stages were to consist mainly of a great hall and an aisled chapel. The first floor was to include a single-storey hall heated by wall fireplaces and a crypt. The ceiling of this hall was to be supported on an arcaded wall.

B. In 1070 or 1071 building work begins according to the original plan. The ground floor is finished, including the Lucas vault and the sub-crypt. Work stops in 1075 during a rebellion backed by a Danish fleet. Battlements are added to the tops of the walls as they stand. There are as yet no doorways so the north-west and south-west towers are heightened to overlook the sites of the intended entrances.

C. Building work resumes in 1076. The intention is still to build the castle as originally planned with four stages. The battlements are not removed but become part of the heightened outer wall. The first floor, including the chapel crypt, is completed. A shortage of building materials then forces a major rethink.

D. One stage is to be omitted. Rather than build a hall and chapel at second-floor level extending up a further two stages, only one more stage is added. The great hall is now built on the existing first floor. A passage is built into the outer wall one stage lower than originally intended. At the same time, the doorway on the north side is blocked up, and the doorway on the south side is replaced with a wider, more ornate one directly below, on the ground floor. The chapel is not built, the crypt being used instead. The castle is finished by 1080.

E. Wheeley gives up his attempt to demolish the castle when he reaches the base of the mural gallery where the wall is much thicker and thus more robust than elsewhere.

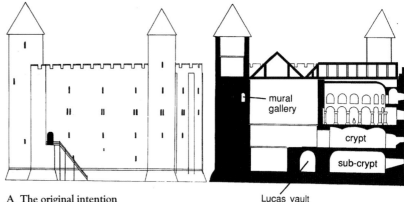

A The original intention

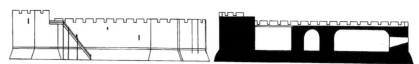

B The early castle

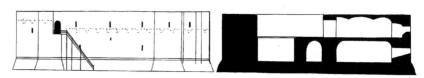

C Major change of plan at this stage

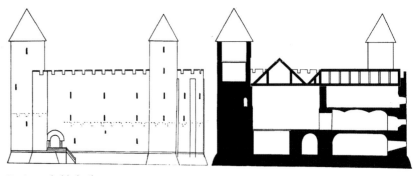

D As probably built

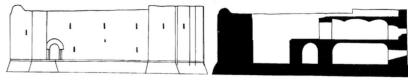

E How Wheeley left it

Incipiunt carte 7 confirmaciões 7e omnibz possessionibz 7
bonis tam ecclesiis q̃m mūdanis 7 libtatibz eccē sc̃i Johīs
Bapt̃ 7e Col̃t̃a ab illust̃bz regibz Angl̃. q̃m catholicis p̃tribz
Archiep̃is. ep̃is 7 alii̇x̃ fidelibz p̃de eccē 7 monach. p̃ie idul
n̄. i p̃mi tuic̃ 7e carta p̃ie mem̄. sub dapif̃ fūdatorī p̃de eccē.

Udo Dapifer domini Regis
totius regni Anglie. Omnibz
dei fidelibz p̃sentibz 7 futuris
salm̄. C̃um largiflua divi
ne miseracionis clemencia me
licet immtum multis in hac
ura donauit b̃ñficiis. Et de
nichilo creatum amplissim̃
honore ditauit donatus 7 di
uuiax̃ copul̃ taritu memor b̃ñficii quid regi regum d̃no
potissimum possem retribuere p omnibz que retribuit
in puigili sep̃ animo reuolui. Pie ig̃ tauritis deuo
tōnis mee studiositati supna insinuauit pietas. Hoc si
bi fore acceptabile hoc michi salubre. si religionis stu

*From the first page of the Cartulary of
St John's Abbey of Colchester. It records
the founding of the abbey by Eudo.*

*The excavation of Siric's chapel
on land that was once in the
grounds of St John's Abbey.*

formed the vaulted roof of the crypt underneath. No internal features of the chapel survive but the positions of the columns forming
the aisles can be deduced from the shape and
size of the existing walls. The resulting plan
turns out to be very similar to the chapel in
the Tower of London, with more or less the
same internal dimensions and the same number of columns.

As a result of the investigation, it was clear
that, in the 18th century, the surface of the
floor had been removed and replaced with
'crazy paving' made almost entirely of reused
Roman building materials. More to the point,
no stumps were found where the columns
should have stood, and there were no visible
traces of a floor surface which could have
served the chapel. In fact, all in all, there was
little good evidence that the chapel had ever
been built. The remains on the roof give the
impression that the builders had intended to
build the chapel, but that they changed their
plans at the last minute. This change of plan
was to have a major impact on the building,
for it meant that one complete floor was
never built and the castle was topped out one
storey lower than originally planned.

If the castle had been completed as initially
intended, it would have provided Eudo with
a huge fortified residence. The sheer scale of
what was emerging may have prompted last-
minute changes. Alternatively, it may simply
have been an over-ambitious project which
was so large that it needed more local building materials than could be supplied at the
time. As we have already seen, the castle
needed huge amounts of stone and tile, in
fact twice as much material as the Tower.
The volume of material was so great that it
would have been too expensive to import it
from somewhere like Kent where suitable
stone was available. The vast bulk of it had
to be obtained locally from the ruins of the
Roman town, and that may have amounted
to as much as a quarter of all the suitable
material that survived.

St John's Abbey

Quite a lot of written detail exists about the
foundation and early years of St John's
Abbey. The sources are not completely reliable and in some places they are contradictory. However archaeological excavations in
the 1970s showed that there is much that
must be based on fact. The main essential
'facts' are as follows. The monastery was
founded in 1095 on a site where, it is said, a

priest called Siric had his house and a church which was made of wooden planking and dedicated to St John the Evangelist. The church, which stood on the northern slope of a little hill, was the scene of a miracle and a place where inexplicable voices were often heard and strange lights frequently seen. Abbot Hugh, tired of the noise and bustle of the town, decided some time between 1104 and 1115 to transfer the offices and workshops and the monks' dwellings to the south side of the abbey church. This involved the removal of a little hill which overshadowed the abbey church and the dumping of the soil thus generated on the north side of the church to form a cemetery. (Some sources suggest that the relocation of the monastic buildings followed a serious fire in 1133 which badly affected the abbey and town.) The abbey church was completed in 1115. The parish church of St Giles was founded in the cemetery of the abbey some time in 1171.

The construction of St Botolph's roundabout in the early 1970s meant that the north-east corner of the abbey grounds had to be removed, and the ground greatly reduced in level. As a result, not only did we find the remains of Siric's church, but we also located the dumped soil and the early cemetery, just as they are described in the written sources. The church was aligned east-west, with an apsidal east end. Its foundations were made of reused Roman rubble which, on the face of it, seems to contradict the idea that it was a wooden church like the famous example at Greensted in south Essex. However, it may be that the building incorporated wooden elements in the above-ground part of its structure. The remains of the demolished church were sealed by a layer of dumped soil which seems to have extended down the hill so that it was piled up hard against the inner face of the early stone wall forming the boundary of the abbey precinct. A number of shallow graves cut the dumped soil and penetrated the remains of the church below. The earliest of the graves were very distinctive in appearance. Each had its sides lined with rubble to form a crude coffin with a niche at the west end for the head. The later graves were plain and not lined in this way.

In 1973, part of the cemetery of the former St Giles' church was lowered to form a car park and, as a result, it showed that the burials in the graveyard had been cut into a thick, dumped deposit of sand and soil. This material contained much burnt debris, including the remains of burnt clay buildings. The historical narrative seems to be confirmed: the burning, the primitive buildings, and the dumped soil are matchable in turn with the fire of 1133, the monastic buildings to the north of the church, and the spoil from the 'hill' which was levelled to provide a new site for their replacement.

St Botolph's Priory

St John's Abbey was not the only monastery in the Norman town. St Botolph's Priory was founded on a nearby site between 1100 and 1104 but it had little to do with Eudo. It was formed by a small group of priests who were probably serving an existing church and had decided to adopt a monastic order. St Botolph's has the distinction of being the first Augustinian foundation in Britain and as such was granted authority over all later houses of that order. But the priory was not wealthy, which explains why the church was not finished until 1177.

Like monasteries everywhere in England and Wales, St Botolph's Priory was destroyed as a result of the Dissolution in the 16th century. However, the nave of the priory

The west front of the church of St Botolph's Priory as it might have looked in c AD 1200. The west end was probably completed in 1177.

The west front of the ruined St Botolph's Priory church.

Conjectural ground plan of St Botolph's Priory.

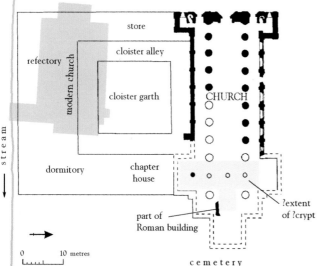

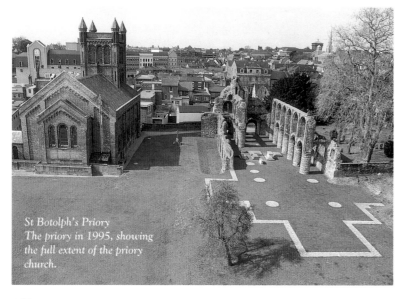

St Botolph's Priory
The priory in 1995, showing the full extent of the priory church.

church was preserved and used for parish and civic services, but this practice stopped when the building was reduced to its current ruinous state during the Siege of Colchester in 1648.

In 1991, excavations were carried out on behalf of Colchester Borough Council on the site of the eastern half of the priory church. This was done so that the positions of the missing parts of the building could be marked out on the ground to help the visitor understand the standing remains better. It turns out that the building had a square, fairly short, east end. The excavations were limited and confined to recovering the plan of the missing parts of the church. However there were two discoveries of interest, both of which need to be investigated further to understand them properly. One was a crypt or basement, and the other was a late Roman building.

The crypt or basement lay under the south transept and extended northwards under the crossing (which is under the central tower). The backfill of the crypt contained the upper part of a collapsed column which had supported a vaulted roof. The church was built on a sloping site, and it is possible that somehow our 'crypt' is no more than a product of the changing levels. However, should it prove to be a real crypt, then this would be a significant discovery since it would suggest that the priory church contained a relic, presumably of one of the saints to whom it was dedicated (ie St Botolph, St Julian, or St Denis).

Of all the religious institutions in Colchester, St Botolph's Priory is the most likely to have been based on the site of a Roman church or a 'martyrium' (which was a building, a tomb, or a piece of ground associated with an important Christian). Being outside the walled town, it lay in just the right place for a Roman cemetery church. And as a foundation, it clearly had early roots since it was formed out of a pre-existing college of priests. Thus the discovery of a late Roman building under the east end of the priory church is an exciting one, and raises the possibility of another Roman church. Unfortunately it was not possible to uncover enough of the building to tell what it had been used for. However the short sections of wall which were seen in 1991 included some heavily-burnt areas suggesting something like a bath-house rather than a church. If true, then its presence under the priory church would be coincidental.

St Mary Magdalen's church

Medieval hospitals were charitable foundations for the sick and the poor run on semi-monastic lines. There were four in Colchester, the earliest being St Mary Magdalen's hospital which was founded by Eudo around 1100 as a home for lepers. By the end of the medieval period, leprosy had declined to a point that the hospital would accommodate the poor and infirm when no lepers could be found.

Excavations in 1989 and 1994 provided information on the layout and history of the hospital. The heart of the community was a dormitory and a small chapel. The foundations of these buildings had been badly affected by later graves, but enough survived to provide some information on size, plan and structural development. Five graves inside the church included one with a pewter chalice indicating the probable burial place of a priest who had been a master of the hospital. With the establishment of the parish of Mary Magdalen in the early 13th century, the chapel became the parish church, and the hospital was relocated on the adjacent site to the north. Here the inmates were provided with a new dormitory and a new place of worship, the so-called 'Maudlin chapel'. The new chapel proves to have been so much bigger than the original chapel (six times), that it may have provided living accommodation too.

When outside, lepers were supposed to ring a bell to warn others of their approach and to wear distinctive clothing which covered their bodies. This widespread fear of contagion (although largely unfounded) explains why Eudo's hospital (like all leper hospitals) was in a secluded area, well away from the built-up areas of the town.

St Helen's Chapel

The Colchester Chronicle tells us that Eudo restored St Helen's Chapel and gave it to St John's Abbey. 'Restoration' suggests that the building was already old in the late 11th century. Archaeological investigations in the 1980s showed that at least three of its four walls are not only founded on parts of the underlying Roman theatre, but the lowest parts of some of them may also be Roman. Moreover later records prove that St John's Abbey did indeed own the chapel, just as the Colchester Chronicle says. Thus the Chronicle is shown to contain yet more elements of truth. We cannot say if the building

had actually been a Roman chapel, but at least the idea that it had been restored seems to fit what is now known about the building's origin. Chapels were sometimes inserted into public buildings in late Roman times, so it is just conceivable that something similar happened to the theatre in Colonia Victricensis. However, given that the Colchester Chronicle describes the Temple of Claudius as the palace of the mythical King Coel, it is not surprising that the same source should see a surviving part of the adjacent Roman theatre as the place of worship of his saintly 'daughter' Helen, regardless of whether or not it really had any Christian connections in its earlier form.

Moot Hall

Colchester's Moot Hall was demolished in 1843 to make way for a larger town hall which, in turn, was replaced by the present town hall little more than half a century later. The Moot Hall is a great loss because it was the most lavishly-decorated urban secular building known in the country. Two round-headed windows and a round-headed door date the building to c 1160—too late for

The church of St Mary Magdalen (demolished in 1854).

St Helen's Chapel. Medieval legend has it that the building was a Roman church restored by Eudo Dapifer.

The reverse of the first common seal of the borough of Colchester probably dating to the 13th century. It shows a castle in reference to Colchester's own. The fish and water under the arches symbolise the fishery which was held by the town's burgesses under the terms of their charter.

Eudo—and were carved by the same sculptor (or sculptors) who worked on such important buildings as Rochester Cathedral and the Priory Church at Dover. The intricate carvings on the windows included figures on the column-shafts which was a French innovation of the mid 12th century. As at Rochester, the figures may have represented King Solomon and the Queen of Sheba. Their presence would be appropriate at the Moot Hall since Solomon was famous for his judgement and wisdom.

Although the people of Colchester received their first charter in 1189, the wording of the document shows that they were already enjoying elements of self-government by that time. The Moot Hall seems to corroborate this deduction, since the building would appear to have predated the charter by a few decades.

Stone houses

Although by Norman times Colchester had developed into a successful and flourishing town, we have not as yet been able to excavate any houses of the ordinary people. Other remains have been found in plenty: pits, lime kilns, pottery kilns, and robber trenches for Roman building materials. This is partly because of a lack of opportunity to dig the most promising sites, and partly because the construction of later buildings (especially cellars) has damaged what remains there were of Norman houses.

The one exception is the stone house excavated at Lion Walk. Part of one of its walls survived above ground until its demolition in 1971. The building had been of two storeys, with the hall at first-floor level. In common with the other stone buildings in the town such as the castle and the churches, the walls of the house were made of reused Roman building materials salvaged from standing Roman ruins or quarried from the gardens and fields in and around the town centre. Records show that there were at least seven early medieval stone houses, and no doubt there would have been many more. There were very many stone houses at Canterbury, where they are associated with Jews. The same may be true at Colchester where there is a reference to two stone houses in St Runwald's parish being bought by Aaron the Jew in 1275. The unpopularity of the Jews in England at the time culminated with their expulsion in 1290, and stone buildings were presumably favoured by them for the security they offered.

The Hythe

The most important and far-reaching of all the developments in early medieval Colchester must have been the building of the Hythe. Until then, the main landing facility had been at Old Heath which stood

Far right: impression of the Moot Hall c 1200.

Right: reconstruction drawing by A.J. Sprague of 1845 showing one of the windows of the Moot Hall.

near the bank of what is now a dried-up meander of the Colne. Two miles upriver from here, the water-course was straightened and a timber wharf was built along the west bank to form the core of the Hythe we know today. The construction of a new Hythe was to pay dividends in the years to come, particularly because of the cloth trade for which Colchester became famous.

Old Heath takes its name from *Ealdehethe* meaning old landing place. The earliest reference to the name is in 1272, but we can confident that there was a 'new' Hythe much earlier. At a guess, the Hythe was probably built in the 12th century, since this is the sort of investment we would expect from the people (burgesses) of Colchester, rather than somebody like Eudo. Like the Moot Hall, the Hythe was probably another expression of the new powers of self-determination which Colcestrians were beginning to enjoy.

The Romans could have built something like the Hythe. Claudius' massive constructions at the port of Rome (page 29) show the technical feats which the Romans were capable of. The Hythe would have been very minor by comparison and, indeed, a larger version of such a scheme was built at Londinium as archaeologists in London have shown. Excavations near the Hythe in 1995 on a site opposite St Leonard's Church failed to produce a single sherd of Roman pottery. This is hardly proof that there was not a Roman version of the Hythe since the site is 200 m from the waterfront. Clearly the wharves at the Hythe need to be investigated to be certain, but the omens do not look good.

As always, the narrowness of the Colne was a problem. The existence of good wharves at the Hythe made no difference to that and, as records show, cargoes still had to be transferred on to smaller boats at the mouth of the Colne for transportation upriver. Near the beginning of this book, we argued that the position of Colchester in relation to the river had a critical bearing on the subsequent development, not merely of Colonia Victricensis, but of south-east England—a big claim for what is now a small town. The burgesses of 12th-century Colchester tackled the problem in their own way with some success. But they could never overcome the root of the difficulty— Colchester is in the wrong place. As we have seen, the location of Colchester was fixed over two thousand years ago when Claudius and the Roman army built their legionary fortress next to Cunobelin's works depot at Sheepen. A few miles closer to the mouth of the Colne could have made a lot of difference.

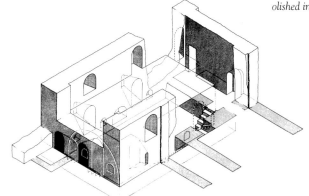

Isometric drawing of the surviving parts of the Norman stone house in Foundry Yard, off the High Street. Demolished in 1886.

Left: the remains of the Norman stone house demolished in 1972 at Lion Walk. Only one original wall of the building survived. It had been much altered and repaired. Note the part of a 12th-century round-headed doorway in the middle of the wall.

Further reading

Readers are spoilt for choice when it comes to books on the history and archaeology of Roman and later Britain. Some standard works are *Britannia: a history of Roman Britain* (3rd edition 1987) by Sheppard Frere, the *Oxford illustrated history of Roman Britain* (1993) by Peter Salway, *Anglo-Saxon England* by F.M. Stenton (3rd edition 1971), and the *Oxford history of Britain* edited by Kenneth O. Morgan (1993). Useful books which are particularly relevant to Colchester include *The towns of Roman Britain* (2nd edition 1995) by John Wacher, *Fortress into city* (1988) edited by G. Webster, and *Boudica: the British revolt against Rome AD 60* (1978), *Rome against Caratacus* (1981), and *The Roman imperial army of the first and second centuries AD* (1969) all by Graham Webster. And to come in 1997, in the Shire Archaeology series, there is to be *The Boudican revolt against Rome* by P.R. Sealey.

Colchester has been well served by archaeologists and medieval historians over the years and it can boast a long tradition of publication going right back to 1748 and Philip Morant's *History and antiquities of the Borough of Colchester*. For example, the county journal (now called *Essex Archaeology and History*) has since its beginning in the mid 19th century included a great many important and useful articles about the archaeology and history of Colchester. Clearly it would be unrealistic to list every publication, but we can at least pick out a few key works which someone new to the subject might wish to consult. These are: *Roman Colchester* (1954) by M.R. Hull, *Camulodunum* by C.F.C. Hawkes and M.R. Hull, *The Roman potters' kilns of Colchester* (1963) by M.R. Hull, and *The Trinovantes* (1975), *Sheepen: an early Roman industrial site at Camulodunum* (1985), and *Excavations in Colchester, 1964-8* in the Transactions of the Essex Archaeological Society, 2 (3rd series), (1971) all by R. Niblett (formerly Dunnett). More recently there is the *Victoria history of the County of Essex, IX: the Borough of Colchester* (1994), which is an excellent history of the medieval and later town edited by Janet Cooper. For those wishing to explore the archaeology of Colchester in serious detail, there is an article in *The archaeology of Essex: proceedings of the Writtle conference* edited by Owen Bedwin (1996) (pages 69-75). This is a survey (plus brief commentary) of most of the archaeological publications between 1977 and 1992 which cover some aspect of the archaeology of Colchester. On the other hand, as a lighter read, there is *The Colchester Archaeologist* which is a magazine published annually by the Colchester Archaeological Trust for members of the Friends of the Colchester Archaeological Trust. The magazine mainly features articles about the year's work in the town.

Finally it should be noted that the detailed results of most of the excavations over the last twenty-five years including those at the Balkerne Lane, Culver Street, and Lion Walk sites have been published as a series of twelve volumes entitled the Colchester Archaeological Reports. These are the basis for many of the reconstruction paintings in this book. The reports are as follows:

1: *Aspects of Anglo-Saxon and Norman Colchester* by Philip Crummy (CBA Research Report 39), 1981 and 1995.
2: *The Roman small finds from excavations in Colchester, 1971-9* by Nina Crummy, 1983, reprinted 1995.
3: *Excavations at Lion Walk, Balkerne Lane, and Middleborough, Colchester, Essex* by Philip Crummy, 1984.
4: *The coins from excavations in Colchester, 1971-9* by Nina Crummy (ed), 1987.
5: *The post-Roman small finds from excavations in Colchester, 1971-85* by Nina Crummy, 1988.
6: *Excavations at Culver Street, the Gilberd School, and miscellaneous sites in Colchester, 1971-85* by Philip Crummy, 1992.
7: *Post-Roman pottery from excavations in Colchester, 1971-85* by John Cotter, publication 1997.
8: *Roman vessel glass from excavations in Colchester, 1971-85* by H.E.M. Cool and Jennifer Price, 1995.
9: *Excavations of Roman and later cemeteries, churches and monastic sites in Colchester, 1971-88* by Nina Crummy, Philip Crummy, and Carl Crossan, 1993.
10: *Roman pottery from excavations in Colchester 1971-85* by R.P. Symonds and S. Wade (eds P. Bidwell and A. Croom), publication 1997.
11: *Camulodunum 2* by C.F.C. Hawkes and Philip Crummy, 1995.
12: *Animal bone from excavations in Colchester, 1971-85* by Rosemary Luff, 1993.

Acknowledgements

A book like this about the archaeology of Colchester would not be possible without the hard work, enthusiasm and dedication of hundreds of people who over the years have devoted much of their time towards the study of the town's past. It is therefore a pleasure for me to thank and acknowledge the invaluable help that I have had from so many people both on and off the various sites since 1971. Similarly the Trust has enjoyed the support and co-operation of many organisations and commercial companies over the years. There are lengthy acknowledgements of all this elsewhere, especially in the Colchester Archaeological Reports, although in this book I have had to restrict personal acknowledgements to those people who have been directly involved in the production of this book.

I am indebted to Peter Froste for all his hard work in producing his illustrations for this and other publications. I am also grateful to the following people who have helped in various ways with the preparation of this book: Gillian Adams who did most of the design and layout and produced plans and drawings; Alison Colchester who took most of the photographs in the book; Stephen Crummy who prepared some of the drawings; Nina Crummy who provided the research basis for the reconstruction drawing of the Lexden Tumulus; Susanne Atkin who prepared the index; Ernest Black and John Wilkes for their comments on the text; and Janet Cooper for her comments on the last chapter. I am also grateful to the staff of David Holland Graphics and Bath Press for their support and help on the technical aspects of the production of the book.

I am also grateful to the following people and institutions who have kindly provided illustrations: Paul Sealey (Colchester Museum); Ralph Jackson (British Museum); Paul Coverley (Essex Record Office); Editions Electo; and Dr Paolo Liverani (Vatican Museum). In particular I am grateful to Paul Sealey and the Colchester Museum for providing facilities for the photography of some of the objects in the museum's care.

I much appreciate the invaluable financial support provided by the people who subscribed to the book in advance of its publication. I am very grateful for the support of the Friends of the Colchester Archaeological Trust and, in particular, to Nick Hines for his efficient management of the pre-publication subscriptions. Similarly the Trust is indebted to the Essex County Council, the Essex History Fair, the Friends of the Trust, and Colchester Borough Council for grants towards the production costs of the book, and to Tarmac Southern Ltd for supporting the book launch. The Trust is especially indebted to the Colchester Borough Council for the financial support which has been provided on an annual basis and for the council's support and encouragement generally.

Picture credits

(PF= Peter Froste; SC Stephen Crummy; CM Colchester Museum; BM British Museum)

Cover drawing: PF
Pages 6-7: large aerial photograph by Edward Clack; page 9: © (and kind permission of) the Vatican Museum; page 10: PF; page 12: SC; pages 15 (bottom right) and 23 (bottom): photographs © CM; page 17: PF; pages 24-25: reconstruction drawing by SC; page 26: PF; page 31: plan by SC; page 32: © (and kind permission of) Professor R.R.R. Smith; page 35: SC (map); page 37: photograph by James Fawn; page 38: illustration of the arch reproduced with the kind permission of Professor A.A. Barrett; pages 42-43: PF; page 53: © (and kind permission of) the Vatican Museum; pages 62-63: PF; page 67: PF; page 71: plan by SC; pages 75-77: PF; page 86: glass bowl, BM; page 88: PF; page 89: PF; page 90: finger-ring, BM; page 90: SC; page 92: 'mithraeum' photograph, CM; pages 94-95: PF; page 95: mosaic by Bob Moyes; page 96: PF; page 97: mosaic by Bob Moyes; pages 98-99: PF; page 100: finger-ring, BM; page 100: PF; page 101: PF; page 102: gladiator, BM; page 102: PF; page 103: PF; page 103: aerial photograph by Edward Clack; page 104: PF; page 104: aerial photograph by Edward Clack; page 105: high view of excavation by High Rise Totem Photography; page 105: PF; page 107: figurine, BM; page 108: expanded view, CM; page 110: samian mould, CM; page 110: boar, BM; page 119: © reproduced courtesy of the Essex Record Office, Colchester branch; page 123: PF; pages 126-127: PF; page 130: CM; page 131: reconstruction from Roman Colchester; pages 138-139: PF; page 144: © Editions Electo; page 146: SC; page 146: aerial photograph by Edward Clack; page 148: Cartulary, © reproduced courtesy of the Essex Record Office; page 149: PF; page 150: bottom, High Rise Totem Photography; page 152: bottom right, PF.
End papers: part of a mosaic from the Culver Street site painted by Bob Moyes.

Subscribers

Mr D.H.F. Blowers
Mr Arnold Peter Bobby
Sir Michael Holt
Elizabeth & Peter Mackenzie,
  Timothy & Jonathan Mackenzie
Ashley Cooper
Mr S.H. Sheppard
Miss A.C. Turner
Mrs Jean C. Blowers
Mr D.G. Preddy
Larry Marshall
J.F. George
Mr A. Kenny
Mr L.C. Leach
Mrs F.B. Alexander
Mrs R. Oliver
Mr A.W. Nicholson
Mrs Blanche Hudson
Franziska Dovener
Mrs Gabrielle Chadwick
Mrs Irene Bayes
Mr Colin Bellows
Mr Ian S.E. Bellows
Dinah James
Maureen Jones
Mrs Brenda May
Mrs Lavender Buckingham
Mr D.P. Tripp
Miss V.M. Ellis
A.N. Jenkins
Mr P.E. Croucher
Shirley Durgan
Bill & Dorothy Adams
John Lingwood
Alan Davies
Mr A.J. Fawn
E.P. Mount
Nick Shelton
Mr P. Andrew Borges R.I.B.A.
Mrs M.C. Lugg
St Mary's School, Colchester
Mrs R.E.G. Perrins
R.D.G. Perrins
R.C.G. Perrins
Mrs Margaret Berry
Chris Dowsett
Miss V.S. Spence
Mr & Mrs R. Whybrow
Dr Colin F. Davies
Francis Nicholls
Mr P. & Mrs J. Gill
Mrs J.A. Allen
Mr & Mrs H.J. Downing
Michael Beattie
Mrs J. Hamblin
Mr J. Fryer
Mrs Noreen Proudman
Mrs S.G. Stannard
Mrs L.M. Jansma
W.M. Abbott
Mrs Susannah J. Futtu
Mrs A. Carver

Mr Martin Knowles
Nigel A. Chapman
Mary E. Chapman
Mrs Kythe Read, B.Sc.
Anna Moore
Miss Edna M. Willis
Mrs K.A. Evans
Mrs Ida McMaster
P.D. Hewitt
Kenneth Burstal
Mrs Susie Starke
W.M. Dixon
Mr & Mrs P.A. Kievenaar
Dr L. Spooner
Betty Miller
Mrs M.E. Nicholas
Paul Warner
Miss P. Seamer
Mrs M.J. Harbord
Ian Dodd
Dr John Barnes
Mr J. Firmin
C.A.W. Evans, B.A., F.I.Diag.E.
Nicholas Bond
Mary F. Jones & Charles R. Jones
Mrs C. Catchpole
Owen B. Hay
Jonathan O. Hay
Rebecca Hay
Anthony Beeson
R.A. Spanner
Mary Squire
Donald A. Scott
F.S. Pearce
Mrs Emma G. & Mr Max J. Lambert
Gill Newman
Stephen, Karen & Gemma Brown
Neil Pugh
David A. Judge
Alan V. Rowley
Mr C.M. East
Mrs Betty Nevitt
Malcolm A. Armstrong
Margaret & Mike Eames
Mrs R.J. Harrod
Jess A. Jephcott
Mrs Olive Hazell
Mrs Lesley Stock
Mrs Sally Carter
Mrs L. Basker
Mr & Mrs S.C. Surey
Mrs J.E. Collier
Mrs Janet Wright
Mrs E. Hermon
Mr Vic Scott
Mrs Margaret Pilkington
Mr Mike Napthan
Mary & Kit Hughes
Miss Deirdre Fordham
Mrs Jaki Collison
Warwick R. Lewis
the Richard Jackson Partnership

David Cook
Mr M.J. Corbishley
Mrs Pauline A. Sturgeon
Sue Aldridge
Hannah Hearsum
Zara Matthews
W.G. Drake
Mr J. Yates
Mrs R. Shaw
Alex Scott
Robert H. Sheppard
Mrs F.M. Hoare
Dr & Mrs R.D. Jurd
Patrick Denny
David Anderton
Kate Hughes
John Nicholson
B.A.B. Barton
Jonathan R. Seddon
Mr R.M.C. Harden
Mr & Mrs M.H. Hardy
Mrs Avril Farahar, B.A.
Mrs D.O. Goddard
J. Austin
Mr & Mrs S.A.M. Hines
Nick Hines
Miss Carolyn Hewes
Miss Susan Jacques
Mrs Anne Crook-Williams
Dr Adrian Clark
Dr Christine Clark
Mrs M.J. Claydon
Harry Carlo
Susan Dale
G.M.R. Davies
Mrs U.H. Hammond
Kenneth Neale O.B.E., F.S.A.
Mrs M. Butcher
Hugh Gunton
J.A. Bullard
Mark Hassall
Mr A.J. Doe
John Hedges
Cecil J. Minter
Mrs Christine M. Mabbitt
Mr Gordon Dean
Stephen Fuller
Mrs Nina Crummy
Philip T. Beeton
Stanway Fiveways County Primary
  School
Mr H.W. Palmer
Ms Jo Lynch
Roy Waters
R.R. Yearley
Mrs A.M. Bartholomew
Mrs B. Jonsen
Monkwick Junior School
Mrs J. McCarthy
Colin Baddeley
Ian B. Hay
Miss Bridget Russell

Paul Bowen
Stephen Smith
C.F. Robbins
Keith W. Francis
Mr E.A. Huxter
Peter Yeates
John Roche
J.R. Steele
Cyril Meadows
The Revd J.C. Hardy
Mrs Ida Blower
Bryn Walters
Gerda Frank-Gemmill
Dirck B. Stickle
F.R. Westgate
Karen Laken
Miss R.M. Wall
Graham P. Andrews
Mrs B.O. Barton
B.R. Roach
D. Brown
Mrs Jill White
E.W. Hadkiss
Mrs D. Woodward
Dr John D. Gray
His Honour Judge Michael Coombe
Dennis Thorogood
Mr C.L. Rowe
Rosalind Niblett
St Helena School
Mr R.C. Todd
Mrs J.R. Potter
Nick Wickenden
Roger Goodburn
Mr P.W. George
Miss M.L. Clachan
Mrs Patricia M. Monk
Miss E.M. Gosland
D. Harrington
Mrs Elaine Cope
Vernon Edward & Marta Johanna
    Hilton-Bowen
Jennnifer Warren
Mrs B.E. Drage
Ernest E. Gay
Mary Dale
Miss Sharleyne Chaston Scott
Dr Grace Simpson
Mrs Caroline Merriam
Mrs M. Maltby
Ian Dean
Lawrence Chopping
Mrs M.O. Furnival
Mrs Margaret Hatherley-Champ
Mr Anthony Pitman
John R. Chalmers
John Burton
Dr R. Woodd-Walker
John Lepper
City of Lincoln Archaeological Unit
P.E.L. Luxmoore
Mrs B. Chenery
R. Hopkins & W. Moses
G.E. Meller
Mr C.W. Goddard

A. Stokes
G.R. & D.A. Browne
The Revd. Philip M.N. Gullidge
John F. Windsor
Brian Rowe
Robert Tatam
Dr Paul R. & Mrs Julia S. Sealey
Michael George Dodd
Ann & Ralph Newns
Mr F.J. Gaskin
Mrs J.M.C. Rawlinson
Mrs J. Phillips
Mrs Beryl Barr
Mrs S.W. Morgan
Roy Hidson
Ray Gamble
Mr P. Sheppard
Colchester Boys' High School
David Grayston
Peter Dimmick
Mrs M. Gooderham
Mrs H. Pitchforth
Mr & Mrs Williams
Roy & Marion Ward
Mr D. Barbour
Dr R. Bourton
Peter D.W. Bourton
Mr M. Cant
W.E.G. Kirby
Mr & Mrs D.J. Appleton
Mrs D.E. Balchin
Mr E. Black
Dr Reva Brown
J.R. Wightman
Kevin Northcott
Mrs Jennifer Renton
Mrs P.J. Farnell
Mrs Eleanor Mary Haworth
Judith Robson
Mrs J. Crawshaw
Miss E.J. Shearn
Heather Reed
Mr D.C. Miles
Brenda & Ken McLean
Dr Beryl J. Goff
Mr F.A. Tabersham
Mrs M. Durlacher
L.B. Corben
Mr S.G. Reed
R. John Cruse
Mr M.H. Gould
Mr & Mrs S. Duckett
Miss E.H. Maltby
P.J. Cott
Julius Baker
Miss B. Woollings
Mrs April Stride
Mrs J.M. Sully Morgan
Bruce Neville
Mrs Barbara Ann Westmancoat
Geoff Wright
Major P.S.P. Worsley R.A.
The Revd. Paul Davis
Mrs Wendy Smedley
C.J.M. Dunn

R.B. Spooner
Mrs Dinah Beckett
Graham Mather
Mrs L. Rogers
Mark Martin
Richard Shackle
The Rev Canon R.M. Wilson
Mrs Molly Reeve
M.J. Matthews
Dr Janet Cooper
Peter M. Ratcliffe
Rupert Knowles
Margaret Ward
Mrs B.J. Butler
Dr C.P. Biggam
J.D. Black
J. Trent
P.H.K. Merriam
Peter Sargeant J.P.
Mrs Elizabeth White
Mrs J. Singleton
Mr W. McMellon
Major V.A. Freeman
Hywel Edwards
D.H. Spendlove
F.R. Howe
Karen Glanville
Nicola & Michael Pickering
Jean Ashmore
Mr C.H. Sims
Timothy Pennells & Sam Pennells
Rosemary Adams
Michael Yore
A.J. Blaxill
Mrs G.F. Templeman
Stuart Connal
S.J. Pettican
John Bisdee O.B.E., D.F.C., M.A.
C.A. Sacker
T. Locker
B. Cavendish-Tribe
Mrs Jane Bowdery
Mrs Dorothy Archer
Christian Leppich
Mrs Heather Smith
Martin Broom
Mr R.W. Bennett
Mrs Julie Ager
Miss R.A. Castle
The O'Hare family
Melody O'Sullivan
Mrs Y. Beck
Michael & Rosemary Morris
Ms D. Ford
Emily Dodd
Elizabeth Aznar
Mr W.F. Grove
Lesley Groom
Essex County Council Planning Dept
Keith Robert Meredith
Keith Cullen
J.W. Heslop
Wayne Leslie Gillett
Mrs J.H. Richardson
Bill Gore

Index